Storm Prayers

Storm Prayers

Retrieving and Reimagining Matters of the Soul

By Patricia Hoolihan

Patricia Hoolihan (signature)

p. 174

NORTH STAR PRESS OF ST. CLOUD, INC.
St. Cloud, Minnesota

Copyright © 2014 Patricia Hoolihan

All rights reserved.

ISBN: 978-0-87839-773-0

First edition: September 2014

Printed in the United States of America.

Published by
North Star Press of St. Cloud, Inc.
P.O. Box 451
St. Cloud, MN 56302

www.northstarpress.com

This book is dedicated to Chris (who listened to and read endless versions and always cheers me on), Caitlinrose and Kelly James, with deep thanks for always reminding me that this boat/book was and is worth paddling into the future.

This book is also dedicated to the ancestors whose energy and stories have inspired these pages.

Table of Contents

Prologue ix

Part One
Swinging Back and Forth

1. At the Hour of Our Death 3
2. Self-Consciousness & Dissonance 13
3. Canning Peaches on Second Avenue 17
4. Saying Goodbye to the House on Second Avenue 34
5. Uncle Dan: Wildness & Piety 41
6. A Good, Home-Cooked Meal 51
7. Where Did the Wild Woman Go? What Went Wrong? 56
8. Cracking it Open 65
9. Meditation on Mary Magdalene 72

Part Two
Reaching Further Back

10. The Mary Statues 83
11. The Centennial & My First Home Mass 96
12. Bernie, Gert, & BVG 104
13. The Bridge to Peterborough 112
14. The Jig is Up—The Farm 124
15. Storm Prayers 146

Part Three
Faith Takes: Reorienting Faith In My World

16. Storms & Sanctuaries 155
17. Faith for the Roadblock 160
18. Five Takes on Faith 171

Part Four
Lifting Off & Leavetakings

19. Lift-Off & Eagle's Wings 185
20. Uncle Dan's Final Flight 197
21. Gert's Surgery 207
22. The Rescue Mary Mission 210
23. Goodbye to Gert 214
24. Leavetaking of the Last of the Tribe (Goodbye to Dad) 219

Part Five
Landings

25. Canadian Retreats 233
26. From Cavan-Blazers to Controversy 239
Epilogue 242

Prologue

WHEN I WAS IN GRADUATE SCHOOL in the 1980s, I wrote my thesis on what Chaucer's *Canterbury Tales* tells us of the fourteenth century. In particular, I focused on how the Catholic Church and its representatives were involved with bribery, money laundering, adultery . . . and many other abuses.

I had grown up intensely Catholic but had no current involvement with Catholicism—except that I had nearly died a few years before. And (Catholic) prayers recited at my bedside by my aunts, uncle and parents (the faithful) had brought me inexplicable comfort during a time when I floated between living and dying.

That was a warm memory, a memory I still hadn't fully mined and did not yet (and perhaps still do not) know its full implications and impact. I did know it had cracked open the wall of anger between me and the religion, and by extension the family, I had been born into.

Yet enough of me was still at a great distance from the church so that I found it strangely satisfying to trace corruption in the church back six centuries. "See?" I wanted to say to someone (who?). "Bad things happen in the name of the church. People are cheated on, hurt, wounded, robbed, judged, violated, gross injustices happen and then are ignored, in the name of the church. If it happened six centuries ago and is still happening today, then it most likely has always been happening."

Did I want to hold this up to my parents, aunts and uncles, whose faith had always been steadfast and rock-solid? Did I want to hold it up to priests who I had known over the years? Was this the voice of my own inner Doubting Thomas, the one wanting proof, the one quick to sniff out anything less than 100% in authenticity and integrity?

Who, indeed, was at the other end of this ongoing conversation inside me, this never-quite-extinguishable, question-filled debate? It's as if at some profound level I was programmed to question my every motive, thought, and decision; from a young age we Catholic children memorized rote answers, but what has stayed with me long past the memorized answers is the idea of questioning.

Some questions have so many threads of potential explanation that a book is written in the hope of meandering toward answers. The questions here are about who we are to one another, streaming through decades and generations. What truths resonate through such time travel, and what of the old forms must die in order for us to truly meet the challenges and changes and evolution of time? What of the past is worth retrieving?

Why not just walk away from a form, a system of religion that has been willing to enable and hide sexual abuse, that is only now in the twenty-first century beginning to remove predators, make amends to those who have been ravaged—and then often only because of intense efforts on the part of the victims through legal channels? Or a system that in some cases will deny communion to people based on their sexual preference, a completely private matter which creates no harm to others? Why not just walk away from a church that denies ordination to women and whose official position on birth control bespeaks allegiance to a system that is often unjust to women? Why not just walk away from a church whose public position on these and other issues I disagree with?

WALKING AWAY (although running away and slamming doors behind me would be more accurate) was not enough. I also eventually needed to walk *toward* something. In the complex journey of walking toward experiences that moved and touched my spirit, my soul, I have been surprisingly led, eventually even drawn to retrace the roots and rituals of this religion I grew up in and to find comfort there. To find what works for me has been more surprising than the catalogue of what's wrong. I have come to appreciate the depth and breadth of what the community of Catholicism has to offer, even as the questions, although sometimes abating, continue to resurface.

These stories, then, are about my teachers, the authentically and deeply faith-filled members of my family who loved me even in my angriest phases, whose deep well of empathy has provided comfort and softened life's blows for so many of us in the family. What this book is ultimately about is sifting through what is, for me, redeemable, even laudable, about Catholicism—what aspects of it have called me to reconciliation, forgiveness, and acceptance at the other side of my anger. Recovering a relationship with my religious past braided itself into other paths of spiritual recovery for me: thus the twelve steps of AA/Al-Anon and other spiritual paths enter into this river of the spirit. Religion was so intertwined with my family life; therefore, these stories are about sifting through family life as well. Since matters of the soul and spirit happen not only in church, but in communion with others in many ways, these stories also trace rituals, relationships, and roots. I mine them for timeless truths as well as minefields.

The word "truth" is one to pause over. "Thou shalt not lie" is one of the ten commandments. And yet, when one traces corruption back in Chaucer's day and into today, the roots of harm to others (evil?) often lie (no pun intended) in untruths or half-truths. Covered up, swept-under-the-rug abuse has created horrors and scars for many victims. The abuse is caused by sickness, yes, but the further pain is the cover-up—the inability and unwillingness to face and deal with the truth. It seemed to me the church's rhetoric could too easily be used (misused, abused) in service of not facing the truth, hiding the truth in order to "look good" or protect the status quo. The church's reliance on image over substance trickled down into my own family. It takes a lot of sorting out to know what one wants to keep and throw away. It's more complex than just throwing it all away, which is a route I traveled for a while.

I sometimes wonder if the past doesn't create its own magnetic field that pulls us in or forward at key moments during our lives. In a strange twist of fate or destiny or magical serendipity, my husband's family bought a very small, "wee" Canadian island in the 1950s. My husband and I now own and run this island where we spend most of our summers. It is 1,200 miles from our Minneapolis city home, and roughly about the same distance from my hometown of Grand Rapids, Minnesota, but less than three hours from where my paternal grandparents were born and lived before they immigrated to Minnesota. In less than a morning's drive, I can visit gravesides of great- and great-great-grandparents and walk the sites of the childhood homes of my grandparents. The past calls out, waits, and reaches out in mysterious ways. Canada, northern Minnesota, my city home in Minneapolis: these are landscapes that surround and filter the stories here. The path unwinds from northern Minnesota north through Canada and back to Ireland.

Many of these stories were written as I fell into the pulsing magnetic pull of my past. But it's a collective past. It traces a family, an Irish family, an evolution from an immigrant's journey to a modern story through the lens of the role of faith, and examines how its form changes as the culture around it changes: religious anthropology, as one of my early readers called it. My father's family is the central spine here, his siblings, his heritage—its gifts and its burdens. For me and for many of us raised intensely Catholic, the religious thread is inextricably connected to personal and cultural history. Faith is difficult to define. Its definition and applications take up four columns in the Oxford English Dictionary, followed by another column devoted to defining "faithed" and "faithful." It is deeply interwoven with people (loved ones) and place—homes and natural settings that have shaped me. Its practice is both timeless and very much affected and shaped by the times we live in.

My mother's family gets short shrift here. For this I apologize to her. As it is, the numbers of characters are hard to track. I was very close to my maternal grandmother but by the time I was reflecting on these issues, the elderly who remained were my father's family. I was able to spend more time with them and hear more of their stories. My mother's life was intertwined with theirs for almost seventy years of married life and so she is very much a part of this shared legacy.

Part One

Swinging Back and Forth

Chapter One

At the Hour of Our Death

GREEN SUMMER AIR lingered on the white cotton between their fingers as Bernie and Gert snapped the sheet taut between them. With freckled arms, they folded the top corner over toward the garden side of their spacious backyard, the same direction they always folded their sheets outdoors. July sun soothed their skin through worn, short-sleeved pastel cotton blouses and light cotton pants. Gert squinted under her wide-brimmed straw hat, but Bernie's wrinkles rested lightly under her prescription sunglasses. Beside them in the garden, tall, green stems of onions rose in a tidy row, next to rows of sprouting leaves of bush beans, corn, and tomatoes. A few clumps of chives and parsley shot out a brilliant green against the dark earth.

The sound of the ringing phone floated out through the screened windows, halted the flow of their bodies, the rhythmic pulling tight of the sheet, the folding over, the easy meeting in the center. Instantly, Gert's movements quickened. She thrust her end of the sheet into Bernie's rough, sturdy hands and scurried, brown oxfords moving quickly over the grass, toward the side door of the house. Bernie finished folding the flat twin sheet by herself, the last of the day's wash, and set it on top of the pile in the laundry basket. Hefting the wicker basket to her hip, she trailed Gert through the black-framed screen side door, up the five wooden stairs, and took a right turn into the foyer.

Gert's voice was sinking low with concern, a tone of sympathy Bernie recognized could mean only one thing. "Oh no, not Alice. We'll be right there, Jim." Bernie, her heart in her throat, thought immediately of their brother Jim and wondered what could be wrong with his usually healthy wife, Alice.

But in this family of multiple names, her initial guess was mistaken, a rare wrong turn down the well-traveled road of her intuition. Gert turned her now-pale face to Bernie. "Alice, Jerome's Alice, has had a heart attack. She's on her way to the hospital," she said. Alice—widow of Jerome, who, until his death ten years earlier had held the prestigious position of eldest male in the family—had been parked in front of the drugstore on Main Street, reaching for her nitroglycerin tablets, when she slumped over the steering wheel. The pharmacist phoned the ambulance and then Alice's son Jim, the town mayor. From his office, my cousin Jim called Bernie and Gert, his wife, and his sisters before he raced off to the hospital.

Bernie's and Gert's sheets lay folded and forgotten on the piano bench next to the phone. The aunts reached for their purses, which were always ready, holding prayer books and rosary beads. They clambered into the white Oldsmobile inherited from their cousin Rosemary and worriedly drove, with Gert at the wheel, the mile and a half to the hospital.

AT ALICE'S FUNERAL a few days later, Bernie told me, "She was already gone when we got there. They say the spirit hangs around the body for a while after death, so we stayed in the room and prayed for quite a while. Look at her in that casket. Doesn't she look like she's going to sit up and start talking?" Then Bernie said wistfully, "She was always so full of energy."

When my Uncle Ted, their youngest brother, neared the end, the phone rang in the middle of the night at *the house*. *The house* is what my father called the family homestead, the one that his siblings, Bernie, Gert, and Dan, lived in for seventy-five years. Every time my father said *the house*, I saw it in italics, his emphasis granting it mythic proportions. That night when the phone call came in from Ted's daughter, Bernie wasn't feeling well, so Dan and Gert went to the hospital and prayed with Ted's four children from four until six o'clock in the morning, when Ted took his last breaths. Fortunately, Dan was home for that one; as a bush pilot and salesman he spent a lot of his life in the skies over the western U.S. and Canada. He sold grease to mining companies, for a company Jerome began decades earlier. For Dan, *the house* was home base.

At the cemetery after Ted's funeral, I stood near Bernie and Gert, looking at the family plot, the names already engraved on stones, the empty spots waiting to be filled. It was a cool fall day. Both of "the girls," as my dad called them—Uncle Dan often said "the gairls" with an Irish twist—had on long rain coats: Gert's a dark gray, Bernie's a tawny gold. Bernie was clutching her small, no-longer-shiny black leather purse, looking at the plots in front of her. Shaking her head thoughtfully, she said to me, "It's going to be a long, drawn-out affair, getting all of us buried."

After a wistful moment, Uncle Dan began singing, "When Irish eyes are smiling, all the world is bright and gay." Most of us joined in, for even though it was a moment of loss we—the siblings, cousins, remaining aunts and uncles—were all gathered and the song, its fierce Irishness, connected all of us. The thread woven among us all began with sadness at one end and traveled to joy at the other. Uncle Dan had many ways to remind us that we were all connected—singing "Irish Eyes" at that moment was one way. He also had a knack for connecting us on a plane of joy. (No pun intended, although he was the pilot!)

The line-up of siblings in that family read like a litany: Sherman, Mary, Bernadette, Eleanor, Jerome, Margaret, William, Gertrude, Daniel, James, Matthew, and Theodore. As the other sisters and brothers married and moved out of *the house*, Bernie and Gert— along with Dan—shared the common historical practice among the Irish of at least one child remaining unmarried and living at home to care for eventually ailing parents. They helped their mother care for their Papa, as they called him, when he was sick, setting up the hospital bed in the front living room, where he stayed until he died. Years before, they had nursed their younger brother Matthew, a mere lad, still in his teens. He suffered from nephritis—at that time an untreatable disease—for months before he died in the same room.

Years later it was Mama's turn. Bernie and Gert bathed her, fed her, and prayed with her as she grew weaker and weaker. They held her hands and murmured the rosary as she took her last breaths on a quiet Sunday morning.

I became particularly attuned to Bernie's, Gert's, and Dan's deathbed presences, not because they were with me for the death of a parent, as with some of my cousins, but because they came to me when I was close to death. Twenty-seven at the time, I was a "fallen-away" Catholic, not having been to church more than occasionally in about ten years. It was just after Christmas, when I was home from my life in Seattle to spend the holidays with my family.

The first collapse happened in the kitchen of the home I grew up in. One early morning I came downstairs, sick with fever and a sore throat. I pulled an old blue plaid robe of my father's around me and sat on a high stool near the telephone where I, with no warning, passed out. When I came to, I was being carried by my father and younger brother, Bill. It was such a relief to be carried. They placed me gently on my parents' bed, the only bed on the main floor.

In the following days I felt death near me. Instead of getting better, I got worse. My body's resources, my usual resiliency, lay on the other side of a thick curtain. No amount of effort or will on my part allowed me to reach it. I had had plenty of fevers and sore throats in my life, and I knew what it felt like to be weakened by them.

But this was different. This was beyond weakness. The possibility of not ever getting better hovered beside me as a slice of consciousness, a strangely foreign yet entirely palpable shadow. I began to understand that death has a presence. I felt its darkness and its power. I feared it.

One evening, they moved me into the back seat of my parents' roomy gray Chevrolet as snowflakes fell in a mad flurry around us. A multitude of designs melted on the window and piled up thick beneath the windshield wipers. The white, swirling, spinning magic glowed under every familiar streetlight as we drove to the hospital I hadn't stayed in since I was born.

Days later, my appendix removed and all of us certain the worst was over, I was scheduled to go home. I stood to pack my few belongings into the duffel bag my mother had dropped off the day before, when a familiar heat and weakness rose up in me. A quiet sensation at first, it flushed and prickled its way across my skin within an hour. The nurse's thermometer read 103 degrees, and the doctor shook his head, no, when I asked if I could still go home. All day I watched the alarm deepen and echo in the eyes of my parents, the nurses, and the several doctors who poked and prodded around and into my body. An eerie sense of distaste for smells circled around me. In the middle of my torso, an intense pain expanded like a slowly inflating balloon.

Although the day was long, the night stretched interminably. Muted lighting and bodily pain were haunting companions as the clock on the wall ticked its slow way to my next scheduled dose of pain medication. I forced myself to buzz the nurse. She unwrapped two round pills out of their silver foil. The silver caught and reflected the light, reminding me momentarily of a fish jumping on a moonlit night. She put her hand to my forehead and I felt briefly soothed. After she left, I was alone again. I returned to my sense of a dark presence, waiting and hovering.

By morning, it hurt to breathe and my stomach felt rock-hard beneath my fingertips. My parents were at my hospital bed at 7:00 a.m. when the family doctor entered, slid a tube down my throat, hooked it up to a whirring machine to pump my stomach out, and announced he would be taking me into surgery in an hour.

When he left the room, my mother leaned over to me and quietly asked, "Can I call Father Jerry?"

Father Jerry was the parish priest, a good Catholic's last bastion between God and mortality.

"Yes," I was surprised to hear myself answer. Impulsively, intuitively, I added, "Would you ask Bernie and Gert to come, too?"

Within fifteen minutes they were all there. My mother and father, Father Jerry, Bernie, Gert, and—this was a surprise—Uncle Dan. "I was supposed to fly out this morning," Uncle Dan said. "But the cloud cover was too thick. I guess the Lord wanted me here." His words lifted the wings of my soul. A wave of happiness, enormous comfort in their presence, rippled through my pain.

They shut the door behind them and closed the curtain between me and my roommate, forming a circle around my bed. Someone held each of my hands. Gert pulled out a small, very worn prayer book and a scapular, which she put around my neck. A scapular is made of two small, one-inch square cloths, often covered in plastic so as not to get it ruined in the shower, held together by a bare-bones necklace of thick brown thread. The front cloth, to be worn on your chest, portrays

Jesus, red heart bared. On the back is inscribed the promise: "Whosoever dies wearing this scapular shall not suffer eternal fire."

I had always thought the scapular business a silly one. The idea of those two small squares being able to save me from hell and send me—or anyone else—straight into heaven seemed absurd. At any given time I wasn't sure if I even believed in hell, and I'd been through many metamorphoses of my view of what heaven could or might be. In cynical moments, I imagined Richard Speck, mass rapist and murderer in the 1980s, at the last minute throwing the scapular around his neck. Would this save him from a kind of hell I thought should exist just for him and his kind? Would the scapular around his neck catapult him into a space in heaven populated by those who had done nothing but make life on earth better for those around them? If so, what kind of deal was this, this scapular deal?

But that morning, deep inside the heart of a Minnesota winter in the twenty-seventh year of my life, deeper inside a long-practiced, family death ritual than I had ever expected to be, I questioned nothing. I noticed only a delicate tenderness, beautiful and airy as lace, wrapping itself around me as my mother helped Gert get the scapular settled on me. The back side stuck down behind my neck and the front rested lightly over my hospital gown. Everyone else pulled rosary beads out of purses and pockets. I heard the familiar and lightly musical sound of beads on beads.

When I was a child, I resented the rosary. Down on our knees every night after supper before we could go out to play, our friends waiting outside to play kick-the-can. They learned not to wait on our front steps after having been invited in by my mom or dad to join us for the rosary. They were definitely there for the games and not for the prayers; there were so many of us that our presence was needed for such games. On road trips, we dreaded the snap of our mother's purse ten miles out of town, the clatter of the beads. "Time for the rosary, kids!" No matter how hard I wished, she never forgot. We would wait until she turned back around to roll our eyeballs and stick out our tongues for only each other to see. My parents always attributed their no-car-accident record to this ritual of saying the rosary at the beginning of every road trip.

That morning, I watched each set of beads. My dad had the same black ones I'd seen him use for years, the ones that usually hung on the crucifix in our living room. He kissed them reverently before wrapping the beads around his hand. They all did. Mother's beads were a soft pink, Bernie's silver, and Gert's white. Dan's were black like my dad's. Such gentleness from my uncle surprised me. Usually he was gruff or jovial. He held my right hand. A patch of red hair curled on top of his sturdy hand. My mother was on my left. Her hand felt dry and papery, like my grandmother's used to be. Next to her was my father, then Gert, Bernie, Father Jerry, and around to Dan. Their hands pulled me into the circle. The rest of the world faded away while the faces around me grew larger, filling my world.

Often during church, my mother's voice had rung out above all the others, embarrassing me. That day, their voices rose and fell in unison. I breathed in and out to the rhythm of these prayers I had known all my life. It wasn't the words I heard at first. It was a motion. An old, old motion. A rhythm my body knew deep in its bones. They intoned, "Hail Mary, full of grace, the Lord is with you. Blessed are you among women and blessed is the fruit of your womb, Jesus."

Each of them had his or her own inflection, own particular word they accented, yet what came to me was a peaceful, murmuring chorus. There was an intake of breath with each prayer and each response. They exhaled for the length of the phrase, "Holy Mary Mother of God, pray for us sinners now and at the hour of our death. Amen."

The ache in my throat encompassed the tube and all the fear and love pooling around it. I was too weak to do anything but receive. This weakness, this raw need, rendered me wide open. Words filtered in. *Fruit. Womb. Sinners. Death.* Their hands moved methodically down the row of beads. Bernie's, Gert's and my mother's hands, worn from years of household work. My father's long, slender fingers, sprigs of white hair on them. Dan's thick hands, a woodsman's hands. I wanted their prayers to last forever: the ups and downs of their voices, the familiar words, their inhaling, exhaling. The words entered me in a way they never had before. "Pray for us now and at the hour of our death."

Was this it for me? *The hour of our death. Amen.*

Surrounded by this circle, a light went on inside me in a room that had been dark for a long long time. The stone wall of my anger at my parents' strict religiosity, my anger at the heavy doses of judgment I had experienced and witnessed through religion was crashing inside me. Rising out of the dust was the rhythm of their voices, the pulse in their hands, the feeling of my palms inside theirs. I felt for the first time the power of their faith, of this circle of brothers and sisters all worshipping in the same language. The faith of their ancestors, surviving years of famine in Ireland, the "coffin-ship" journey to North America. The faith that had pulled them through years of poverty on the farm, when there was not enough rain for the crops.

This same faith brought them to my bedside. From their hands and prayers came a solace which I could not reach deep enough inside myself for. When they finished the rosary, Gert read special healing prayers from her tattered prayer book while the priest sprinkled holy water on me. Even then, I felt amazement at how she knew just what to do, how comforting the words were that came out of her mouth. They all ended with a communal "Amen." Gert, her voice thick with concern, asked if I wanted to be left alone, but I said no. The big, dark hole, the great unknown I was facing, seemed lighter while they were around me.

When the orderlies opened the door and came in with the stretcher to move me, another aunt of mine, Theresa, wife of my youngest uncle, Ted, burst into the room, rosary beads in her hand. She had been praying out in the hallway. She must have received the second round of phone calls and didn't feel like she could interrupt whatever was going on behind the closed door. Her head was covered with a scarf because of her chemotherapy. Only when she died of cancer six months later did I realize how close to death she, herself, must have felt that morning. As I was wheeled away, it was those faces I wanted to etch forever in my mind as they watched me down the long hall: Mom, Dad, Bernie, Gert, Dan, Theresa, Father Jerry, holding their rosary beads, readying to await news of my surgery in the meditation room, perhaps after a cup of coffee.

The surgery went well, although they watched me very closely for days afterward. A bowel obstruction was discovered and unobstructed. I spent five days in intensive care, days when being able to shuffle from my bed to the sink to brush my teeth was a major feat. There was always a nurse at my side for these outings, and I felt a deep appreciation for the kindness and care of these nurses. They lightened my days of being hooked up to tubes, days when all I was allowed to ingest were ice cubes, melted slowly on my thirsty tongue. Days when the administration of morphine, moving from one end of my body to the other, signaled relief and a route to a surreal dreamland.

On my fifth night in intensive care, Chris Fisher, the man I had, impossibly, fallen in love with half a year earlier, appeared by my bed. I hadn't seen him in months—and had never mentioned him to my parents—for a whole host of complicated reasons. He had told the nurse he was my brother and when she asked me if I was up for a visit from my brother, I said, "Yes, of course!" I remember puzzling through my five brothers and thinking it didn't seem quite like any one of them to show up at the hospital at nine o'clock on a Friday night. In Chris came, and he was carrying a white rose. I was wildly happy and surprised to see him. After a wonderful, brief visit, he left and I confided in the nurse that he wasn't really my brother. I still remember her smile when she responded with, "I know. And I know what's good for my patients."

The next morning, I introduced him to my parents and watched as the three of them left to go out for lunch. I lay back in my bed, feeling the fresh dose of morphine move through me. My need to witness their meeting each other, my need to smooth over the details of his impending divorce, his acting career, his young child, his not being a Catholic—not even a churchgoer—disappeared. I couldn't possibly carry that weight into the land of dreams.

What my parents saw on the day after Chris's arrival was that I moved, for the first time in weeks, significantly outside the reach of that dark presence of death. Any of their other concerns paled in comparison. After five long days in intensive care, I was moved into a regular hospital room, where I spent five more days. The expected Catholic rigidity in my parents was overpowered by their joy and relief at my resurrection, and what they saw as Chris's inextricable contribution to my rapidly improving health.

On January 21, 1981, I was released from the hospital, on the same day the U.S. hostages were released from Iran. I tied a yellow ribbon to the tree in front of our house and walked to the corner and back on my dad's arm, which winded me. When I sat down to play the piano, my hands were shaky.

Still, I was on my way to healing.

When I told Bernie and Gert years later that I saw their comforting presence at the moment of illness and death as a gift they had, they were surprised. Bernie had just told me she thought God had shorted her in the talent department.

"We just do what needs to be done," Bernie said.

Gert added, "Mary guides us. We just do the praying." My admiration rolled right off their self-effacing shoulders.

Having taken neither religious nor marriage vows, along their way they vowed to help their loved ones enter the next world and to pray for them diligently and fervently in this world. Uncle Dan, when not circling heaven from the cockpit of his airplane, took part as well. When they entered my room that morning in the hospital, there wasn't a wrinkle of hesitation in their bones. All it took was a phone call from my father, and they were on their way. The few props they needed—rosary beads, extra scapulars, special healing prayers—were close at hand. The ritual, familiar to everyone in the room, was launched without a shred of self-consciousness.

In my generation of questioners, who will know what to do and say at the bedside of the dying ones? Who will get called to these bedsides?

Chapter Two

Self-Consciousness & Dissonance

IN THE DECADES after my surgery, I traveled a long way down the road of my spiritual seeking. I became an urban dweller, except for the summer months. Yet, when I crossed the wide expanse of steps up to the beautiful Basilica of St. Mary that I slowly became a member of, I glanced out at the busy Hennepin Avenue in the heart of downtown Minneapolis and wondered, "If someone sees me here, climbing these steps on a Sunday morning, will they think less of me? Will they judge me as having 'bought in', as being 'less than intelligent', as having blinders on? Will someone assume (wrongly) that I agree with the church's public position on, say, gay marriage or birth control? Am I promoting the church's position by crossing its threshold?"

Such questions would never have occurred to my parents, aunts, and uncles. They were immersed so solidly in their faith and spent their lives sharing this bond, so it was almost as natural to them as breathing. They spent most of their lives living in a small town in the northwoods (Grand Rapids, Minnesota), surrounded by family and mostly likeminded friends. They believed in, and practiced, all the tenets of the Catholic Church.

On the other hand, I have struggled with self-consciousness around and about the religious elements of my faith, and am plagued with periods of questioning it from multiple sides.

I wonder why I am still concerned about being judged for going to church. Perhaps because during my angry period, I, myself, was very judgmental of the "blind" churchgoers. Everyone seemed to do the "right thing" without questioning—I leaned for a while toward the Marxist view of religion as the "opiate of the masses." Many people I knew and loved and thought highly of were not churchgoers. I was not, in all areas of my life, surrounded by fellow practitioners of faith, as the generations before me were. Immigrants came, and still come, to this country for religious freedom, I reminded myself. Yet something lingered, some idea that it was "uncool" or a "sell-out" to belong to a church. I felt a sense of loyalty to my role as a questioner, and in truth, that questioning self occasionally shot to the forefront and I faltered on the steps of the Basilica, even as I was drawn to what I so often found inside.

A friend of mine, who also grew up Catholic, told me she tried but cannot sit in the pew knowing her daughter would be denied the chance to become a minister; knowing that birth control is still considered to be wrong, yet surmising that many of those in the pews at the very least do use birth control. It doesn't feel honest to her.

I have another friend whose son is gay. Although she had been a devout Catholic and still considered herself so, she could no longer enter the church. The exclusion of her son, the judgment of her son, was too painful.

So I sometimes still questioned how it was that I could slip into the pew and find comfort and inspiration in the music and the prayers and the kindness I found in the community. The intellectual part of me wondered and questioned. But the life of the spirit is mysterious and perhaps only peripherally intellectual. Sometimes the mind says one thing and the heart says another. I was touched, deepened, and transformed in very distinctive ways by the music and meaning I experienced in church and by the loving community of people gathered with the shared intention of prayer and spiritual sustenance.

THE 1960S AND '70S changed us all. Directly or indirectly. The bumper sticker "Question Authority" succinctly captured what was happening at deep, echoing levels with far-reaching reverberations. This questioning spread like wildfire: government's (authority's) involvement in Vietnam was not only questioned but protested against; feminism came to the fore; the old ways broke down. They broke down because too many people had been hurt and damaged by the system as it had been. People began to fight to rectify the injustices—racially, politically, religiously, sexually.

Leaving the Catholic Church was part of my response to this era. The sexual abuse by priests that had been covered up appalled me. A good friend of mine and her family had been treated poorly by the parish priest when her parents divorced due to her father's alcoholism. Where was the compassion for the underdog, the less powerful, the hurting?

And so, when I started coming back to the church, I felt a reverse judgmentalism. Toward myself. And I half expected to receive it from others. A great part of my reticence and years of blockage about this book has been about "coming out" as a Catholic. I know that I am such an imperfect one that the real Catholics will not be impressed with me. I fall way short in the "truly practicing" Catholic category. But I also know that the non-religious—especially the ardent ones—could easily see me as weak, blind, having capitulated, for being involved to the extent that I am. And beyond how others see me is the dissonance of belonging to a church whose rituals are a deep part of my spiritual history and who I am, but whose public stance I disagree with on numerous important issues.

One of the beauties of the older people in my family was their lack of self-consciousness, which I think was inextricably connected to their complete belief and the times in which they lived. They not only belonged to the church, they also believed in it. Fully. Without reservation. They were securely, deeply rooted in their faith, which was inextricably connected to their religion. They talked about God and prayer easily. They received regular phone calls from the in-town prayer chain. They prayed. They went to church often and said the rosary daily. I knew I could count on their prayers and when I was in need, I went to them. They took my requests seriously. My Aunt Gert was known to carry the names of my friends, who I requested prayers for, on small slips of paper in her purse so she could always pray for them by name.

Slowly, I realized, in a self-conscious sort of way, I wanted to be a person loved ones could call when they needed prayers. A person who was comfortable praying, in whatever form, for the needs of her loved ones. A great portion of my life had been spent in training for this—the early years in boot camp, then years of fighting this role, then slowly re-entering the training camp, studying with the great teachers, the homegrown mystics in my family.

Self-consciousness may be the curse or the natural byproduct of my generation of questioners—or perhaps one day I will shed it. For now, I work on not letting the self-consciousness and dissonance stop me from what I feel drawn to.

Chapter Three

Canning Peaches on Second Avenue

WHEN I HOVERED close to death in January of 1981, it made perfect sense to have my mom and dad beside me. But what surprised me was how important it was to have Bernie, Gert, and Dan there as well. I had always been drawn to Bernie, Gert, and Dan, always loved visiting them. But after my experience with death's presence, I felt drawn like a magnet to their energy.

After a two-month convalescence in my parents' home, I returned to Seattle for another year, then moved to Minneapolis, where I've been ever since. I began to think of my visits to Bernie, Gert, Dan, and my parents, during the 1980s and 1990s, as a modest pilgrimage, and it always involved what was a romantic notion for me—heading north. Romantic mostly because I thought of myself as a northwoods woman, having grown up in the northwoods town my elders spent their lives in. Romantic because heading north always felt like a return to my roots, to fresher air, cleaner water and the cleansing scents of the woods.

On one such pilgrimage visit on a hot July afternoon in 1991, I noticed the scent of sun-baked pine needles hanging thick in the air. As I stepped outside the door of my parents' modest three-bedroom home, the home ten of us used to live in, I breathed deeply. *Sunburned pine needles.* The potency of the scent careened around inside me and swept into the farthest reaches of my body, laced with layered memories of moments spent among pine trees, gazing at deep greens against endless azure blue and the smell, the incredible smell of summer.

Strolling west a half block, I turned onto Second Avenue. Into my line of vision came the large white home I was headed for, the spacious corner lot dotted with pine trees, apple, and lilac. It was my portal into a different world—a world where the past was always honored and fiercely maintained. A world that seemed innocent, even naïve to me, cloistered, in a way and yet—what did I really know of the human complexities grappled with within its walls? The ones we go to for prayers are also often the receivers of information, the keepers of family secrets.

If it had been a cool or cold day, a plume of smoke would have been rising from Bernie, Gert, and Dan's chimney, rising from the woodstove in the kitchen or living room. If they were napping, the front curtains would be closed—a code everyone in the family knew. But the curtains were open, so I walked up the narrow sidewalk and climbed the five white-painted steps, crossed the painted planks of the porch and rang the doorbell. The wooden bench, painted a bright turquoise, glowed vividly against the white of the house and the porch railing.

Gert opened the rectangular glass door inside while I opened the black-framed screen, and her whole face lit up at the sight of me. She called to Bernie, who came scurrying from the kitchen.

They hugged and kissed me in the small entryway, as if they just couldn't wait for me to come in any further before greeting me. Bernadette and Gertrude were their given names, but we all called

Entrance to *the house*.

them Bernie and Gert—their names rolled off our tongues and were always spoken and thought of in tandem, like the childhood Sesame Street favorites, Bert and Ernie. They were equally inseparable.

"We're sorry we can't just sit and visit," Bernie announced at the doorway after the hugs and kisses. She looked at me ruefully, "We've got ourselves in the thick of a project here." She looked down briefly, then back up at me and added, "But isn't it grand to see you—it's been too long since we laid eyes on you."

"Too long, indeed," Gert said and added, "Now come on out in the kitchen, Patty, and tell us about your life while we work."

From the front entryway we stepped across a threshold into the foyer, the piano on my left and a long living room on my right. Behind the piano, which before I left I would be asked to play, was an open, beautiful mahogany staircase leading to second floor. On top of the piano, as always, was a blue-and-white porcelain sculpture of the Virgin Mary, babe in her arms, and pictures of the two family priests, my cousins. Bernie, Gert, and Dan's nephews and nieces number in the thirties, yet the only two displayed on the piano were the two who became priests. We passed the desk with the black dial phone (most likely one of the few remaining dial phones at that time in North America) as their sensible brown oxfords and my Nike tennis shoes padded over a small tiled crossover into the kitchen.

As we entered the kitchen, I slid my right hand across the smooth woodbin that always held neatly stacked split logs of oak and maple and birch. Next to it was the woodstove. Uncle Dan still split wood regularly, his solid, sturdy body poised over a stump he used as a chopping block. When I showed up to visit, he always proudly pointed out the huge stacks of wood in back, next to the garage. He remembered that in my college years I did an independent study with a woman friend; we lived in a cabin on the north shore of Lake Superior and split our own wood for heat. All of his life he had been splitting wood and only as he slid into his late seventies had he hired a neighbor boy to help him with the splitting.

Gert told me, "Dan and your father are really impressed with Charlie, the neighbor boy. They stood at the window and watched him line up and split log after log—so clean and solid, faster even than Dan."

"I STOPPED BY *the house* this morning," my father often said. It is the home my father's family moved into shortly after their farmhouse burned down. My father, the tenth of twelve children, the fifth of seven sons, was twelve at the time. The family homestead since then, it was at the north end of town, a twenty-minute drive from the forest of birch, pine, oak, and maple their father came from Canada to log in the late 1800s. Their family life was delineated into two time periods: before the fire (on the farm) and after the fire. The heartbeat of family life after the fire was felt most clearly in *the house*.

My parents, seven siblings and I lived a block and a half away from *the house*. Jerome's family two blocks the other direction. One aunt of mine, Mary, left town: she and her husband raised their seven children in Duluth, eighty miles away. Aunt Eleanor and her family lived in Florida for years but always returned to the hometown for summers, and returned to live there in their later years. The rest of my aunts and uncles and numerous cousins (while growing up) all lived within a mile's radius of *the house*.

All these homes and families and lives connected to one center, its common pulse emanating from *the house*, from the unmarried sisters and brother. We, the streams of nephews and nieces and our children and our children's children, were like veins and arteries flowing away from but always returning to the center of the heartbeat, Bernie and Gert and Dan. They were the keepers of the family stories, history, even secrets, as well as the family home and hearth. Bernie, Gert and Dan—when he was not flying—were always there, greeting us with a kiss on the cheeks, a hug and exclamations over how long it had been since they laid eyes on us or how beautiful our children were. Every child was celebrated, anticipated, and prayed for by Bernie and Gert (and Dan), who had no children of their own.

FOLLOWING BERNIE AND GERT, I reached the heart of the kitchen, the table.

Gert pulled out a chair at one end and said, grinning, "Now, have ye a sit-down and don't mind us working!"

Above: Sidewalk leading to *the house*. The author's father is at the porch.
Below: Author's father entering the kitchen at *the house*.

Aunt Gert and Uncle Dan in the kitchen at *the house*.

Bernie added, "Yes, God love ya, today is canning day, so we have to keep working!"

A huge vat of peaches simmered on the stove with thinly sliced orange rinds floating on top. The smell in the air was so fresh and so sweet I wanted to spend the rest of the day just breathing it in. The two of them examined the vat, Bernie giving it a slow stir and then a nod to Gert.

"It's ready," she said.

Gert moved a box of mason jars from the counter to the table. She looked at me, "How's Chris's work going? How's Caitlin?" They always wanted to know about my husband's work. He taught in an inner city high school and they listened intensely to his tales of teaching kids whose lives were marked not only by poverty but also by guns and violence, genuine concern etched in the lines of their faces as one of them exclaimed, "Oh, mercy, so young and they have guns? Drugs? Doesn't anybody love them?"

The other would echo, "Isn't it a fright? The world just isn't the place it used to be, is it?"

Headshaking and a palpable, puzzled sadness filled the room during such discussions.

When I first told them the man I was in love with was divorced, Bernie's face fell. "Oh no, Patty," she said. "How could you?" I cringed at the genuinely stricken tone of her voice and the disappointment folded into the wrinkles across her face. But that wasn't the half of it. When Chris and I first fell head over heels in love with each other, he was not yet legally divorced from his first wife. I entertained the thought of saying to Bernie and Gert, "Better divorced than married," but opted to keep it to myself.

Bernie and Gert met Chris the night his theater troop performed in our small hometown, about six months before I ended up in the hospital. Chris, who I barely knew yet, although we were definitely eyeing each other, didn't have a clue these two white-haired ladies were related to me. But after the performance, which everyone in town turned out for, the actors mingled with the audience. Dressed in full Shakespearean costume, Chris took Bernie's hand into his own and dramatically kissed the top of it. For days afterward, each time Gert would tell the story, Bernie blushed like a schoolgirl.

I hated to tell them about the divorce but knew I must—for how else could I explain the young boy who came with Chris? The moment I told them was a strained one. I don't know what moral dilemmas they weeded their way through in the months after this encounter. Their strict Catholic morality hadn't ever been so close to a divorce, although in the years to come there would be quite a few divorces among their nephews and nieces. Perhaps "judge not and you shall not be judged" won out, or remember to have "faith, love, and charity, and the greatest of these is love." Perhaps, quite simply, their love for me was stronger than their need to question my choice. Four years later, they drove the two hundred miles south to my wedding, and helped my young stepson who was distraught at the last minute over dress pants with a falling-down hem. Bernie and Gert, just down the hall in the same hotel, worked alongside my mother to pin up his pants at the last minute, smooth his hair, and calm him down—a memory of our wedding day he often talked about in the following years.

In the kitchen I sat at the wooden table, my elbows rested on the worn-smooth, yellow vinyl tablecloth. Light streamed in through the large west-facing window above the double sink. If I stood at the sink

Aunt Gert and the author in the kitchen at *the house*.

I looked out on their lush backyard vegetable garden: tall stalks of corn; thick leaves around budding tomato plants; rows of carrots; and a row halved between purple-veined beet greens and tall wisps of onions. At the north edge of the garden, stacked against the garage, were the neatly layered, criss-crossed piles of split wood. The window above the sink, as always, was sparkling clean, making the experience of looking through it crystal clear, heightened almost like a hallucination.

White cupboards and light yellow walls, partially covered with a subtly patterned wallpaper, made the room feel airy, uplifting, and pleasant. The small shelves above the sink were lined with prayer cards and a small, three-inch plastic statue of the Virgin Mary, her arms held open at her side in what Gert informed me was her Miraculous Medal position. As Gert told me, the Virgin Mary appeared to St. Theresa of Lisieux in the 1200s and asked her to have a medal made in her honor, in this pose. Gert added, "Endless rays of grace flow from her fingertips."

Over the years I became fascinated with their devotion to the Virgin Mary and found myself collecting small Mary statues. One of my favorites glowed in the dark and sat (and still sits) on my writing desk. Her hands are outstretched at her sides, palms open, and I love the thought of endless rays of grace pouring out—toward me, toward my writing, toward my family. But for so many years, I shied away from this part of Bernie and Gert.

During my wild years, I didn't ask questions about Mary. We talked then about the weather, the classes I was taking, the camp for mentally handicapped children I worked at in the summer, their garden, other family members. Always, I kept at bay the thought: *if they only knew who I really was.* Why was I still so drawn to them, I, who out of so many nephews and nieces, was in some ways the wildest? I was proud of my wildness, but I also struggled with Catholic guilt and a haunting sense of sinfulness.

Bernie and Gert never spoke of my having left the church, although I'm sure my parents enlisted their prayers on the behalf of my soul. But even then, hiding so much of myself, slip-sliding toward them and away from them into a world so removed from theirs, I still wanted to see them. And there was always the piano to connect us. I played and, loving the music, they gathered around the piano, or they broke into jigging behind me. My uncle, when he was home and not flying the skies, played his seemingly effortless jazz. I loved and admired his ear for music and natural talent for jazz piano. Our mutual love of music was always a common meeting ground, one that drew us close and sustained us.

I was happy that in their aging years, I was a married woman, with children, who had found her way back to the church. I was, however, what my father would call a "cafeteria Catholic," meaning I took (and take) what I want—the beauty, ritual, liturgy, the music—and leave the rest, like my political disagreements with the church. These older relatives of mine were conservative in most ways, including politically. When they would get going on the evils of homosexuality or right to life issues, I would get quiet. I knew there was no changing them.

I did let slip a couple of years later that I'd voted for Bill Clinton. For the second time in my life Bernie looked at me and asked, "Oh, Patty, how could you?" The familiar stricken look flashed across her face again.

But the day of the peach canning, no controversial issues floated to the surface. We just enjoyed each other's company. I was a married woman with a troubled college-aged stepson and a young daughter. I was still raw in my grief over a recent miscarriage. My son was not yet conceived and Ronald Reagan, whom they loved and voted for, was at the country's helm. Bernie was on duty in front of the stove. With a large aluminum scoop, she ladled the hot, sweet peaches and juice into a jar, took two steps away from the stove and handed it to Gert who, with lithe quick movements, set the hot jar on the table, wiped it dry with an old dishcloth, then set it off to one side of the table, the side away from where I was sitting.

By the time Gert set one jar down, Bernie had another one ready for her. Bernie's space was at the stove, Gert's at the table. Bernie would step away from the stove and hand the next jar to Gert just as Gert turned back from the jar she had wiped clean and set in place. Bernie was adept with the ladle, knowing just how much to scoop, how to get the right combination of peaches, juice, and orange rinds.

Laughing, Gert advised me, "Now, listen for the popping sound, Patty, it's coming soon."

Pop!

"There it is now," Bernie said. "Now we know it's sealed."

Bernie continued talking, without slowing her canning pace a bit. "Our favorite thing, you know, is to bring out a jar of these peaches in the middle of winter. They smell sweet now, but come a January evening, it's like having a breath of fresh summer air."

"We'll send you home with a jar, Patty," Gert added. "Save it for a special night in winter."

There was maybe four feet between the stove and the table. They never bumped into one another. They never stood idle. Their movements were relaxed and fluid. A peacefulness floated in the air, a camaraderie, a focus toward the task at hand, that settled into some deep place inside me. The lyrical rhythm of their movements, separate yet together, lulled me, along with the sweet scent in the air, the angle of midafternoon sun streaming in through the spotlessly clean kitchen window. Overhead, dishtowels and rinsed plastic bags hung, pinned to a clothesline strung above the stove to the far corner. It was this detail of their kitchen that always struck my husband, an eccentric detail I was so used to I didn't notice it the way he did.

As we visited, the two of them waxed poetic about how perfect the peaches in the store were for canning. "We couldn't help ourselves, Patty," Bernie said, shaking her head at herself and letting the full force of her clear blue eyes rest on me. "We had to buy two crates. Then we had to wait for Dan to come home so he could carry them in." As she spoke, Gert murmured, "Perfect for canning, so smooth and plump."

Dan, no matter what his age, was always their younger brother. His role vacilated between being the man about the house they couldn't do without and an irritant without which their lives would be far more serene, although way less interesting. "The thorn between two roses," Bernie called him, laughing. Her eyes lit up; the angry edge in her was delighted with this image. Gert's smile was more subdued, but irrepressible.

They both complained about Dan, but Bernie was more vociferous, that edge would creep into her voice. "That Dan, he wants to know why we don't read more. Well, if I weren't so busy cooking and cleaning, I would." She was taller than Gert, bigger boned, quicker with her opinions. Her short white hair curled close to her head, accenting her ruddy complexion and sturdy stature. Freckles and wrinkles rippled across her fair skin.

Gert was smaller, more softspoken—her job, it seemed, had always been to smooth out the rougher edges of her older sister. But there was no question: they were on the same team.

"Yes," Gert added, quietly. "He sits and reads in the living room, while we make dinner. He's always giving us books." She wrinkled her nose at this. "You know, political books. Pat Robertson. Phyllis Schaffley. You know how he loves Phyllis Schaffley. And Pat Buchanan. We're interested but we just don't have enough time to read."

She shrugged her shoulders, gestured to the kitchen at large, as if it should be obvious how much time all these tasks took: the cooking, cleaning, canning, gardening, not to mention all the time they spent helping out at church, and, most of all, praying. Gert's silvery gray hair, cut close to her head, settled in small curls near her ears.

Of course they also delighted in telling me about Dan's flight plans. "He's in Canada, up at his camp right now," Bernie told me. "He's supposed to come home Friday for a few days, but you never know." Here there was another shoulder shrug and a knowing look, because we all knew there was no predicting exactly when Dan and his plane might reappear in the skies over our heads.

Gert added, "He's got a load of priests up there right now and then next week he's got some of his mining people coming in." Uncle Dan opened his fishing camp to relatives, business friends and always to the priests who needed a place to "get away" from their parish roles and duties.

I noticed the freckles splattered up and down Gert's long, thin arms. Steam roiled up from the huge vat and lost itself in the clean air of the high-ceilinged kitchen. Interspersed with their comments about the plump and irresistible peaches was their concern for me.

"We heard you lost your baby. We were so sorry to hear that," Bernie said. She was not afraid to bring up the hard things in life. She carried on, "We're praying for you."

Gert's gentle voice added, "We're praying the good Lord will give you another one." They didn't use the word "miscarriage" and I was strangely grateful to them for that. It was as if "miscarriage" was too modern a word, too technical. The truth was I had lost a baby, that is exactly what I had lost, and there was a moment of shared grief in that kitchen as I sat and they passed the jars. It comforted me to know they were praying for something I was at the moment too afraid to let myself want again.

"We're praying for Caitlin, too, for her bladder condition. How is she?"

"Much better," I said. "She hasn't had an infection in almost a year now."

"Oh, we're so glad to hear that," Gert said.

Bernie added, "Thank the Lord."

Then Gert told me she used to get recurring bladder infections too but when she went to Lourdes twenty years before, she was healed. Hadn't had one since.

Off to the side of the kitchen table waited their small, black, well-used prayer books, with typed sheets of special prayers, frayed from so much use, inserted here and there. Besides praying for my daughter's health, my stepson's tendency to let drugs and alcohol get in the way of him keeping up at college, and for my husband and I to have another child, were endless other intentions among my aunts, uncles, cousins, brothers and sisters, as well as close family friends.

Bernie's head was going from side to side, "Yes, " she said. "There's never a shortage of things to pray for in this family . . . so many people."

"Yes," Gert echoed. "There's always something."

They shook their heads in a good-natured way. This was their calling, praying for all these people. And if they shook their heads at how busy it kept them, if they complained a little about the sheer size of this fold of sheep, they also exuded a genuine sense of caring. A sense they could do nothing better with their lives than sit at the kitchen

Gert's eightieth birthday. Seated: Aunts Eleanor, Mary, Gert, Bernie, Margaret, Uncle Dan. Standing: the author's father.

A family get-together in the early 1990s. Standing: Uncle Dan, Uncle Ted, the author's father, Aunt Gert. Seated: Aunt Margaret, Aunt Eleanor, Aunt Bernie, Aunt Mary.

table with their prayer books and list off the litany of Hoolihan-related needs: there were marriages that needed bolstering, a depressed cousin who needed a change of career, another cousin who was unemployed, a cousin who lost her daughter to a heart condition and needed prayers to help her through her grief. There were the ailments among the original clan, increasing as they aged, and this list, incomplete as it was, was constantly changing and being added to.

Bernie and Gert echoed each other, finished each other's sentences, affirmed what one said while the other was still speaking. There was no sense of competition between them, only a friendly and natural tendency to spill one's version of a story onto the other's version. No exclamation, no point of view, no story, would have been complete without the other's input.

Before I left they took a short break to pour me cranberry juice with a slice of lemon in it. From the corner of the counter, Gert pulled out a round tin and opened it. It was one of my favorites—her homemade oatmeal raisin cookies.

"Play us a tune before you leave, will you, Patty?" Bernie's eyes were bright as she asked.

"Oh," Gert chimed in, "would you? Would you play our favorite, you know, the *Doctor Zhivago* one?"

Months would go by without my playing it, but I could still sit at a piano and play "Lara's Theme" from memory. For years it was the favorite request from these aunts of mine, as well as from my parents. I learned it well and deeply. Another song I had memorized along the way, "Song of the Soul," was written by a feminist, lesbian singer and songwriter, Cris Williamson. She was a musician I discovered during my years of listening only to female musicians, and reading only books authored by women, during my early to mid-twenties. Those were the years I eschewed marriage and motherhood and organized religion as conventions I would never take part in. When I finished "Lara's Theme," I played it for them.

Enthusiasm lilted its way into Gert's voice. "What is that song?" she asked.

"It's called 'Song of the Soul,'" I replied.

Bernie's hand slapped her thigh, "I *knew* it had to be a soul song."

"Yes," Gert echoed, "it feels like a spiritual song. It's lovely, isn't it?"

I smiled happily and nodded as I played the chorus one last time, on the edge of both laughter and tears. I remembered discovering this song at a concert, surrounded by women holding hands with each other—a sight which might well horrify Bernie and Gert. I remembered conversations with women during those years of my life when people who were narrow-minded or conservative were considered harmful. Yet there was not a trace of harm in my conservative and "narrow-minded" aunts. I remembered another time I played this song while a room full of women sang at a twelve-step retreat. It had been a weekend of tears and laughter, and the song was part of a final celebration and ceremony. "Let in the light it will heal you, and you can feel you, sing out a song of the soul."

The joy I felt on that retreat I felt again with my aunts. Bernie and Gert felt it too, the joy in the chords, the melody, the spirit of the song. It was our own private, intimate retreat.

Something shifted inside me. I felt the different worlds I had lived in converge toward a common center, a common connecting thread. Music of the soul transcended dogmatic Catholicism, diehard feminism, political liberalism, the conservatism of old-world religion. Music of the soul underscored and encompassed the best from all the "isms" I had known, fought, misunderstood, cherished, run from.

Music was the bridge, the soul connection. That day, the piano and I were its conduit.

Too soon, late afternoon sun struck the stained glass window behind the piano at the bottom of the stairs. Reluctantly, I slid off the piano bench, hugged them both, and kissed their freckled cheeks. Bernie felt thinner than she had ever felt before, closer to Gert's size.

"Give our love to Chris now, and Kaleb, and Caitlin," Gert said.

Bernie added, "Tell them it's been too long since we laid eyes on them."

I crossed the threshold to the outer door as Gert exclaimed, "Your peaches, Patty. Don't forget your peaches!"

The author and her two children with Gert and Bernie in front of the piano at *the house* in 1995.

She scurried back to the kitchen table and returned to gently hand the jar over as Bernie reminded me, "Now, open that some night in winter and think of this warm summer day. The peaches are delicious on vanilla ice cream."

I opened the screen door, crossed the painted planks, and clattered back down the stairs before I turned to wave. They both stood in the doorway, waving back.

The peach jar felt warm in my hand as I headed north down Second Avenue, the sweet scent of peach and orange floating up and down every hair on my wild, unruly, unpredictable head of red hair. I pulled a clump of hair towards my nose and breathed deeply, letting the smell enter every cell of my body, wanting the scent—its freshness, its innocence, its hints of love—to float in my hair forever.

Chapter Four

Saying Goodbye To the House On Second Avenue

"The dead are only one song away from the living."
 –Louise Erdrich (*The Master Butcher's Singing Club*)

*T*HE HOUSE HAD a good long run—for seventy-five years it housed Hoolihan family life. As much as the whole extended family would have loved for the house at 835 Second Avenue to always be there, its trio of welcoming loved ones greeting us at the front door, offering visits around the woodstove or the kitchen table, time changes everything.

INEVITABLY, AFTER BOTH Dan and Bernie had passed away, *the house* was too big for Gert alone—and too lonely. This was obvious to my father, who worried about Gert, his older sister, and *the house*. He checked in on both daily.

Over the course of months, perhaps a year, the sorting out of seventy-five years of belongings and history happened. Gert hired an estate person (a devout Catholic, of course). She and my dad, and sometimes me or my mom or a cousin of mine, helped. But Gert really wanted to be hands-on. Until near the end of the process. Running out of time and energy, she began to let go, to lose track of things. At that time, the only ones left of the original clan of twelve were Gert, my dad, and their sister Margaret, who was in assisted living in Duluth. Gert was in the process of moving there—eighty miles away—and the two of them would be inseparable for the next few

Grandparents' fiftieth wedding anniversary. Standing: Uncle Ted, Uncle Dan, Aunt Gert, the author's father, Aunt Bernie, Aunt Margaret, Uncle Bill, Aunt Eleanor. Seated: Uncle Jerry, Grandfather, Grandmother, Aunt Mary.

years. Gert had a remarkable ability to partner up with siblings. For so long it was Bernie, then she and Dan became very close, and then it was Gert and Marg, peacefully side by side, twenty-four hours a day.

THE DAY of the estate sale for family only we gathered: cousins, siblings, Gert, my parents. Out of the thirty-two of us in my generation, only a few were missing. There were price tags on everything: furniture, tablecloths, jewelry. It was a Saturday, the first of October, and the autumn sun was brilliant, lighting up golden and auburn leaves all around *the house.*

A few of us gathered in the kitchen with Gert. She was especially bright-eyed and reminded us it was the anniversary of Ma and Pa's wedding. The estate date sale had been chosen for a number of reasons, but there we were in the kitchen realizing that the legacy that began on October 1, 1901, with their marriage, was coming to a close with all of us gathered on October 1, 2005. It was an unplanned and powerful synchronicity. She told us stories of their wedding day: "I wasn't there, of course, but Mama always told us it was so warm the men were taking off their jackets and walking around in their shirt sleeves. In Ontario, Canada—imagine that. Warm like it is today." She looked out the kitchen window wistfully. The Mary statue still held her post in the side yard just outside the kitchen. Tall pines whispered in the mild breeze.

The author's paternal grandparents, "Ma" and "Pa," in *the house*.

I fingered tablecloths. Chose a few things: a shamrock-covered teapot with matching creamer and sugar bowl, a couple of Bernie's and Gert's hats, a jacket of Uncle Dan's. Then, there was a brief discussion about the piano. I was contemplating it when a cousin

The author and Aunt Gert at the piano (along with a family friend). Taken during the last days of *the house*.

came by. "Patty, you should have that piano. You played it more than any of us."

That's all I needed to decide to take the piano.

When I told Gert, she said, "Oh good. Except this means I'll never hear you play it again." She looked longingly, wistfully at the piano.

I FLASHED ON the five days I stayed at *the house* with Gert after Dan died. Every evening after dinner she and I sat at the kitchen table and said the rosary together. Then she went upstairs to get ready for bed, which always took her awhile. I played the piano then: her favorite songs, my favorite songs. I imagined the music swirling upstairs, comforting her, she who was the last one living in this house. I imagined the melody floating two miles away and easing my father's loss of this brother he had been close to all of his life. I knew my dad was sleeping better knowing I was with Gert. Dad was with my mom, and I was with his sister, in the days between their brother Dan's death and burial. The first night when I played "Danny Boy"—a song Dan sang with me many times and which made us all think of him—the tears rolled down my cheeks as I played.

"You'll come and find the place where I am lying, kneel and say an *ave* there for me."

Oh, how I missed him. His voice. His jovial presence. So there I was at the piano, quietly weeping and playing, and Gert was upstairs, listening, getting her ninety-year-old body ready for bed.

For the next few years I went to Duluth for St. Patrick's Day

Uncle Dan at the piano, with Aunt Gert and the author behind him, at *the house*.

and my parents met me there. My dad, even close to ninety, was still driving. We would take Gert and Marg out for lunch and return to St. Ann's, their assisted living place, where there was a piano in the main room. I would make arrangements ahead of time with the recreation director, and we gathered around the baby grand piano while I played a few tunes. My dad would rise to sing "When Irish Eyes Are Smiling" ("When your sweet lilting laughter's like some fairy song and your eyes twinkle bright as can be..."), "Galway Bay" ("But they might as well go chasing after moonbeams or light a penny candle from a star"), followed by "Danny Boy" and "My Wild Irish Rose." Residents wandered in, sat in the chairs, and listened. When I looked up from the piano, I saw smiling faces. But the tone of the piano was different than the old family upright. The room, instead of being a cozy and extremely familiar foyer, was large and open to many. The sound, instead of surrounding us, floated out into all that space. Still, the songs comforted and inspired us, the music entered us, and for a moment the sensation was timeless. My dad was still singing, "When Irish hearts are happy all the world seems bright and gay."

My dad, always happy to sing, said to me on one of those visits to Duluth, "Patty, we should take this show on the road." He cracked

Author's father at the piano in *the house*.

open a wide grin and laughed. He was all of eighty-nine when he said this. I absolutely loved it when I could get him singing, just like I loved it when I could get my uncle to play the piano. And I was grateful in the days after Dan's death to bring a small piece of comfort into Gert's loss and mine by playing the songs we had shared with him so many times. It was through song that I could most feel a connection to Uncle Dan's spirit.

Back at the estate sale, I knew Gert spoke the truth. The piano was moved to my home in Minneapolis. She moved to assisted living in Duluth. And she never would hear me play that piano—the Hoolihan piano since 1902—again.

There we were, my cousins and I, wandering around the house that had been the center of our shared extended family life. Nobody was in a hurry to claim specific items. We were wandering, letting memories flow between us. Gert was the grande dame, mostly holding court in the kitchen, telling stories about items we asked about. My mom and dad were there for a while but then they left. I think it was too painful for my dad to watch for too long, whereas Gert's maternal instincts wouldn't let her leave. She was the last remaining guardian of *the house*.

As I moved toward the front door, something unexpected happened. One of my cousins came up to me and asked, in a whisper, "Do you go to church?" There was an intensity to the question that gave me pause. I answered yes, that I belonged to the Basilica in Minneapolis. And she said, "That may be one of the few places I could go."

"What about you?" I asked.

She shook her head, no. She added, "It's too painful. I watched my dad all his life feel like he wasn't good enough—and the church was always part of that. It's just too painful for me."

I have thirty-two first cousins. Three cousins joined religious orders, devotedly practicing their vocations—two priests and a nun. Some have been faithful churchgoers all their lives, those who have consistently and continually found sustenance and comfort there.

Others have left the church for a whole host of reasons, most of which boil down to feeling wounded, misunderstood, angered by injustices, or too constricted or judged by religious tenets. Some have joined other denominations, which carry less "emotional baggage." Some of us have left and returned, taking time to sort through what it means to us, then and now.

Collectively, we cover a wide continuum—from fervently religious to fallen away and many points in between. Yet we are all direct descendants of an intense, familial practice of Catholicism.

"Do you go to church?" Whispered in the entryway to 835 Second Avenue, this place of warm welcoming hospitality, crucifixes, and rosaries in every room. The dining room hosted more home Masses than one could count. The phone rang often with someone on the other end requesting prayers.

The question, and all the unspoken questions behind it, rattled around inside my heart and mind.

Chapter Five

Uncle Dan: Wildness & Piety

"In a spirit of appreciation and gratitude we give thanks for the attitude Uncle Dan has lived by—that life is an adventure, a sacred adventure."
–Bidding prayer spoken at the celebratory Mass in honor of Dan's eightieth birthday

WHEREAS *THE HOUSE* gave us the hearth to gather around, Uncle Dan's personality, his airplane and his Canadian camp gave us adventure, flight, nature, wilderness, joy. *The house* grounded our spirits, but camp and Uncle Dan embodied opportunities to free our spirits, to connect on a deep level with the natural world. While Bernie and Gert were rooted, Dan's form of faith and spirit took to the skies. He was, as my brother Matt so aptly said to me, all about possibility.

WHEN I WAS a child, we often played softball or kickball in our backyard. Our yard was long and ringed with pine trees at the northern end of town, just down the block and around the corner from the house on Second Avenue. I sometimes wonder how much of our cellular structures are embodied in one clear, vivid memory of childhood, for more than once I remember being on third base, ready for my breakaway to home, when I heard the sound of a small airplane—the one and only sound that could pull my attention away from the need to run to home base and score.

When the airplane sound drifted into our auditory awareness, my brothers and sisters and I stopped our play and turned our eyes skyward. Our friends, used to the routine, joined us in scanning the horizon. Were we looking for God, looking heavenward? The moment of pause, of searching the sky always had that larger-than-life feel to it, tinged with a hint of reverence. As a small airplane cleared the distant treeline we began to wave our arms wildly and shout, "Uncle Dan! Uncle Dan!" Of course, if it was him he couldn't hear us, but that didn't matter. As the airplane flew closer, we could see its defining feature: floats hanging beneath. Next, we recognized the distinctive hum of the engine: the Stinson. And finally, we could see its beige coloring with a white stripe along the side.

The whole field was now filled with youngsters jumping up and down, waving and shouting. Uncle Dan circled above us, flying as low as he could. Then he tipped his wing to us, a final salute, and flew off toward Lily Lake, the airport pond.

When we returned to our game, adrenaline pumped in our veins, especially the Hoolihan veins. Among our friends, we lived in one of the smallest houses, wore our neighbors' hand-me-down clothes. But that was our uncle who had just tipped his wing to us.

Uncle Dan on the right with a friend, ready to take off in the Stinson on skis.

In this memory, which is really a series of memories, my feet were planted firmly on the ground. Yet the way Uncle Dan suddenly appeared in the skies overhead was close to godlike. And the way he got in his airplane and flew anywhere made the wider world feel more accessible. To sell grease to mining companies, he flew and landed on lakes all over Canada and the United States. In the winter he put skis on his plane and flew to his camp, deep in the Ontario wilderness. Once there, he put up ice for the icehouse. He told me about taking off from camp when it was fifty degrees below zero after using two blowtorches to warm the engine. "The cold air gives great lift, though, great lift," he said, lifting his arms to demonstrate.

Uncle Dan's day-to-day life from his airplane was dependent on weather, wind patterns, and the geography of the land and water beneath him. He always had a general plan for where he was headed next, but when he might arrive was an entirely different matter. If the weather was clear, he could fly all day, covering hundreds of miles of wide-open space, landing only to fill his gas tank. If a strong wind or storm blew its way into his path, he eyeballed what was beneath him and landed to outwait the storm. He always found shelter of some sort and always had an incredible ability to trust in finding his own way—rarely the same way twice. You could say he flew on faith, on wings of trust in the ways of the world, and his own skills. Or perhaps, in the words of a favorite family hymn, "on angels' wings."

Once I was having a conversation with Bernie and Gert about their angels when Gert leaned toward me and said quietly, "You know, even Dan has talked recently about having an angel with him when he's flying. And I've always thought he must, because he's always been so lucky up in his airplane."

I often think of Uncle Dan as a "seer". From the air he could see way out in front of him, and that seemed true of him in so many ways. The property he bought in Canada beckoned to him from the air over sixty years ago. Did he see what potential joy and sanctuary could be there for so many of his loved ones? What drew him first was a long stretch of sand beach, perfect for pulling a seaplane up on. He started out landing there just to take a swim. Imagine flying over Canadian wilderness, looking for a good place to touch down and swim. Imagine

Canoe trip with friends to Uncle Dan's camp in the late 1970s. As we paddled hard, he landed and visited us! From left: Anne K., Kay C., Sue S., author, Uncle Dan, Andra P.

maneuvering through wide open skies, surveying the beauty of undeveloped wilderness. Imagine envisioning a place he could build, run, sustain and share with his family and friends. What an amazing combination of freedom and self-direction (from a northern Minnesota farm boy). I could spend years studying it.

Sometime in the 1960s, he bought the land and began to fly in guys and supplies to build the camp. Today, there are still two storage sheds, an icehouse (with authentic chunks of lake ice buried in sawdust), a fish house, and the camp itself. Nothing fancy: open shelves in the kitchen, bunk beds, a woodstove, a cooking stove, a pump at the sink. Every summer from the time I was ten until my twenties, my parents drove our station wagon as far as Atikokan, Ontario. There Uncle Dan would meet us on a small lake nearby and fly us to camp, in two loads, for our annual week of wilderness life. We swam, fished, picked blueberries, longed to see moose and worried about seeing bear. Full moons out on Mabel Lake, with nobody else around, just a ring of trees and water, were spectacular. Thanks to

The Stinson, safe in its Grand Rapids Harbor, with the author's father and Uncle Dan.

Uncle Dan and his floatplane, I developed a deep and abiding love for wilderness.

One of my cousins said of Uncle Dan, "It seemed to me like he was almost an extraterrestrial." I could see what she meant—there was something almost other-worldly about his personality and how he lived. He also really knew his business; he was smart and capable. Sharing what he had was important to him; he opened up worlds for all of us—his huge extended family and numerous friends—and created a space in Canada that brought joy and a connection to the Canadian wilds to everyone who went there. He flew in many of us family members, priests and friends over the years.

Sometimes he came over to our house on a Saturday morning and asked if any of us wanted to go flying. I always said yes. Out we'd go to the airport and up into the sky to check out our hometown from the air. I could always pick out Deer Lake, the turquoise one north of town. Once, in later years, when my siblings and I were staying at a nearby resort with our children, Uncle Dan landed and took all of our children up for rides. He had small squares of duct tape smattered all over the plane. "Hail damage," he casually informed us. Every small hail dent had been covered with that gray tape. My brother told me about a month later that the FAA had caught wind of the duct tape and grounded his airplane until he replaced the Ceconite fabric. My brother and I looked at each other, gulped and then grinned. And to think, we had sent our children up in that plane!

That's the kind of trust I always had in my uncle—and particularly in his flying. Incredibly skilled, he never had an accident in more than fifty years of flying.

In the summer of 1999, Uncle Dan met me, my children, and several other family members on Perch Lake outside of Atikokan. We were just unloading our gear from the car when we heard the Stinson beyond the trees. We stopped what we were doing and watched. A float plane landing is a beautiful sight—the spray swooshed up on either side as the airplane gracefully slid onto the water. It's a movement from fluid air to buoyant water. An airplane held up by currents and windstream is suddenly, almost magically, a water voyager. There's that moment of contact, when the long floats switch from riding air to riding water, that makes all things seem possible.

When we flew out of camp days later, I sat in back with my then-three-year-old son, Kelly, in my lap, my daughter, Caitlin, beside me and my sister, Jane, up in the copilot's seat. After the long, slow, meditative positioning of the plane in front of a long stretch of water, all of us gazed at the wild, unpopulated beauty around us, Uncle Dan pulled both doors closed and revved up the engine. The propeller went into a dizzying spin and my son plugged his ears as we

Duct tape repair job. The author and her daughter Caitlin with Uncle Dan in 1991. Just finished a great flight!

Camp, located in the Canadian wilderness.

moved full speed across the water. There was the arc of white spray on either side, the majestic view speeding by the window, and then, liftoff! Suddenly, we were airborne, riding currents of air and wind and mystery, rising higher and higher over the trees.

Behind my sunglasses, tears fell down my cheeks. I wept for the sheer beauty of flight, with regret that I hadn't flown much with my uncle in my busy adult life. I wept in memory of all the joyful flights in and out of this special Canadian camp with him. I wondered if it might be the last time I flew out with Uncle Dan as the pilot. It was an incredibly beautiful August day, and I felt wildly lucky to be airborne with my pilot uncle in the eighty-second year of his life.

During my rebellious late teens and early twenties, I sometimes misinterpreted Uncle Dan's free-spiritedness. I wanted to liken it to my own need to break rules, but he didn't have the need I did to break rules. Instead, he created his own rules. He created a life for himself which in some ways was beyond and outside of so many small rules. One of the stories about him is what a bad driver he was. He had several car accidents in his youth, and the story goes that this is part of

The author and her parents beside the Stinson on the beach at the Canadian camp.

why he started flying. Maybe that's why he was such a bad driver—because he was out there making his own rules. In contrast, he was an almost flawless pilot. And he was so often flying over wilderness that the factors of wind and weather shaped his flying, the rules of nature rather than man. On joyrides he dipped and rolled the plane to thrill (or terrify) his passengers. But he was also cautious, wise, and respectful of the power of natural forces: if conditions were questionable, he landed or stayed grounded.

Because so much of my rulebreaking was about church and religion, and because Dan made a point of teasing Bernie and Gert about their piety, I once or twice gravely misread his own relationship to piety. The most memorable of these times took place when I was a senior in college. My younger brother, Bill, was in high school and a rising star on a team working its way to the state hockey tournament. I came home from college and my best childhood friend, Kay, and my sister, Jane, and I drove with Uncle Dan the thirty miles to a regional tournament. We chose to drive with Dan in part because we loved him but also because we knew that in my parents' car we would have to say the rosary, as we did on every road trip with them. I counted

Uncle Dan in his Elmer Fudd hat.

on Uncle Dan being too fun-loving and rebellious himself to insist on praying while on our way to a rollicking good hockey game.

But I was wrong. And to further complicate things, neither Kay (who had gone to Catholic school with me) nor I had been to church since we left high school (the 1970s!) and in the small confinement of Dan's car, with him leading the prayers and the three of us responding, something froze up in me and her. I actually forgot certain lines of prayers, which is astounding to me because back in church, after many years away, almost all of the prayers flowed back into my memory. He reprimanded us for not knowing our prayers better. It was clear he was disappointed in us. Years later, when he came to my near-deathbed along with Bernie and Gert, I felt differently about his piety. But the night of the hockey game, his wild-renegade persona unveiled in a way I had never seen before his own fierce relationship with faith and prayer and form. A part of me was shocked and a little disappointed. Deep inside me, I felt chastened. And alongside that feeling, there were threads of loneliness, aloneness, confusion.

The hockey game was incredibly exciting. We won and a week later, Uncle Dan joined our family in Minneapolis/St. Paul for the state tournament. Every time the marquee in the middle of the huge arena flashed goal or assist by Bill Hoolihan, the section that housed our clan went wild. We jumped up and down, cheering with a wild and deep frenzy, hugging and high-fiving each other. It was a thrilling time in our family. In face-offs, the chants of the cheers would pierce the quiet concentration of the players and I would watch my brother, stick in one hand, eyes on the puck, as he took his right hand and made the sign of the cross before the referee threw the puck down.

Hockey has been close to a second religion in my family. That year when my brother was star defenseman, leading scorer and captain of the team that won first place at State, hockey was at its peak. The night of the final game, the hotel management came to our room and told us to quiet down. My father was perfecting his enthusiastic rendition of "Oklahoma," joined by Uncle Dan and a group of my siblings and in-laws piled on beds and on the floor, giddy with excitement. In shorthand, "alcohol was involved." There I was, immersed in my wild college years and busted by hotel management—but I wasn't the rowdy one; the ringleaders were my dad and older brothers. I was just trying to keep up with them!

For the most part in my extended family, alcohol was an accepted way to "let loose." Practiced with some regularity, there existed hugely differing degrees on the continuum. On the whole, women were more restrained. My memory of that night in the hotel is a joyful one. We were celebrating together. But it was tinged with an awareness of the multiple levels of breaking out of the confinement of our ordinary lives and roles. My breaking out was more hidden, less acceptable. The drinking was acceptable to a point which was often invisible from the outside until it was way past its mark.

Its problematic legacy shows up somewhere in every branch of my family tree.

Chapter Six

A Good, Home-Cooked Meal

Two of my father's and Uncle Dan's brothers disappeared for days on drinking binges. When they did return, they returned to *the house*, to Bernie and Gert.

I wonder when the knock on the door came. At night? In the early morning hours? Late afternoon? Did they come to the front door or the side door? Bernie and Gert would be expecting the knock, having heard through the grapevine that one or the other was gone again, had been for days. Bernie and Gert would be lighting votive candles in church, down on their knees, praying for the safe return of the wayward brother. I imagine that Bernie was more impatient than Gert with this ritual arrival, the red eyes, the slightly apologetic, hangdog look, the flannel shirt soaked in days of whisky-scented sweat. This smell announced the condition of the beloved brother and all that condition meant about and for his life.

And when Bernie and Gert answered the door to one of their brothers, he probably said something like, "Ah, girls, you're a sight for sore eyes. Would you mind fixing me a cup of tea?"

In her gentle way, Gert opened the door further and said, "Come on in, then." Bernie, in her blunter way, said, "Go on up to Dan's room and find some clean clothes. We'll have to wash the stink out of the clothes you're wearing."

And "the gairls" busied themselves washing clothes, fixing tea, directing their brother to a bed to sleep it off. They sprinkled holy water on him, recited prayers, made every effort to exorcise the demon drink. I wonder if one of them called his wife and said, "He's here and we'll be sending him home soon." Or did they just leave well enough alone?

When they did send the sober brother back to his wife, they must have said, "We're praying for you," or "May she forgive you," or throwing it all to divine intervention, "God bless you."

They had already nursed two brothers to their deaths—shouldn't they nurse the living as well?

Y<small>EARS LATER</small>, both of these brothers gone on to the next world—both of them heavy drinkers until the day they died relatively young deaths in their early seventies—a cousin of mine took Bernie and Gert to Al-Anon, the twelve-step program for family members of alcoholics. At that time, I had been trained as a chemical dependency counselor and had been working in the field for several years. I had also been going to Al-Anon for a few years. I asked them what they thought of the meetings they went to.

"Nice people," Gert murmured.

Bernie looked up at me, shook her head sheepishly, and told me, "We learned that we probably did the wrong thing. We thought we were helping but we were . . . what is that word again, Gert?"

"Enabling."

"Oh, yes, we were enabling, we found out."

We talked a little bit about how it can be hard to tell the difference between helping and enabling, when a defiant edge crept into Bernie's voice. I sensed the presence of Pretty Weasel. Pretty Weasel folded her arms in front of her, sent her eyes thoughtfully down to the floor and back up to me and said, "I don't know. I still think when a person's down and out what they really need is a good, home-cooked meal."

We were all quiet, letting her words hang in the air, vibrating and resonating with years of memories.

I <small>HAVE NEVER</small> forgotten her words, nor the quietly fierce passion with which they were spoken. Her words were utterly sincere, understandable, and compassionate. Perhaps her words represented Mother Teresa's way—"Feed the hungry, clothe the poor." Perhaps they were the words of a lost, sheltered innocence, a no-longer possible naïveté in a face-off with what is known by millions of us as a cunning, baffling, powerful disease.

When I first learned this story of Bernie and Gert taking care of the drinkers, I was shocked. Cousin Rosemary, my father's cousin, told me one day as I interviewed her on family history. I had interviewed my parents and all my aunts and uncles and asked the same questions of everyone,

Uncle Ted, Rosemary, Aunt Bernie, Aunt Eleanor.

but only Rosemary told me this story. She turned the leaf of the family tree upside down so I could examine the underside, the pulsating veins, usually hidden from view. As a cousin she was intimately involved, yet one step removed. She questioned the perfect family image. And when I asked about the role of alcohol in this family, she gave me a lot of information the others had closed their mouths around.

My father's response had been to tell the story of a moment just days before his father died. Pa was in the living room hospital bed, his body pushed up on pillows where Ma, Bernie and Gert, and Dan had been caring for him since his last heart attack. My father sat by his bed as Pa held aloft a glass half full of whisky, its amber liquid a centerpiece for both of their eyes. He looked at my dad and said, "Watch out for this stuff. It can take you by surprise."

A bedside warning. It was a story I heard my father tell numerous times over the years.

An Irish friend of mine says that those who drink too much "have a touch of the weakness." The only clue I have about my grandfather having a touch of the weakness himself was his bedside warning and the story about his two-year stint running a small bar. According to that family story, Ma made him quit that job because he was "spending too much time working both sides of the bar."

There were also stories about my father's drinking when he returned from World War II and the large amount of time he spent in bars when my older siblings were young. But by the time my younger siblings and I were growing up, he was more homebound. He had ten mouths to feed, and work to get up for every day. He drank at home, mostly on weekends. Although it's a subject cloaked in silence, I have heard faint whispering stories of my mother and other aunts trying to usher their unwieldy husbands out of family parties before they got one more drink in them or before they said one more thing they would later regret.

As I neared my thirtieth year, one quiet morning I called my mother from my small apartment in Minneapolis. The phone call was an assignment from my therapist—the modern day version of a priest and a confessional. I was nervous. We chatted briefly, and then I told her that I was going to Al-Anon. I was going for two reasons: one, because Chris, my love, was a recovering alcoholic, and two, because I had been affected by Dad's drinking. How uncomfortable I was around him sometimes with his maudlin mood shift after a drink or two, the way having a drink or not having a drink affected his temper. Not one word had ever been spoken between us about this. There was a long, deep silence at her end of the line. And then she said, "Well, you're not the only one."

It was a powerful moment. In the short silence that followed, the truth of her words penetrated me. Inside my cellular structure, something shifted—a realigning of mind and body.

In that moment, her honesty, her validation of my experience meant a lot to me. Then, her loyalty to my father kicked in and we didn't speak of it again. My father, in his older years, and in part due to digestion issues, became a moderate drinker—a beer or glass of wine before dinner, and then only occasionally. One of my brothers went through treatment and has been sober for over thirty years, as has my husband. Now my daughter has joined the ranks of the sober. Their sobriety adds an important balance to our family ecosystem.

I PUBLISHED A BOOK with Bantam in the early 1990s of daily meditations for mothers in recovery, called *Small Miracles:Daily Meditations for Mothers in Recovery*. No one was more enthusiastic about this book than my parents. The edges of their copy were tattered from daily use over the years, and they regularly told me how much they loved and appreciated my words. They came to my book signings in Minneapolis and in my hometown of Grand Rapids. Bernie and Gert, and my aunts Eleanor and Margaret, who were still alive and living in Grand Rapids at that time, came together, in a pack, to my hometown book signing. The Hoolihan women, the sisters (in their seventies and eighties then), clutched their purses and looked at me with their four sets of bright blue eyes. I could see pride in them—and excitement. I gave Bernie and Gert a signed copy, thanking them for all the ways they had nurtured me. Aunt Marg and Eleanor bought copies for their daughters, and I signed those, too. They mingled with the others who had come downtown for the signing. It was great fun, and as Bernie said, "We all had a jolly time."

A few days later, when I asked Bernie and Gert what they thought of the book, they were just a tad bit tentative. "There's a lot of wisdom in there . . . but we did have a hard time with that word 'Higher Power'. Why don't you just say 'God'?" I tried to explain that the word "God" is hard for some people—but this was beyond comprehension for them. I told them "Higher Power" appealed to a wider group, to those who don't go to church or who find God more out in nature or in twelve-step meetings. They shook their heads at this, stymied.

I couldn't begin to explain to them how at one time I cringed at the word "God," that I had traveled far away from it. I couldn't even explain it to myself. I didn't speak of my years of being immersed in the open and accepting concept of a higher power, surrounded by people struggling to find spiritful ways to live through difficult situations. Years before I had walked, scared and nervous, into my first Al-Anon meeting because of all the issues coming to the surface in my writing and therapy work. Issues about the drinking in my family, about my growing relationship with a recovering alcoholic, my need to take care of everyone around me at my own expense. Those years in Al-Anon, from my late twenties on, gently, slowly, and deeply led me back to a comfort with the word or concept of God. A God who lives in the middle of the river of complexity, rather than on the separate black and white banks of right and wrong.

With my brief explanation, I tried to bridge their world with the path I have traveled, and though I knew in some small way I had disappointed them, they nodded their heads in assent.

Chapter Seven

Where Did the Wild Woman Go? What Went Wrong?

Before I ended up on my twenty-seven-year-old deathbed, I had trained to be a chemical dependency counselor. The field was at the beginning of its boom, and something about it ("duh," a therapist might say) intrigued me. Part of the training consisted of a two-day marathon group therapy, where the eight of us who were in one group and two facilitators took turns diving into and hopefully excavating and exorcising some deeply held personal pain. The youngest in the group, I was surprised and moved by each person's experience in the "hot seat." I wasn't sure what would come up for me—or if anything would.

What came up was how suffocated I felt by religion. For a whole host of complex and interwoven reasons, this was intricately connected to my relationship with my mother. My mother's mother had converted to Catholicism because she married a Catholic. Her sponsor? My dad's mother, Ma. My mother married into the Hoolihans, known for their Catholic fervency. She admired this, aspired to it. Perhaps she felt it her motherly duty to facilitate our spiritual lives in the way she believed in. The rules in our house around adhering to Catholic expectations were huge and she was the daily rule enforcer, although fear of our father was also a powerful rule enforcer. Church, and all it stood for, had been crammed down my throat so much that it was difficult for me to breathe around the issue. At that time, I was unable to separate my relationship with God from this overwhelming and oppressive experience.

Where did this need to question come from? My younger sister asked me why I had to cause so much trouble. I think she took a quieter path in the wake of my unsettled one. My need to question, explore, and rebel rendered judgmental responses, edged with fear. I felt separate from my siblings. It was not an easy path, and often lonely, but I felt like I had no choice. I felt my life path had to be carved in this way or I would end up living a muted, compromised life. Perhaps I questioned earlier than others or more vociferously, for certainly others in my family have questioned their relationship to the church, at different times and in varied ways. Quite possibly my questioning was a factor of my being a writer, someone who questions and observes. Another factor most likely was the times, the culture, in which I grew up.

There was a wild streak in me, and this wild streak was acted out in a whole host of ways in every generation and branch of my Irish Catholic tribe. It makes me wonder about the role of wildness on a spiritual path. Certainly, Uncle Dan embodied and expressed a wild edge in his flying, his Canadian camp, his refusal to be tied down by everyday obligations. And my grandfather, striking out from Canada to start a whole new life in Minnesota. Before him was the generation that put their faith into huge unknowns, into crossing the oceans and building a life in North America. And then there has been the continuous wild streak expressed through the excessive consumption of alcohol in every generation, sometimes letting loose harmful behaviors which eventually become much more cagelike than freeing. The "spirits" of alcohol, that longing for more, often tricks and truncates the spiritual longing process.

How did it happen that I needed to leave a deeply rooted tradition, a family bond, Catholicism, and leave behind what was most familiar to strike out across unfamiliar terrain? Certainly I am not the only who left or walked away, but others did stay, firmly rooted in the tradition they grew up in. I wonder what creates the dividing line between those who decided to leave and those who stayed. Is it personality-driven? Birth order? Influence of friends? Cultural history that surrounds us? A combination of inner drives and outer influences? Who immigrates to new lands, new ways of thinking, unsettled territory? As we cut our way through the bush, how do we not hurt others around us? How do we decipher what needs to be thrown out of the way and what would be most helpful to carry with us?

My wildness was catalyzed by leaving home for college. I was out from under the thumb and watchful eye of my father's intimidating presence. He put his military training to use in raising us, and wasn't afraid to use fear or force to get his preferred results. Also, it was the 1970s, and I was headed for a college campus (not a Catholic one!) on the edge of the Mississippi River, lined with green grass and tall trees. I threw my suitcase and a duffle bag into the back of the family station wagon and watched out the rear window each mile that flitted by between the home I had always known and my freshman dormitory room. The drive, with my parents in the front seats, was laced with the allure of anticipated freedom and the taunting thread of trepidation. Each mile represented degrees of longed-for change—180 miles from my hometown, 180 degrees of change. And yes, at some point, I am sure we said the rosary.

At home, I had become the horse held back at the starting gate, held back by all the rules and regulations. The one I chafed under the most was church every Sunday.

"One hour a week for God," my mother and father said. "It's not much to give for all the gifts you have in return."

My younger sister said years later, "I watched you cause so much trouble I just wanted to make things peaceful. I went along with whatever they wanted—it wasn't so bad, you know."

"As long as you live under this roof," my father roared at me at one of the rare times I tried to openly fight the rule, "you will go to church on Sunday."

Knowing I would be grilled on who said the Mass and the point of the sermon, I usually went, cursing my cowardice, shrinking under the weight of ritual resentment. Occasionally I kept driving and headed for the forest at the edge of town, then walked among the sanctuary of tall silent trees, felt the splatter of sun across my arms, and thought *This is what feels spiritual to me.*

Decades later, I considered myself lucky to be in church sitting next to Mom and Dad. They were then in their late eighties and early nineties and I so admired how gracefully and lovingly they aged. Going to church together allowed us to hug and wish each other peace, gave us a chance to hold hands and say the "Our Father" together, allowed us a quiet space to be side by side, in prayer or meditation.

We came so far down this road together that one time when I visited them in Grand Rapids, they asked me which route I drove from Minneapolis to Grand Rapids and then reminisced about taking that same route themselves once many decades before—with us younger four children in the car—and missing the turnoff. We had been in the midst of the usual car-ride ritual of the rosary. When the turn was missed, I muttered from the back seat, "That's what you get for saying the rosary." My dad actually laughed as he told me this story. I am quite certain he didn't laugh then. I don't remember the specific moment but I do remember my, for lack of a better word, attitude. We were able to laugh about it, many decades later, because of the incredible healing that had happened between us over the years. My younger self knows this to be a miracle.

What Went Wrong?

In my impressionable grade school years, I was extremely pious, fervently memorizing my *Baltimore Catechism*.

> "Who made the world?"
> "God made the world."
> "How many kinds of actual sin are there?"
> "There are two kinds of actual sin—mortal sin and venial sin."
> "What is mortal sin?
> "Mortal sin is a grievous offense against the law of God."
> "What three things are necessary to make a sin mortal?"
> "To make a sin mortal these three things are necessary: first, the thought desire word action or omission must be seriously wrong or considered seriously wrong; second, the sinner must be mindful of the serious wrong; third, the sinner must fully consent to it."
> "What is venial sin?"

"Venial sin is a less serious offense against the law of God, which does not deprive the soul of sanctifying grace, and which can be pardoned even without sacramental confession."

"How does venial sin harm us?"

"Venial sin harms us by making us less fervent in the service of God, by weakening our power to resist mortal sin, and by making us deserving of God's punishments in this life or in purgatory."

The end of this section reads, in bold print, I presume to leave no doubt as to the importance of the message: "Mortal sin deserves the everlasting punishment of hell," accompanied by a sketch of a human with face buried in hands, surrounded by red, licking flames.

Pretty heavy stuff for elementary school kids. I recently brought a copy of the *Baltimore Catechism* to a family gathering and my older sister said her stomach still tightened up just looking at the book. As kids, we memorized page after page. Then we were tested by the nuns and priests. Underlying the sheer intellectual challenge of memorizing so much material was the pressure of everlasting hell.

I fervently racked up indulgences (a kind of Catholic spiritual insurance) by perfect attendance at the first Friday Mass of the month and by praying nightly for various causes and purposes. Parochial school, which I attended through eighth grade, automatically included a morning Mass. Every single morning, I knelt on the slightly cushioned kneeler and followed the day's gospel in the little black leather prayer book.

In seventh and eighth grade, it began—a rising up in me of an umbrella of anger and disillusionment with the Catholicism I had been so immersed in all my life—an umbrella both shrouding and illuminating many of the following years of my life.

A sense of feeling left out, unfairly discriminated against, snuck up on me. Why was it that all my brothers could be up on the altar, serving for Mass, but I could not? Today, this is different—young girls get to serve alongside the boys. But not back then. And, of course, women are still denied the priesthood—that began to bother me then and still does. The way priests were put up on a pedestal throughout my extended family also irritated me—there were one or two who I felt were mean to us Catholic school kids or ineffectual, but still they were venerated. The sanctity of priesthood was inviolate.

I was also attuned to the social hierarchy in the church. "Important" members donated above a certain level, a level unattainable for my parents during their years of raising eight children on a Bell Telephone electrician's salary. When I was feeling sensitive about these issues, groping in my awkward adolescent way to find my place in this culture, I began to suspect the parade down the aisle on Sunday mornings to communion. Into new suits, dresses, and stylish hats I read subterranean themes that had everything to do with class, relative wealth, a jockeying for position and power—all of which felt to me like a complete antithesis to the life of the spirit. I was practicing skepticism. I suspected our own familial parade into the pews on Sunday morning, the image we were expected to project glossed over the "dirty laundry" no one was wont to air in public.

Although numerous experiences fed my sense of disillusionment with what I saw as double standards or hypocrisy in Catholicism, there was one memorable trigger. My older sister, as a college student, spent several summers working on an Indian reservation. She began to date a Native American man who helped run the program she worked for. Out of a deep sleep I was awakened one night, groggy, shocked, then shot through with an electrical current of fear. It was my father's voice, his anger bouncing off the walls of the kitchen below me, ricocheting its way up the stairs and penetrating what was, just moments earlier, a warm blanket of sleep. Jolted awake, every cell in my body raced with adrenaline, my heart beat with fear.

"You will not see him again, do you understand?" Each word was punctuated, a staccato accent unto itself, each word emphasized, amplified, resounded, echoed within the walls of our small home.

In contrast were my sister's muffled words, tears, vain attempts to argue.

My father's anger spilled out of him again.

Like the tide, it splashed into every heart in the household. A natural tenor, my father's voice rose like a symphonic crescendo. building in pitch and emotional complexity. When my sister crawled into the double bed we shared, weeping, I didn't know what to do. Eight years her junior, I wanted to hold her, brush back her hair, whisper comforting words, tell her I was on her side. As she wept quietly beside me for a long time, I ran my hand across her shoulder, told her I was sorry, then turned to face the ceiling. For hours I stared at the many little holes in the white squares of cardboard tile barely visible in the moonlight shining in our window. All my life, in various rounds of Baltimore catechism, I had been reciting the line, "All men, women and children are created equal in the eyes of God."

I could hear glass breaking inside me, tiny shards crashing to the floor, splintering in tiny pieces. What I thought was whole and intact, a philosophy, a way of thinking, believing and living, was broken. There were as many holes in this philosophy, in the living out of this religion I had been born into, as there were holes in the ceiling above me, as there were holes in the image of God I had once believed in.

WHEN I WAS in high school, I picked up Herman Hesse's *Siddhartha*. Reading this, the concept of and quest for truth took on wider dimensions for me. I questioned how Catholicism could be the one and only way, as I had been so indoctrinated, when ancient tribes danced their dreams under holy moonlit skies. I questioned how the religion I grew up in had, for the most part, not honored native beliefs and rituals here in our country but rather imposed a foreign worship and language as the one and only way, essentially robbing the indigenous people of their roots, history, and language. In many ways, I felt more drawn to the native worship of the natural world than to Catholicism.

Then, of course, there was the issue of the church and the body—a lot of rules there. "Don't touch until you're married." Even impure thoughts were considered sinful. From my perspective, it seemed that anything to do with sexuality was deemed impure, and impure equaled sinful.

From the *Baltimore Catechism*:

> "What is the sixth commandment of God?"
> "The sixth commandment of God is: Thou shalt not commit adultery."

"What are we commanded by the sixth commandment?"

"By the sixth commandment we are commanded to be pure and modest in our behavior."

"What does the sixth commandment forbid?"

"The sixth commandment forbids all impurity and immodesty in words, looks, and actions, whether alone or with others."

"What are the chief dangers to the virtue of chastity?"

"The chief dangers to the virtues of chastity are: idleness, sinful curiosity, bad companions, drinking, immodest dress, and indecent books, plays, and motion pictures."

It wasn't until college, surrounded by the heady taste of freedom, my inner sense of having broken free of a cage, reading books like *Our Bodies, Ourselves* and *The Feminine Mystique* that I began the long and ongoing journey to find what was spiritual within rather than separate from my body. My college years also coincided with the Vietnam War. That war touched off a whole generation to question forms of authority and ways of being—to question our government, our churches, our roles as males and females.

I flung myself headlong into college life. Drugs, sex, rock 'n roll, and studies. The curly head of hair I had spent years trying to tame became a symbol for me. I let it go wild, unfettered, electric, noticeable. Denim overalls, khaki pants, flannel shirts, and headbands were my favorite apparel. Putting myself through college on scholarships and part-time jobs, I was a good student. But when my studies, papers, and work for the day were done, Party Patty came out to play. She was full of pent-up energy, fueled by her anger, and spurred on by a need to break all the old rules as she longed for that elusive quality called freedom.

Sexual freedom was part of the times and, of course, this was pre-AIDS. My first serious boyfriend was an Eagle Scout who had a side business selling drugs. I loved both sides of his personality and was thrilled by the hidden, dangerous side of his life. No way was I ready to settle in for long, so after we broke up I found my way into the lives of interesting men on campus. It was especially challenging to gain admittance to the house of the black brothers, to be accepted there, to try to break down the racial barriers of my childhood. Tony sat across from me in my English class and on many days we talked after class. He invited me back to the brothers' house at the edge of campus. We became friends. With strobe lights flashing, James Brown singing low and throaty, we shared a pipe reverently between us, his black, long, graceful fingers handing the soft wood over into my pale, midwinter hands. The passing continued as he told me what it was like to come, alone, to this nearly all-white town (on a scholarship) and walk from the bus station to campus, heads turning to stare at him as cars drove by. I felt a real kinship with him, and admired the lone explorer and trailblazer in him.

    I became friends with a female instructor who was a feminist and openly bisexual. I took many of her courses, which focused on political, social, and feminist issues. For a time, feminism replaced Catholicism for me. For years I was convinced I would never marry or become a mother because those roles would "trap" me.

    Daughter of Eve, I explored, tasted, entered worlds ripe with forbidden fruits. I found wonderful, interesting, kind, and intelligent people in those worlds. I found pieces of myself I had never known before. But there was a strange, subtle hum of dissonance inside me. I cringed when I heard the word "God," and felt ill at ease while attending the baptisms of my older siblings' children. Party Patty knew how to have a good time, but she kept herself busy, too busy to pay attention to internal confusions, deeper questions.

Chapter Eight

Cracking It Open

THIS BURIED PART of me emerged at my first writing workshop, several years after college. At the time I was single, and what I wrote startled me with its images, its fierce loneliness, longing, and guilt wrapped in self-loathing. One of the women in my workshop was a nun. Her black habit, and her presence, affected me.

> I want to reach across the table to this nun. Tear at the cloth of her clothes, on my knees, pleading . . . why, why did your religion pull you when it pushed me so far away? The explosion began in seventh grade, slowly fermenting until it blew me across the earth. I vomited all the way, page after page of *Baltimore Catechism*. Most of all the don't ask whys, just get the answer right, accept it. Don't you see I have to ask?
>
> I recognize you, Sister, there is the same kindness in our eyes. We are not so different, yet I feel so far away.
>
> Sometimes I feel so evil. Swimming single in a black sea of marriages. I belong to no order. Men marry women in white, I know that. And I have been black a long time now. Evil enough to be interesting. Too evil to be lived with. Sister, you wear black on the outside. I wear it inside.

Until I wrote and read these words, I was unaware of how I judged myself at deep levels by all the old standards. In my conscious life, I was oblivious to my continual subterranean sense of self-as-sinner. The nun in my writing workshop became a symbol for me. Although around this same time my cousin was becoming a nun, my cousin the nun seemed much further away than my writing partner nun. It felt to me like my cousin was too holy, too traditional, too conservative for us to have a relationship. It was decades later when she and I grew close as we cared for an aging Gert that I began to see her in a new light. The new light had little to do with her changing but much more to do with me opening my heart to see her in new ways.

As I woke up to these parts of me, I dreamt often in black and white. I realized I had been incredibly well-trained in my youth to view myself and the world in polarities: good/evil, right/wrong, black/white. Hence a wild personality, something that stood out a little, was often called a black sheep. At times I was sure I was one. Even as I traveled away from my childhood, I carried inside me an inner judge pounding her gavel—right, wrong—based on all the old rules.

One of the sayings to emerge from the civil rights movement was "Black is beautiful." At a personal level, I needed to embrace that. What I called "black" inside of me was all about what Jung would call my shadow side, parts of me that were hidden or nonconformist explorations into the unknown.

It was also about shame, and the only way to let that go was to shine a light on it.

THE NEXT COUPLE YEARS after college were very intense for me. The writing opened me. After working for a couple of years with teenagers in my hometown who had drug and alcohol issues, I moved to Seattle for a year. The physical and geographical distance from my family gave me emotional space which was useful for opening a wider perspective on my life. In the middle of that year, I returned home for Christmas vacation and ended up on my deathbed. Even the universe was conspiring to crack me open. Was it all part of my personal destiny? Writing and the way it led me was a huge factor, but perhaps my path was destined to be that of an emotional explorer—perhaps I was deeply a part of my times or just more and more curious about what really made me, and makes me, tick.

DREAMS ALSO LED ME during this time. In Seattle I was part of an ongoing dream group for most of a year. It was a remarkable experience. In one group session, with the guidance of the facilitator, I became mother to myself and I called myself (out loud) black inside and a whore and a sinner over and over again. I did most of this with my eyes closed. I still remember the man across from me—the shocked look on his face when I later looked up. He was shocked at what lived inside me, and I was, too.

On a relativity scale, I really had never been *that* bad in my "acting out," but I was a very harsh judge when I got down to it. To this day I struggle with harshly judging myself.

I peeled away enough layers to see the mud-slinging going on inside me—this is not easy work. But alongside the shock, a strange relief flooded my body. I had been carrying that mud around for years. The shadow of it cast itself across my days—I held people at a distance, for fear they get too close and see me for what I really was. I felt like a fraud no matter what outer successes I had. I kept my love relationships shallow and then called myself a whore for keeping them shallow. I took my cues for how to act and what to think from other people. I told myself I was too empty and too shallow to be an artist (writer). No matter what, I kept myself down, down, down.

During this period I went to great lengths and explained to my mother how put down and ashamed I had historically felt with how she pushed her religion and religious values on me. She was puzzled, saying, "I was trying to help. How did I make you feel this way?" She actually thanked me for sharing with her and said, "Go ahead and write about it, publish it if you can. You came through, that's what is important. Maybe it will help someone else."

Generous spirit.

Sometimes, even with the best of intentions, we hurt those we love.

I SPENT A YEAR doing family-of-origin work. I interviewed all my aunts and uncles, asked many questions, saw a therapist regularly to process what I learned from answers given and withheld. I lived alone at that time, although my love (now my husband) and I were doing this work at the same time and supporting each other through it. It was not uncommon for one or the other of us to hold the other, weeping. I needed to cry a lot. The work was difficult—very difficult—but in the long run, liberating. In the long run I have felt cleansed and able to pursue a life of harmony, not discord. The deeper questioning went against all my training ("just memorize the answers, don't question"). I had felt invisible in my family, and one of the ways I compensated for that was by making myself very visible in other ways—dressing weird, wearing my hair wild, fighting family rules. Writing was—and is—my way of coming out of invisibility. I found it terrifying at first, and often still do.

As I was digging around in the family trenches, it was suggested to me that I might find support in Al-Anon. I did so, tentatively at first. It wasn't long before I felt at home there; issues people spoke of resonated with me. Many of us were struggling to work our way out of shame, to learn healthy ways to take care of ourselves. The twelve steps work slowly on a person: I was unaware early on of how deeply the steps were transforming me, slowly, a bit at a time. Being in a group of people week after week, together studying the deeply wise twelve steps, and working and learning to live honest thoughtful lives through them was a huge part of my healing.

Edges of bitterness, resentment, and shame were slowly peeling away, like pieces of armor flaking off. It took years, but it was in these meetings where I slowly moved into being comfortable with the word and the concept of God. I felt such real authentic spiritual struggle and growth there that I became a believer. At first I became a believer in the concept of a higher power, which slowly and deeply helped me return to believing in God, which eventually led me to re-examine through a new lens the rituals and faith of my childhood and heritage.

I also loved and cherished (and still do and always will) one of the basic principles of Al-Anon, read before every meeting: "Take what you want and leave the rest." Having come from a background where I was painstakingly instructed on a whole repertoire of specific beliefs and behaviors, I found that so freeing. Another aspect I found incredibly freeing was the reference in the twelve steps to "God, however you understand God." It was practically earth-shattering to me to find a spiritual program that allowed multiple versions of God. In my youth, we were trained to a certain vision of God, and to a God whose message was set in stone—black and white. For instance: when I was twenty-eight and decided to move in with Chris, even though we didn't feel ready yet for marriage, we told my parents. I was in the brutally honest phase, which one of my friends jokingly says, "Yeah, brutal for you." I was choosing to be honest; I did not want to be secretive and shameful about a decision I was making thoughtfully. My father's response was to tell us that right and wrong had been handed down since Moses, and what we were doing was wrong, and God would punish us. I can't imagine saying such a thing to a beloved child of mine. In later years, my parents mellowed on all these fronts and found ways to love their children more and judge them less, for which I give them a lot of credit. But their response to our moving in together was a moment where the judgment was crystal clear and very painful. They, and most of my siblings, had little to do with me for about a year in response to this and also in response to a "brutally honest" therapy session I had done with my parents. I was shunned. (Mary Magdalene?) To my parents' credit, they eventually called me up and asked to get together for a cup of tea. A very Irish form of healing, I think. It was the beginning of my slow reconnecting with them, and with my family—a reconnection I am deeply grateful to have had.

My parents did keep surprising me, especially in their later years, with an elasticity I didn't see in their youth. When I was in my thirties, I trained to run a marathon. When my Dad heard this he actually pronounced, in his magisterial way, "Girls shouldn't run that far." It set off echoes for me of all the messages I had received about what girls could and could not do. He did call me the night before the marathon and wished me well, albeit with a reminder that I could drop out at any point if I needed to. And when he congratulated me the next day, relieved to know I had survived, he added, "You won't do it again, will you? Once is enough." Running and my running friends have provided me with much sustenance and spiritual fortitude over the years; thank God I didn't listen to that limiting voice and instead surrounded myself with people who believe, easily, that girls *can* run that far.

Along my seeking way, well into raising both of my children, I found myself in an auditorium full of people listening to the Dalai Lama, an internationally recognized spiritual leader. The main message I took away from him that day was: " The foundation of all major religions is compassion." I love that belief and find great comfort in the concept of a shared, universal foundation: compassion.

The eighth and ninth steps of the twelve steps are about making amends where we have harmed others, except when to do so would create more harm. The concept of a spirituality that refrains from harming others, that makes amends for harm done, really touched me. I began to shape my thinking about a spiritual life around these concepts of compassion, of not harming others.

I also began to see connections in other ways. A spirituality group I went to once talked about the common connections between prayer beads in other parts of the world and rosary beads. In fact, the prayer beads in India hold the same number of beads as does the rosary. This helped me to see the rosary in a new light: I began to think of people all over the world using prayer beads to comfort themselves, to re-center themselves toward a higher being, a higher frequency. If I were in India I would think that was pretty cool, so why not take a second look at the way my parents and aunts and uncle reached for their beads on a daily basis? If I could strip away my own judgmentalism, I could see the teachers right in front of me.

Practicing the principle "take what you want and leave the rest" has made it possible for me to revisit Catholicism, to take what I want and leave the rest, in a thoughtful way.

Even during the years of my rebellion there was something about Bernie and Gert's faith I admired and was drawn to. After college, but before I moved to Seattle (during what I sometimes think of as my "penance years"), I lived in my hometown and worked with high school students in the area of chemical dependency and drug abuse prevention. When I took the job I made a commitment to myself to not use or drink. But I still felt my wildness in other areas, and I still stayed away from church.

During this time, Bernie and Gert were into the charismatic phase of their lives. Besides regularly attending Mass, they were going several times a week to services at the church for the charismatic fringe. They attended charismatic celebrations in the Twin Cities and developed a whole group of friends around this, many of them in their twenties and thirties.

One of the teachers at the high school where I was working was into this movement, as well. She raved to me about my aunts, how much everyone loved them. Other members of the family were shaking their heads. According to my parents and other aunts and uncles, this was going a bit too far. The charismatic service focused on worshippers speaking in tongues, raising their hands, chanting—in general, getting carried away and swept up in a certain kind of group prayer. There was a wild edge to it that mildly intrigued me.

One day Bernie said, "We keep waiting for the gift of tongues, Patty, and it hasn't happened for us yet. We see it happen to others around us, so maybe we haven't been good enough."

"Yes," Gert added slowly. "We haven't spoken in tongues yet, but we have met some of the nicest people. And you never know, it could happen to us at the next meeting."

Their desire to speak in tongues was passionate, full-fledged. I saw in this a desire, a quest for letting loose, freeing up their form a bit. A quest I could relate to.

Their charismatic phase went on for a year or two and then gradually died. They told me that the meetings were always in the evening and it was getting hard to drive at night. They began to prefer their own quiet prayer time together, after dinner, at the kitchen table or in the living room, or on a warm night, outside on their front porch.

Although I was tempted, I never checked out a charismatics meeting. There was a similar spiritual longing in our quests, however.

Chapter Nine

Meditation on Mary Magdalene

When I began opening the door to my inner life it was the image, the story, of that other Mary that initially brought me comfort. Mary Magdalene. Long-haired, veil-less Mary Magdalene entered my dreams. Here was a sinner, known for her prostitution and her life of carnal pleasure. Here she was sitting at Christ's feet on his way to his death. She washed his feet and he kissed her, absolving her of her identity as a sinner. This was a compassionate God I felt it possible to move toward, across what had become a wide crevasse.

Sexual shame has been huge in the Catholic Church, at least in the time when I was growing up. When a young child was told that even thinking about sex is a sin (which was how most of us interpreted the *Baltimore Catechism* and to the best of my memory is how it was interpreted for us), then that very natural process of curiosity about our bodies became twisted. We either didn't know our bodies very well or felt guilty for exploring and educating ourselves. I believe a (quite possibly unintended) outcome is that we were encouraged to separate the life of the soul from the body. This disconnect was huge. Bodies are so connected to our intuitions, to our spirits, to our souls—a connection I have worked hard to relearn. The importance of intuition, of listening to our bodies, got lost when we paid attention only or mostly to outer forms and rules.

Shame about the natural life of the body was communicated through the *Baltimore Catechism* and through an aura of secrecy about sex. That institutionalized shame, I believe, is intricately connected to the cover-up of sexual abuse by priests. This issue exists in many cultures but has been embarrassingly prevalent in the Catholic

Church. Everyone involved is covered in shame: the perpetrator, the victim, any witnesses. Shame paralyzes people. And the aura of secrecy keeps that paralysis in place. If no one is talking or sharing or communicating then the whole system stays stuck. What matters on the outside is how things look, the stories people want to believe. So how people feel gets buried. Intuition gets buried. Feelings of anger and loss are buried and mutated. Recognition of what feels wrong gets lost. The wisdom of the body is lost; the stomach-churning gut is ignored because it doesn't match the desired picture.

A pervading sense of shame is what feeds systems that cover up and enable sexual transgressions and most likely abuse of any kind. If you add to the secrecy of shame a belief in a holy hierarchy, then those with less power are doomed. The perpetrator, who was probably a victim at one time, gets away with pursuit of pleasure (addiction). The victim is silenced by a system that gives her/him no voice. And the image (of holy hierarchy) is so powerful that many, even the victims, cannot believe what is going on. The unbelievable defies belief. So those who might suspect or wonder or feel something is not quite right push it away. Some push it away out of naïveté; others push it away because they do not have the courage and/or energy to break the status quo, especially if they are benefiting from it in any way. Children in these situations suppress their feelings and awareness in order to survive.

The case of the Penn University assistant football coach Sandusky shows a similar system at work. There the holy hierarchy is football, money—lots of it—and fame. Interestingly, some of the main players in this case were Catholic. For years, this man in a position of power took advantage of those weaker than himself for the purpose of his own sexual pleasure. His head coach, Paterno, one of the all-time most admired coaches in college football, covered it up. The victims were silent and silenced for years . . . until they began to speak out with the help and support of the legal system. I am wowed by the courage it took to speak up against that system, which venerated the "holy hierarchy" and those in a position of power.

I am equally wowed by victims of priest sexual abuse who have spoken up. I can only imagine how complicated the struggle to move past the cultural shame has been. As the veil of secrecy is being lifted by victims speaking up and by legal channels of accountability, the numbers of priests who abused and the numbers of victims are heartbreaking. Appalling is the information that priests who had abused others were sometimes simply passed on to other parishes and then they abused again. Sexual abuse at the hand of a priest cripples and scars the victims in many ways, not the least of which is spiritually. God's representative, the priest, has violated them. How do they move on and trust God? And in all cases, the shroud of secrecy made what happened so shameful and painful that the secrecy and hiddenness of the event compounded its damage.

Where was moral fiber and courage? Where is it in all such cases, inside the church and outside of it? Where was the truth? Chaucer's poetry anticipates such a dilemma, hundreds of years before. Just like in Chaucer's time, the belief in a system by many well-meaning people was manipulated to cover up the abuse of power for personal gain. The system itself, unchecked, created a milieu in which abuse could exist and even thrive. It is my personal opinion that when the power system is heavily dominated by men this can happen more easily; dare I say that then power becomes way more important than empathy or integrity or intuition? This is part of why Mary's presence in the church is so important. It is why it would be so helpful if women could be ordained. The church's power structure is sadly lacking in the balance of female energy; without Mary's presence I would not have felt called back.

I have one brother who was flirted with by a priest when he was young. He told my parents about it and to the best of his memory my mother got on the phone and dealt with it. That priest never bothered him again. But he stayed on as a priest. That brother said to me, "It felt wrong. I knew in my gut it wasn't right. I tell my kids to listen to their gut." Another brother of mine was close to being molested by a deacon. He managed to make a phone call to one of our brothers, who came and got him out of a potentially dangerous situation. He was quick-thinking enough (at the age of fourteen) to use the stairs in the hotel rather than the elevator and was able to outsmart his potential perpetrator. To this day he attributes this to the presence of a higher power. So, there was abuse at the hands of a system which trusted anyone on the path to becoming a priest, and yet simultaneously an awareness of God's presence in his time of need.

Unfortunately, the situation was never really talked about and affected him for years. Naïveté? Did my parents simply not know how to talk about this? Ignore it and it might go away? Too hard to believe or deal with the unbelievable? Say a prayer and hope for the best? The problem with such silence is that it further hurts those already scarred: the victims. The lack of talking about it enhanced shame about what happened: the questions of "why?" and "what did I do wrong?" went deep inside of him, as it goes deep inside of most victims. It wasn't his fault and he needed to hear that, but the shroud of secrecy and shame prevented that important conversation. Decades later he unraveled this and its impact on him, with professional help. As painful as the unraveling of all the sexual abuse in the church is, the gift is that it opens the conversation. What is hidden and kept secret cannot heal. A deeper understanding and the gentle light of attention holds out hope for healing.

One of the routes my own personal shame took me down was that when I veered away from the strict Catholic path, I began to see myself as a temptress, as a "mistress". My original "cracking it open" journal entry stated that men married women in white, that I was black and unworthy of love and by extension good for only unholy pleasure. It took me a long time to see myself as worthy of being a full, deserving partner in a loving relationship. It took days, weeks and months of steps, hiking across rough terrain but I eventually made the crossover. That was when I knew I was ready to marry the man I loved.

I WANT TO HONOR my cousin the nun here, Sister El Ann. For so many years I felt I could not relate to her: she was holy, I wasn't; she was conservative, I was liberal. But as the elders in our family aged, she and I were often there together or spelling each other, helping out, taking care. We shared a similar value—taking care of the sick and elderly. And we both had very special and strong bonds to Bernie, Gert, and Dan.

Sister El Ann held Gert's hand all night the night she was dying and I was snowbound in Minneapolis. They were in Duluth, 120 miles away. Her own cancer was painful but she set that aside to be there for Gert.

In the weeks after we buried Gert, Sister El Ann was given bad news. Her bone cancer had progressed and she was given two months to live. She was such a strong link for me to Gert and Gert's dying process that I visited her in Duluth every two to three weeks. I had also grown very fond of her gentle presence over the years.

Somewhere around February or early March, there was a young woman visiting when I came to visit. Her name was Marie. When I asked who she was, everyone said she was a friend of Rene's, a beloved niece of Father John and Sister El Ann.

Suddenly she was there a lot—so attentively and with such care. I began to think of her as the mysterious Marie. Her presence puzzled me; there was something here that I didn't get. My body was processing the veil (shame/secrecy) between my questions and their answers.

On the phone ten days before Sister died, she told me she felt enormously relieved of a burden she had long carried, something about being part of the generation of the sixties, seventies, getting caught up in the times. She felt like she had let go of it, felt at peace, with the help of a good priest friend. She encouraged me to do the same, acknowledging that all of us get swept up by the times we live in. She spoke in generalities and shared no specifics, but I had a pretty clear idea what she was talking about and I was happy to hear the relief, acceptance, and even joy in her voice.

I was struck that for her the best way for this to happen was to confess to a priest. For me, a similar process happened in therapy, years before.

El Ann died ten days later, surrounded by the nuns of her order, her brother at her side, having said Mass for her every day. Also beside her was Marie.

I had begun putting pieces of a puzzle together and then had a long talk with Marie after the funeral. She was Sister's daughter, given up for adoption before my cousin joined the convent. Marie had done her research to track her down. And as she said, "In the last months we made up for lost time."

I think she must have been a source of great comfort to Sister El Ann. But what to do with this information that had been sealed and kept secret all these years? Father John knew; he had held the baby in his arms before she was taken away by the adoption agency. For whatever reasons, Sister El Ann chose not to share this information with me nor with other close family members. Perhaps she felt it would overshadow so much else of what was going on. Perhaps shame kept her quiet. It's guesswork on my part.

What I do know is that collectively, my siblings and cousins and I could not have been more surprised. We were shocked. It had truly been a family secret. Deeply buried. Hidden.

I said to Father John when he and I talked of it some weeks later, "I hope she didn't feel shame all her life about this."

He looked me straight in the eye and said, "She felt shame."

I wanted to personally absolve her of it, what seemed to me such an unnecessary shame. When Sister's daughter took care of her on her deathbed, her daughter was thirty-seven years old.

Her daughter who showed up in time to meet her dying mother, I found to be uncannily like her mother: gentle, caring, spiritual, religious. She juggled three young children, and while being there for Sister El Ann, she exuded a quiet sense of mission and gracefulness. She and I were able to talk openly at the funeral, but she respected her mother's need for quiet around this issue until then. And she has continued to care for Father John, her "new" uncle, who held her at her birth and also held her secret all these years. She is a remarkable and loving presence, and now, a part of our family.

What Sister El Ann and I shared was an inner sense of being Mary Magdalene, whore and sinner. Never would I have guessed that of all my cousins I would share that with her, this kind, gentle, holy, (she could be easily seen as holier-than-thou) nun who served as a nurse to so many. Who had a special gift with the dying, elderly sick ones in our family. Who was outwardly and completely conservative in her views and politics, demeanor and dress.

Bernie, Gert, and Dan all knew. My father did not. The tight family of sisters must have surrounded El Ann's mother, Eleanor, during the crisis. This also sheds light on who would have been left out of this information and felt some strange line drawn they didn't understand. My mother would be in this outsider group, and probably all the other sisters-in-law as well.

As all of this bubbled to the surface, I missed Gert terribly. I would have loved to talk with her. I felt sad that El Ann had passed away without the two of us ever being able to talk about it.

I couldn't help but wonder what other secrets, wounds, scars were held in confidence at *the house* on Second Avenue, received and accepted with the same open arms as the Mary statues perched in miniature on the kitchen shelf and out in the yard.

WHAT I AM TRYING to articulate is my own personal world, as part of a familial and larger, heavily religious culture that has been shattered by shame. The only antidote that I know is shining the light of truth on the darkness—talking about what is most secret. Otherwise the darkness becomes a place one must escape from, and addictions are born.

To have a showdown with shame, one has to do the work of stripping denial and have the courage to be honest, to speak the truth. My grandfather blazed a trail across wilderness, unsettled terrain. These days we blaze trails through thickly wooded emotional truths that became mutated somehow. That "somehow" has many mysterious threads.

For victims/survivors, I believe there are two main keys to exiting a sick (shameful, abusive) system: intuition and support. Intuition is our inner knowing of a true God: the God who wants the best for us, that God who loves and respects who we are and the best of who we are. Intuition tells us when someone is violating us, lying to us. The body does not lie; it is such an incredible tool when you learn to listen to it. It is an underestimated tool of the spiritual life. And we all need support (people who listen to and believe us) in order to speak and hear our own voices . . . especially if we have been silent or silenced for a long time.

Shame silenced my own sense of my spiritual life for years. As long as I always felt unworthy, there was a part of me that wondered, "why bother?" Untangling its power and its tangled roots has helped me to clear the way for my spirit to grow.

For all these reasons I will never rely solely on Catholicism as a form for my faith. I have seen its blindness, its shortcomings and limitations. I need other ways as well to embrace my relationship with a loving God and with God's many presences. I also need other ways to keep looking at the issue of harm. Who is being harmed by my actions? Or the actions of those around me? What can I do to foster compassion, to soften wounds caused by harm? Before I can be of much use as a source of compassion, I have to and have had to look hard at my own darkness. It is the twelve-step program (Al-Anon) and my writing that have provided ways for me to do so. Since high school I have been a faithful runner and I consider it part of my spiritual life. Running has helped me to know my body and to work difficult emotions through and out of my body.

In my dark time, Mary Magdalene was important to me. If Mary Magdalene could be cherished, rather than shamed, then perhaps one day I could be. If she could be given such public blessings, then perhaps one day I could weave together my wild woman, rulebreaker, questioner, with the part of me that longs, always has longed, and always will long to be whole. She gave me hope into the days when I could look elsewhere for hope.

Perhaps there is nothing in this world that is as black and white as it may look from the outside, not even the habit of a nun.

Part Two

Reaching Further Back

Chapter Ten

The Mary Statues

I HAVE HAD people tell me that what they envy or admire about Catholicism is that we have Mary (Virgin Mary, Mother of God). Certainly in many other religions there is no female who has the kind of presence Mary has.

No one was more devoted to Mary than my aunts. As I began to study their pure ability to believe, the relationship to their Mary statues rose in front of me. Bernie, Gert, and Dan kept showing up in my dreams: Bernie and Gert in their kitchen, Dan in his airplane. And so I followed the trail of my curiosity of wanting to know more about them and their ways. And this trail led me from a connection to Mary Magdalene to a connection with the Virgin Mary, even though the word "virgin" made me wince.

In the summers of my youth, on Sunday afternoons, July Fourths, hot and humid early evenings after my Dad finished his day at Bell Telephone, we piled in the black Chevrolet station wagon with its red interior and drove to the cabin. We drove toward the promise of a cool swim. We drove, some days, toward a gathering of aunts, uncles, and cousins, which promised a frenzy of swimming and picnicking. We drove south of our northwoods town, across the long open-vista bridge, where Pokegama Lake sprawled as far as I could see on either side. We drove over miles of winding country roads, through a tunnel carved by the deep green of pine trees, and the flashing white of birch.

Those were the days of no seat belts, and we four younger kids climbed in back, duking it out over the window seats. The cabin was owned by Bernie and Gert, the "gairls," and many of my father's numerous siblings and their equally numerous children experienced the sense of having a cabin at their place. Summer memories of many years center around this lake place.

As we all piled out of the car, my eyes were drawn to the Virgin Mary shrine, which gracefully presided over the western edge of the cabin lot. More than any other aspect of the cabin, the Mary statue pulls me back to the lake memories, the white plaster lit by sunshine through dappled leaves, the green and blue rosary beads draped over her praying hands. She perched on top of a two-foot high wooden shrine built especially for her, to raise her aloft in the midst of the trees. Even as a child playing rock-paper-scissors in the back seat of the car, I felt a mysterious, magnetic pull towards the Mary shrine.

We children spent most of our time on the beach, in the water, lounging at the picnic table in front of the cabin, or at the long wooden table running half the length of the front porch. On special occasions, often the Fourth of July, the old ice cream maker was put to use, with everyone taking turns cranking it. I remember pouring in cream, ice chips, peaches, salt. The result, fresh ice cream, beat anything store-bought!

With Aunt Bernie as the task master, my older brothers and male cousins were hired in the summer to paint the cabin or trim trees. She didn't abide spilled paint or drips or haphazard clean-ups of any sort. At family gatherings the guys often told stories of narrow escapes, of just finishing a cigarette break as they heard Bernie and Gert's Oldsmobile at the far end of the shaded drive, the flurry to bury their butts and wield a wet paintbrush by the time the aunts emerged from their car.

One particularly memorable Fourth of July, the beer was flowing freely among the older set all afternoon. My cousin Tom and older brother Dan left the lake early and headed into town. Hours later, as our Chevrolet rounded a curve in the road, we were all alarmed at the sight of their car in the ditch with no sign of either of them nearby. (This was way before cell phones.) My father drove straight to the hospital, and we found out they were both going to be okay. But Dan nearly had his ear sliced off. Just enough of the ear hung on so that the doctors could stitch it back up.

That nearly sliced-off ear floats in the ether of my memory. In all the talk that swirled around my young ears, the main message was not what a shame it was that the accident happened in the first place, nor the role that alcohol played, nor what a shame it was that his ear was damaged. No, it was that amazing, miraculous fraction of an inch that held on, the way the ear-slicing stopped just short of a complete disaster. The thread of tenacious skin cells was proof of all that was good and intact and hopeful in our world. Proof, perhaps more than anything, of our Irish luck.

In later years, however, Uncle Dan told me that the following year the keg was nixed for the Fourth celebration.

Every visit I ever made to the cabin I couldn't help but glance at the Mary shrine, even during the years I would have walked an extra mile to avoid anything religious. Often a vase of flowers sat at her feet. An air of friendliness emanated from the shrine, no matter how much I wanted to intellectualize the silliness of it all. During my wild years, I hurried by Mary, a tug of guilt pulling at me. Disdain, an old habit that's taken me years to step out of, lay like a thick cloth over my guilt.

And yet, in spite of my long voyage away from the religion of my childhood, that statue of Mary, perched in the middle of a partially wooded expanse of lake property, shimmered in the landscape of my memory. It captured the fervor, the passion, and the unabashed eccentricity of my dearly beloved aunts and uncle.

As Bernie neared ninety and Gert was in her eighties, they sold the cabin. They no longer had the energy for upkeep and didn't use the place much anymore. I suspect that finding a fair way to sell the place to one of their nephews

Mary statue at the lake cabin with Uncle Ray, who built the platform.

and nieces seemed impossible, so they sold it outside the family, to the disappointment of some family members. When the news reached me, my immediate thoughts were of the Mary statue. Did they leave her there in the hands of the new owners, or did they pack her up and bring her into town?

On my first visit with Bernie and Gert after the sale of their cabin, I had to ask about the Mary statue. After their usual spirited greeting of me at the front door, we settled into the soft couch in their more formal living room. When I asked about the Mary statue, both their faces lit up. "Oh," Bernie said enthusiastically, "She's here in the yard now."

"Come and see her," Gert added, motioning me out to the kitchen.

Right away I noticed how the statue was "she" or "her," not a hint of the pronoun "it".

On our way to the kitchen, through the dining room, they pointed out another Mary statue with a gold crown perched on her head, standing a foot-and-a-half high on their oak buffet. "That's the Carmelite Mary," Bernie said in passing. "She's been with us since Ann McHenry died. She's going to be in the Carmelite parade tomorrow."

What? Another Mary statue? The Carmelites, along with being a religious order, are also a modified order for lay people. From the Carmelites:

> Lay Carmelites . . . seek to live their own vocation by silently listening to the Word of God. The members of the Lay Carmelites follow the charism of the Order which takes its inspiration from the figure of Our Lady and the Prophet Elijah. In the midst of their normal family lives, in the work place, in their social commitments and relationships with other people, Lay Carmelites . . . try to live in the spirit of the Beatitudes, humbly and consistently exercising the virtues of honesty, justice, sincerity, courtesy, fortitude.

My parents belonged to this order, as well as all my aunts and uncles. In fact, that morning, there had been a special Mass, always held on the first Saturday of each month, for the Carmelites. Bernie and

Gert had been there, of course, as well as my parents. While they were all in church that first Saturday of October, I was on the road, driving north from my city home through silhouetted trees. I was oblivious to it being a special morning for the Carmelites. Furthermore, a Carmelite parade around the church block was complete news to me. What else had I missed, I wondered, as I followed my aunts.

We moved through the dining room and into the kitchen. The three of us stood in front of the south window next to the stove.

Mary statue in the garden of the house.

They pointed out Mary's new perch in the side yard, which was hard to miss. There was Mary, in front of a grove of pine trees. She was easily visible, cemented onto a foot-high foundation of bricks and rocks built, they told me, by Dan. The red bricks formed a cross in the midst of gray cement and rock. Made of solid white plaster, the statue itself was almost two feet tall. The familiar green and blue plastic rosary beads were draped over her praying hands, her eyes peacefully downcast.

After over thirty years of Mary being exposed to the wind, rain, snow, and the imploring hearts around her, the only sign of wear and tear was a small hairline crack on the back of her head. Gert confided this to me and added, "Her head is a little smudged right now from the flowers El Ann put on her last week." By very virtue of the fact that El Ann was a nun, she was part of an inner sanctum I could only hope to circle around. Gert continued, "But we washed her up when we moved her. She's nice and clean now. We like to clean her about once a year."

Bernie informed me that Dan's shrine was not quite as well-built as the one Uncle Ray designed out at the lake, the one they were unable to move after so many years without destroying it. Dan, in his usual style, had been a little sloppy with the cement and the rock design. Gert added in a slightly hushed voice, "Ray built a beautiful shrine for her and you know, he wasn't even Catholic." Of course I knew this. It was a sore thumb in the handbook of family history, and something I had secretly admired in Ray—his tenacity in the face of the fierce piety with which he was surrounded. But what Ray, many years gone then, was remembered for was that beautiful shrine at the lake he built that housed Mary for all those years. He was also known for the fact that two of his four children chose the religious life—Sister El Ann and Father John were his children.

In Bernie and Gert's roomy kitchen that autumn morning, the larger west-facing window looked out on the tall corn and beanstalks turning yellow and brown with the drying out of the fall season. Tomato vines, brittle at the end of their productivity, still clung to weathered stakes. The woodstove over in the corner was "taking the chill out of the air," as Bernie always said. Gert put tea water on for us, and Bernie stood at the window and began to recite a salutation to Mary. I had never heard it before. My piqued interest made them both laugh, and I asked where it came from. Bernie said, "An old Irish priest taught it to us years ago."

"Will you say it again for me?" I asked, and so they recited it slowly for me, the two of them, together, the slight hum of the tea kettle (or "kittle," as they pronounced it) the only other sound in the room.

> "Ah, Mary, isn't it grand that you look
> like a bride in her rich adorn
> With all the pent-up love in my heart
> I bid you the top of the morn."

I watched the two of them, side by side, words rolling off their tongues in unison, merriment lighting up both sets of blue eyes. Their eyes crinkled as their voices moved up and down together. The words were heartfelt but laced with a mirthfulness directed at themselves, and a deep and thorough enjoyment of the lyric flow. Because of the way the words rolled off their tongues there was little doubt it was a regular invocation they addressed to Mary.

Something about the way Bernie said an old Irish priest taught them this poem made me wonder how far back this lyric prayer went. Perhaps the mother of the old Irish priest taught him this, as she looked out on her shrine on a verdantly green hillside in County Clare. She may have had a small wooden statue in her window sill that looked out on the rocky soil, the rows of potatoes, the two lonely cows in the pasture.

I was struck by the line "all the pent-up love in my heart." A heart full of pent-up love. A priest's heart, an old Irish priest's heart, Bernie and Gert's hearts, my heart. Few of us love as passionately, gently or deeply as we thought we could or would, whether we're living through famine in Ireland or near-prosperity in America. Bernie and Gert were quick to admit their own failings. And I was (and am) well aware of how I fall short of my ideals as a wife, mother, daughter, and friend. Hearts full of love, yet we all love with so much ineptness. Hearts full of pent-up love turning to this presence, this female, motherly presence and greeting her. "Top of the day." What you would say to a friend. Giving her this pent-up love, turning it over, in a sense, to her, unpenting it, letting it go . . . this daily onslaught of imperfection, this wild desire to love more freely and deeply.

Bernie said to me once, "You know, you can go to Mary sometimes when it's harder to go to God, just like how it was always easier to talk to Mama than to Papa. We send many of our prayers straight to Mary."

I imagined these two aunts of mine, after rising early, meeting in the kitchen, their rosary beads and prayer books on the table as one of them puts the "kittle" on and the other slices the homemade whole wheat bread and puts it in the toaster. If Uncle Dan were in town, he would have a pot of steel cut oats simmering on the stove as he liked to do, slowly, for an hour to let the full flavor and nutrition bubble up, puffing out the small chunky bits into a tender mush. They would stand together at the window, those two sisters, looking out at the Mary statue in their yard and recite this prayer every morning, the aroma of toasting bread or cooking oats swirling around them. I wondered if Bernie began and Gert joined in. Perhaps one stood at the window and the other remained absorbed in the task at hand. Perhaps they alternated lines. Some days I imagined them dreaming of old loves. I wondered if they always remembered the old Irish priest and in the weeks after my visit, did they remember reciting it for me?

I HAVE LEARNED that the sighting of Our Lady of Guadelupe in Mexico is on the same ground as the ancient site where the Aztec mother goddess was celebrated in honor of new moons and full moons. In India, her image is said to be the goddess of mercy and forgiveness. Bernie and Gert would have eschewed a connection to anything remotely pagan or staunchly feminist, for that matter—they were not sure the ERA was at all necessary. Yet I was struck by their devotion to a female holy one, in the center of a patriarchal system that didn't seem to bother them in the least.

I thought of all the reading I did in my twenties on goddess mythology and the feminine spirit. Books about Lilith, Gaea, Sophia, and Aphrodite lined my shelves as well as polemics by feminist writers like Mary Daly and Gloria Steinem. If I were to name the search I would call it "Looking for a Feminine Approach to the Divine" or "Looking for What is Spiritual in the Feminine." It was a winding, wending road that led me back to my aunts, to cups of tea around their kitchen table or woodstove, to the family rituals and stories they carried in their bones and hearts, to their Mary statues.

THAT MORNING in October, after they recited their invocation, after Gert had poured three cups of steaming green tea, I asked, "Where did you find the Mary statue?"

"Oh," Gert said, as we gathered at the kitchen table, "It's a wonderful story." Gert was happy to launch into the telling of this story, or any story for that matter. And I was happy to settle into my role as the receiver of these stories.

Gert explained to me that she ordered the Mary statue in 1962. She remembered the exact year. She read an article about the statue in one of her religious magazines. The statues were made by a doctor from Iowa who had been on the frontlines in World War II. Gert's face was flushed as she told me the story.

"One day when he was under shellfire he made a deal with Mary: if she got him home alive, he would build a shrine to her in his front yard." She tilted her head slightly, raised her palms up and shrugged. "Mary took care of him and sure enough, he built a shrine in his front yard to her. Then people started stopping by to ask about the shrine, so much that he began to make and sell them nationally."

Gert's voice moved up the scale as she went from telling his story to her own participation in the story. "When I read about it, I decided we had to have one. I only paid twenty-one dollars, postage and all, and she's lasted all these years."

"Only twenty-one dollars!" Bernie echoed, "Can you beat it? And she's been with us all these years."

I was biting into a tea-soaked gingersnap cookie, baked by Gert the night before, when the doorbell rang. Bernie stayed seated. She was telling me about her arthritis, which had just appeared in the last year. Gert returned with a short, wide woman whose hair was sprung into tight gray, beauty-parlor-permanent curls. Gert announced, "Marcy is here to pick up the Carmelite Mary for the parade tomorrow."

Gert had already patiently explained to me some of the details. Mary, held aloft on her shrine, would be paraded around the church block with all participants saying the rosary as they walked. The parade, Gert explained in answer to my ignorant question, was in October, because it's the month of the rosary. The parade also happened in May, six months later, for May is the month of Mary. This latter part of the schedule I knew for I had not forgotten all of the May Mary processions of my youth—the white dresses we all wore to church and school and later changed out of to deliver May baskets to the boys we had crushes on.

Marcy looked at me and said, a little awkwardly, "If now isn't a good time, I can come back."

Gert disappeared and reappeared with a shoebox and a piece of thick, dark blue, velvety cloth folded under her arms. There was a fairylike quality to her movements, so fast and smooth. Lithe and thin, she took up very little space. She said to me, "We have to dress Mary now, and say farewell prayers to her."

Carmelite Mary with Aunts Eleanor, Bernie, and Gert.

Both Bernie and Marcy were looking at me, although Gert was still in motion, heading into the dining room. I ventured to say, "If you don't mind me joining you, we can go right ahead. It will be a treat for me."

"Oh, that would be great," Marcy said.

Gert added, "We'd love to have you join us."

Bernie echoed, "That would be just grand."

I was not exactly comfortable with this kind of small group prayer, as my nun or priest cousins were. It was not really my thing, but I was amazed, fascinated, awed, and perplexed by my aunts' lively and ever-surprising displays of their faith. When I got to witness its expression at close hand I felt blessed by invisible waters of history, hints of where I came from.

Around the corner, in the dining room, we all stood around the oak table, its surface cluttered with books, magazines, and papers, most of them religious. Gert handed out small prayer books to each of us. Both Bernie and Gert deferred to Marcy as the "leader," as the prayers called for a leader and then responses from the others. Gert called out the page number. We all riffled through to the right page, then Marcy led and the three of us answered. These prayers went on for about eight pages and at least ten minutes, full of invocations to Mary in all her various roles.

"Mary, mother of God."
"Mary, our lady of mercy and forgiveness."
"Mary, receiver of all our sorrows."
"Mary, mother of all mothers."

Page after page of these petitions were read diligently by Marcy, all of us responding each time with, "Pray for us," over and over again.

Every once in a while I looked up from the prayers I was reading and caught Gert's eyes gazing devotedly at the Mary statue in front of her as she recited, "Pray for us."

Such devotion in her eyes. Not a distracted bone in her body, every cell alive, attuned, directed toward this holy image in front of her. If we beside her were to fall off the earth, she may well not have noticed.

I could feel the power in her devotion, her concentration on prayer. In the land of prayer, I was a fledgling—awkward, unsure how to mix the old and the new, unsure what constituted prayer, distracted in my efforts at concentration.

But I knew how to do my part there, joining in with each "Pray for us". And somewhere deep inside my heart I felt waves of good-humored gratefulness to be inside this rather wacky scene with these dearly beloved aunts. When the prayers were over, Gert collected the prayer books and she and Marcy began to pack up Mary. The gold crown was removed from Mary's head and put into the shoebox, along with the small white cloth Mary stood on. Also into the box went the delicate white rosary beads which had been draped around Mary's praying hands. Marcy wrapped the statue in a large plastic bag, which she then slid into the blue velvet bag with a zipper on the end of it.

As Marcy worked, Gert chatted, "Look at that bag Marcy has made for Mary. Isn't it grand?"

Bernie dared me, " Can you guess what it is made from?"

Then, in conspiratorial tones, they told me it was made from the material that used to hang as a curtain in the confessional.

"Not only that," Marcy added, modestly victorious. "But I made Mary's platform for the parade from the rods that used to hold those curtains. I found the material and rods in the basement of the church waiting to be thrown out and told the priest I could find a way to use them."

Bernie and Gert were praising Marcy right and left for her cleverness, her devotion to these details, and in return Marcy told me what a good home Bernie and Gert were providing for Mary. Gert said in an aside to me, "Now, Dan will be here tomorrow night to welcome Mary back after the parade. We always say a rosary to welcome her back."

Gert picked up Mary, safely zipped inside her blue bag. I offered to carry her out to the car. Holding the velvet-wrapped statue close to my chest, it was a hefty bundle, reminiscent of holding my young son close to me. Bernie remained at the door, but Marcy and Gert traipsed out with me, and Marcy directed me to put Mary in the back seat. I laid her carefully across the back seat. No sooner did I get out of the car than Marcy moved her round body in and spent several minutes fiddling with the seatbelt. When she emerged, Mary was buckled in just right, the shoebox of necessary attendant items buckled in beside her. We were decades beyond the days when my siblings and I rode unbuckled in the back seat of the Chevrolet.

When Gert and I walked back in the front door, Bernie was right there in the foyer. She had been watching from the front door. The first thing she said was, "That Marcy, she is something else, isn't she? And you know what?" Bernie spoke in a hushed tone, "She's a convert."

Gert nodded and echoed, "Ever since she got married. And she's a good one too." They imparted this grave news in a hushed tone.

ONE JUNE MORNING, years after this October visit with my aunts, I mentioned, half joking, to my dear running friends in the middle of a long run around Minneapolis city lakes, that I thought my yard might need a Mary statue. My husband and I had spent the previous year embroiled in a property dispute with our new next door neighbors. Although it was over, there was still a lingering sense of having been violated in our own yard. Trees I loved had been cut down. We were trying to rebuild our yard out of a sense of ravaged barrenness. While we were away in Canada that summer, as we had begun to do with our summers, one of my friends, serendipitously named Mary, saw a statue in an antique store window. She was driving by to pick up her kids from day camp. Moments later, her children in tow, she bought it. "It jumped out at me," she said. "It was meant for you."

On a moonlit night in August—while I was 1,200 miles away in Canada—the women, my running friends, gathered. They hauled the hefty statue out of the back end of Mary's car where she had been traveling, unbuckled, but swaddled in blankets. They placed her beneath the oak tree outside my bedroom window, built a shrine around her with sticks they gathered from my yard and lit candles. Rustling oak leaves whispered above them, candles flickered in the summer breeze and scents of summer perfumed the air, enveloping them in a moment of reverent urban splendor. Until Beth's black lab, Boomer, wound his leash around the barbeque grill and dragged it screeching over the patio blocks. A neighbor yelled out, "What's going on over there?"

I was told I had a surprise waiting for me when I returned that summer. And there she was—robed in deep blue, her arms fully extended—graceful and receptive. I loved the way stray morning glories had attached their deep blue beauty to the entwined sticks rising up and around the statue. Part of her nose was and still is missing. My aunts soon supplied me with rosary beads, blue and white plastic to match her colorings, and these beads were draped around her neck.

I suppose some neighbors might wonder at such a display. But her presence still soothes me, reminds me to look for the reverent moments within the chaos of my busy life. She connected me to my aunts and uncle, to devotion, to a rootedness I left long ago and was trying, in my own replanted way, to carry on.

Chapter Eleven

The Centennial & My First Home Mass

THE CENTENNIAL ANNIVERSARY of the founding of Grand Rapids was celebrated in the summer of 1991. Originally settled by loggers and railroad people, the northwoods town of Grand Rapids sits today on the edge of the Iron Range and one hundred miles from the Canadian border. My grandfather Will, one of the founding fathers of Grand Rapids, immigrated from Peterborough, Ontario, in his twenties and set his roots deep into the soil of northern Minnesota. Back in 1891, a "hot issue" in northern Minnesota was the vote to decide if Grand Rapids or nearby LaPrairie would become the county seat for Itasca County. My grandfather was leading a group of lumberjacks through the woods to the voting poll. A Henry Logan met them in the woods and proceeded to convince them why they should vote for Grand Rapids. Logan pointed out that, unlike LaPrairie, "which was owned lock, stock and barrel by the lumber companies," Grand Rapids was

> . . . owned by many people and one man had just as much to say as another about the running of the town. That argument made an immediate hit with the men; the idea of doing as you liked always appealed to the lumberjack. So William Hoolihan and his crew voted for Grand Rapids and had a large share in deciding the election.
> –From *Logging Town: the story of Grand Rapids*

My grandfather, or Pa, as my dad, aunts, and uncles referred to him, worked first as a lumberjack, then a lumberjack foreman, then was Itasca County sheriff for six years, ran a sawmill, farmed, owned and ran a bar, and was a road foreman over the course of his working life. His obituary described him as "one of the most colorful figures in the early days of Itasca County... A man of great physical strength and endurance, he covered much of the county on foot to make his arrests and serve papers." The beloved farm where he housed his family for particularly formative years sprawled on both sides of the dividing line between Grand Rapids and LaPrairie.

An artifact from Pa's election for sheriff.

When Grand Rapids celebrated its hundredth year, many of my siblings and our kids returned home for it. Of course a highlight was the parade, replete with marching bands and candy and bubble gum thrown into the crowd by floats and fire engines. In the midst of a seemingly endless stream of brassy bands came the Founding Families float. There was my father, seated on a deck chair two seats away from Edith Mae Costello, the mother of my best friend from childhood,

Centennial Parade in Grand Rapids, MN. Founding Families float. The author's father is standing.

Kay, and numerous others I had known all of my life. They waved to us all enthusiastically. Two floats behind was my cousin Jim, then the mayor, waving from the back of a maroon convertible with the banner "Mayor Hoolihan" draped along the length of the car.

Part of the weekend-long festivities was an all-school reunion. Bernie, Gert, Dan, and my dad, as members of a founding family and graduates of the local high school, had served on committees and volunteered their time for months. The day I went to sign up for the reunion, since I attended the same high school, I found Bernie and Gert at the sign-up table, greeting people in their side-by-side folding chairs behind a cardboard table full of small boxes of pre-registered names. The sign-up was in the high school gym, the same gym I danced through junior prom in and had the time of my life in leading cheers for our state tournament hockey team.

"You've been busy this week, haven't you?" I asked the aunts. Gert said, "We are having a great time seeing people but we've been so busy we've hardly had any time to pray." Bernie agreed, "That is the truth!" They said it in the way someone I knew might say, "I haven't even had time to do my laundry."

While I was in town for a few days for all these events, my dad invited me to attend what is called in the family a "home Mass." These were small, intimate Masses at a dining room table or in the living room of one of my aunts' homes, said by one of my two priest cousins. This was the first time I'd ever been invited—the usual participants were my dad's generation and from among my generation, the two priests and the nun. I felt like I had been invited to enter the inner sanctum. The anthropologist in me couldn't turn it down, and the daughter in me was honored my dad would ask me, but I was a little nervous at the same time. I was one of them and yet not, not anywhere near as fully or completely or wholeheartedly religious. Would this be a problem for them or for me? After all, a Mass in this setting would allow no escape, no hiding.

I rode with my dad over to Aunt Eleanor's. Her son, Father John, was home from his parish in Wisconsin for a visit and officiating at

The author's two priest cousins with Aunt Bernie and Aunt Gert. Father John is on the left, Father Bill on the right.

the home Mass. Bernie and Gert were there, and Uncle Dan, my Aunt Marg, her husband Milt, and my cousin Sister Eleanor Ann, dressed in her nun attire.

My aunt's living room was small and we filled it, my dad using a folding chair and the rest of us finding seats on the couch and scattered chairs. As the rest of us visited, Father John was donning his floor-length white robe, laying out two candles and setting up a small chalice filled with communion wafers and another filled with wine. He picked up a long, narrow piece of white satin lined with a gold braid and kissed it, then draped it over his shoulders. I noticed how red the skin on his thick, round neck and jowly face was, how his flaming red hair was turning a faded gray. I worried for his health.

When he lit the two white candles on the table and joined his hands together, a respectful silence fell. He said simply, "Let us begin." Sister El Ann had passed around small missals for all of us, which they kept on hand for these events. She acted as his assistant, which indeed she did for much of her life. We followed the prayers in our booklets as he led us. The words fell fast from Father John's mouth—words tripping over each other, racing to get out. I had to listen hard

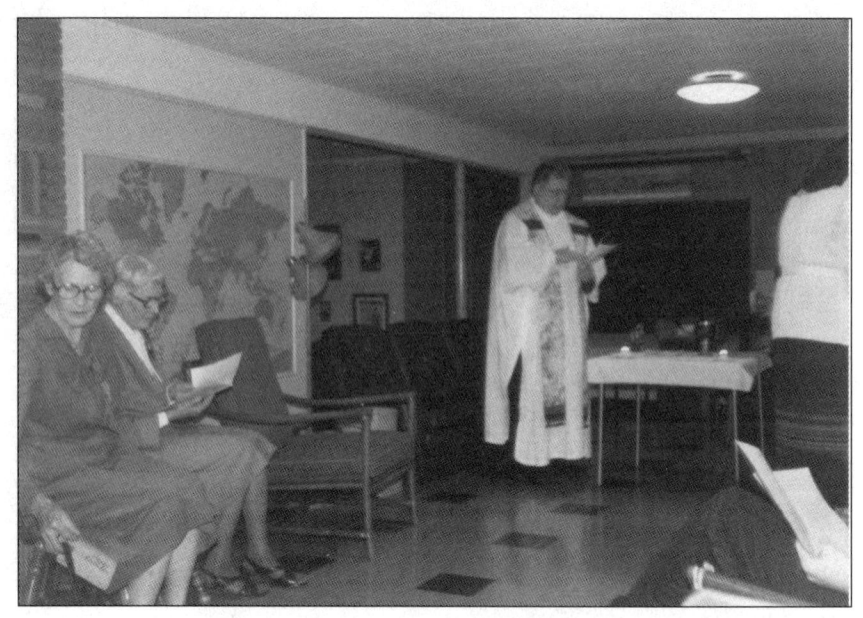

Aunt Gert, Aunt Bernie, and Father John preparing for a home Mass.

to keep up. Sometimes his way of speaking felt to me like nervous energy but that day it was more like a stream flowing downhill over rocks, eddies and curves, a flow even he had a hard time keeping pace with. He had asked me to read the psalm for the day and when the time came, he gave me the nod. I read, "The Lord is my shepherd, I shall not want . . ."

At homily time, he referred to the beautiful words of the psalm. Because the centennial was in the air he talked about Grandma and Grandpa, both long gone. He talked of their hardships and their faith. Then he opened up the floor and there was a moment of quiet—it was a reserved group, in a reserved setting. Then Aunt Marg spoke up in her distinctive, yet gentle voice, "Well, John has really said it all—our Lord is our shepherd. All we need is trust and faith in the Lord."

Beside her, I tightened up. It was not the sort of thing I could get out of my mouth and I was feeling nervous about having to say something. Aunt Eleanor, across the room, picked up the conversational thread, "Yes, John has said it very well. Of all the things Mama and Papa gave us, their faith is their greatest gift. They used to pile all twelve of us in the sleigh and ride to town from the farm for church services on Sundays. Think of how hard that must have been."

Gert entered the story line there, saying, "Mama and Papa's faith helped them so much. And all of us in this room are fortunate to be so rooted in our town and our religion and our family."

Father John was back on. "Yes and I remember Grandpa telling the Blessed Virgin Guide story so many times."

My grandfather died two years before I was born and I envied my cousin for having known him, having heard stories directly from him. I too loved the BVG story and Father John told a brief version of it, then looked my direction.

I felt tenuous as I began, "I can honestly say I don't know very many people who come from a background as rooted in faith and religion as mine." This I could say with absolute sincerity and it seemed to be appreciated. All heads were nodding. I felt like I had somehow passed a test.

Sister El Ann cleared her throat. Her demeanor was gentle and quiet. I remembered the time—her late twenties, I believe—when I heard whispers of her struggle with depression, when her hair was black and short and unwashed. Somehow she made it through that difficult time, made a decision to become a nun, and seemed content in the many years since then. She was trained as a nurse and spent her days taking care of others. She was older than me by about six years, was slightly overweight and wore a matronly beige dress and small black veil on her head.

She exuded care and a kind of quiet comfort. "Father John has spoken very well today," she said, "and today's gospel reminds me of a special intention. When I was in Medjugore [a Yugoslav shrine to Virgin Mary], Mary's message was to pray for the young children. It is very difficult to be young these days, and we also need to pray for young couples. It is also hard to be married and raising children these days."

This was a special intention I could get behind. My daughter was three at the time.

All in the room nodded again. I thought of this head-nodding as the Irish (repressed) version of a gospel church service. Instead of people shouting out "Sing it, sister," they all just nodded vigorously, emphatically, thoughtfully. It was truly their way of participating.

Aunt Bernie then spoke to the room in general, but caught my eye, "It's more difficult these days to have faith or religion, isn't it? Do people have faith like we do?"

I thought of all the different journeys I had been through in my relationship with faith and this religion. Mine had been a rocky route. It had led me back to that small living room with new eyes, an anthropologist's curiosity, and a sense of spiritual quest. There I was, drawn toward the people in that room and the light in their eyes and their connection to my history. And yes, I was attracted to the raw force of their faith.

I looked at Bernie and said, "I don't think faith is dead, but it is different these days. In some ways, yes, it may be harder to have it. Life is faster, more complex."

Father John spoke up, "Life used to be simpler, more innocent. But it really isn't anymore, especially for the younger ones."

Father John moved the Mass forward at this point, reciting the communion prayers. Sister El Ann stepped up to his side to assist him. She took the wine and followed him around the room. He offered a wafer to each of us and she followed with the chalice of wine. "Body of Christ," he said to each one of us individually. Each one of us responded, "Amen." She followed behind him and to each one of us said, "The Blood of Christ." In turn each of us answered, "Amen." The shared simple actions united us, and a sense of peacefulness permeated the room.

Father John, the author's father, Aunt Gert and Sister Eleanor Ann after a home Mass.

There were a few prayers after communion, and then Father John said, "Mass is ended, go in peace." As we walked out I told Bernie and Gert that Aunt Alice told me I should ask them about BVG and their hairnet story. I wanted to hear it from them and in detail. So I told them I'd be over later.

"Oh good," Gert said. "We'll look forward to laying eyes on you again soon, then."

My dad and I got in the car and he drove slowly (as always) home. I thanked him for inviting me, and he said, "Oh, it was good to have you there."

In that moment of shared experience and time, I was aware of my closed heart of the past, and grateful for the heart-opening moments that had reopened this trail—or should I say *grail*—to me.

Chapter Twelve
Bernie, Gert, & BVG

My aunt Alice, in the last few years before she died, was in the habit of bringing me story ideas, like hor d'oeurves on a platter. She had an eye for the story, an observer's eye, a writer's eye . . . and as someone who married into my father's large family, she had an outsider's eye. Married to my Uncle Jerry, my dad's oldest brother, she had been my eighth grade English teacher and always encouraged my writing. She was known in our family as the "other Alice," for my mother's name was Alice, also.

At my father's seventy-something birthday party, Aunt Alice had sidled up to me, both of us balancing paper plates with cake on them, both of us spearing away at the white icing and tender crumbs with our plastic forks. Always thin, Alice's smooth, well-made-up face broke into a smile which matched her eyes, alive with intelligence and humor.

"Have you heard the story about BVG and Gert's hairnet?"

"No," I answered, although the combination of BVG and a hairnet made me smile.

"You ask Gert about it," she said. "I don't want to spoil the story for you."

Aunt Alice

The afternoon of the home Mass, I headed over to visit Bernie and Gert's mid-afternoon. A hot summer day, the three of us were soon sipping from tall glasses of cranberry juice with slices of lemon floating between the ice cubes. Gert had just opened a tin of her homemade peanut butter chocolate chip oatmeal cookies, baked with half white, half whole wheat flour. I sometimes wondered if they ever baked a cookie without throwing some oatmeal into it—"cuts down on the sweetness," Gert would say.

She unfolded a white paper napkin, laying it across a china plate with tiny flowers around the border and set a small matching plate in front of each of us. After deftly moving an ample amount of cookies from the tin to the plate, she gently slid it towards me. "Take a few now, dear, you're looking too thin these days." Unless I was at least ten pounds overweight they thought I was too thin. It was the one place in the world where, for a moment, I genuinely felt "too thin."

As I sunk into the cookie's delicious, wholesome taste, I remembered Aunt Alice's tip. Following a swallow of the bittersweet juice, I asked, "Will you tell me about BVG and your hairnet? Aunt Alice said I should ask you about it."

Gert chuckled, "Alice told you about that?"

Bernie chuckled a little louder, and commented, "Can you beat it? That Alice." She shook her head, grinning.

Gert was perched on the edge of her hard-backed chair, ready to launch into the story.

"I wear a net over my hair, you know, to keep it looking neat."

Her thin, bony, freckled fingers cupped the barely visible strands of the gray net. I saw how the threads blended in with her short silver hair, holding her hair close to her head. I never would have noticed it was there, but when I glanced over to Bernie's shock of white hair, it was clear nothing was holding hers down.

Seeing my quizzical look, Gert added, "It keeps my hair from getting too messy in the wind or while I work. There's a special kind I like, and no one in town carries them anymore. I've talked to Emmie Betts and she can't order them."

Emmie Betts, the mother of nine children, one of whom was a classmate of mine, was the Catholic haircutter in town. She had been doing hair for over forty years in the basement of her home, and if she couldn't order a hairnet, then no one in town could.

Gert continued, "So, I looked at the inside of my last hair net, and I could just make out the words, The Hair Net Company, New York, and a very faint zip code. Well, I sat down and wrote a letter, put my last hair net in the envelope and asked if they were still making it and if so, could I order some. I addressed the envelope to the Hair Net Company, New York, New York, and I put what looked like the zip code on it."

"Can you beat it?" Bernie said, shaking her head again. Her deep blue eyes were bright and looked straight into me as she continued, "No address, just 'New York' and the zip code. And she wasn't even positive about the zip code!"

Her arms, strong and sturdy in a short-sleeved pastel blue cotton blouse, were crossed in front of her, each hand loosely holding on to the other arm.

"That's all?" I asked. "Nothing else?" I asked, even though I could guess the answer. This was my role in the storytelling ritual and it was one I happily stepped into in this home of my father's family.

"No," Gert said emphatically. "In the lower left hand corner of the envelope I wrote 'BVG.' Blessed Virgin Guide." She spoke slowly, letting the words sink in before she continued, "It was always Mama's way of asking the Virgin Mary to guide important mail to its destination. She put it on all her letters over the years, especially the ones between her and Pa when they were courting between Minnesota and Canada."

She paused again, looking down at the tablecloth in front of her, as if the mere mention of Mama sent her into a moment of reverence and nostalgia. After a brief moment, she looked up at me, the wrinkles in her face broke into a smile and she resumed. "Well, about a week later I got a letter back from the Hair Net Company, with an order form and my model circled in red and listed at a very good price. So I was able to order more."

Her smile was laced with thin, durable strands of triumph, even joy. She opened her hands out in front of her, palms up, and her thin shoulders gave a gentle shrug under her white striped cotton blouse. "BVG worked for Mama and it still works for me today."

We all pondered that as she slid the plate of cookies over to me again. I picked one with lots of chocolate chips and set it on the small china plate in front of me.

"Tell me the BVG story again, the one about Grandpa," I prompted. I had heard the story many times over the years, but I never tired of hearing it.

"Oh," Bernie exclaimed, "You mean the story of Pa and BVG and the mail?"

"Yes," I answered, watching the color and excitement pick up in both of their faces.

Gert spoke first, her calmness edged with a quiet fervor, "You know, Papa was still courting Mama when he came down here to Minnesota and lived in the logging camps. She was back in Peterborough, Canada. They wrote letters to one another for a year before he went back and married her and brought her to Minnesota. For the mail to get to Pa it had to cross a lot of land, but the last and trickiest part of the mail route here in Minnesota was across a lake to the logging camp."

Bernie was nodding her head, her eyes flicking back and forth between Gert and me, holding her arms at her sides. Pretty Weasel at attention: she watched everything, missed nothing.

Gert continued, " So, one stormy night the mailman, an old Scotsman—"

Here Bernie pounced. She just couldn't hold herself back any longer. Referring to the Scotsman, she interjected, with four emphatic words: "who had no religion." With one bold stroke she had painted him. The sharp tone in her voice made it clear that there could be no worse indictment.

Gert agreed with a long, drawn-out "Yes, he had no religion . . ." letting the full import of those words sink their way into the story before she continued.

"He had to cross the lake in his small wooden rowboat that day in foul weather. The clouds were dark when he started, but the reward of the end of his job, a night on a bunk, a warm meal, the company of other men, all worked on him to start his trip across in spite of the thick overhanging October clouds. Halfway across the lake, the wind came up so suddenly and forcefully it took his breath away. The sturdy burlap mail bag sat up in the bow as the boat rocked in the waves and he rowed his way across, arm muscles bulging and strained, suddenly terrified he might not make it at all."

Here Bernie gave me a knowing look and added, "He was a big man, you know, like Pa. Those men who worked in the woods had to be big and strong."

"That's right," Gert added slowly, reflectively. Then she continued, "As the waves washed over the top of the boat, a light suddenly glowed at the edge of the dark green mailbag: a light in the shape of an envelope, pushing its way out of a small opening. The light glowed, lighting up each wave before it hit, so he could brace himself. Suddenly, also, the front of the boat was weighted down—the boat felt more steady. Looking at that light, he felt he was going to make it. The light gave him a thread of hope."

Gert took a deep breath, sipped on her juice. Both she and Bernie looked at me, their eyes glowing, Bernie's face a broad grin, Gert in her quiet storytelling trance.

"Well," Gert went on. "When the old Scotsman arrived on dry land, wet through despite his thick rain gear, he peered at the corner of his mailbag. An envelope dangled at the edge, a soft green light fading, draining away, just as he made out the name on the front—Pa's name. As the last of the light disappeared, he reached for the letter, touched it, looked at it and then just tucked it back inside, shaking his head. He slung the bag over his broad shoulder and trudged up to the mess hall.

"Immediately inside the door, he flung his bag to the floor, pulled the no-longer glowing letter from the corner of his bag, cocked his head toward Pa, who was standing in a small group of men near the fireplace, and said, a slight trace of awe in his voice, 'What is it with this letter? It glowed in the dark all the way across the lake, giving me enough light to see my way. It weighed the boat down in front, too, or my wee boat might well have flipped over in those huge swells.'"

"Can you beat it?" Bernie's eyes blazed from across the table. She loved this story.

Gert spread her hands out, palms up, and announced, "In the corner, in Ma's handwriting, were the letters 'BVG.'"

The story out, she relaxed, reached for a cookie, and we all reveled for a few moments in the spirit of the story, its familiar swirls enveloping us.

Written in the lower lefthand corner of the envelope, as my grandmother did with all her correspondence, were three letters: "BVG". Blessed Virgin Guide. These simple three letters of the alphabet were carefully and beautifully penned on every letter sent from Kate Scollard in northeastern Canada to William Hoolihan in northern Minnesota in the early 1900s. The magic stamp of BVG ensured the safe arrival of love notes across miles and miles of wilderness: huge forests of white and red pine, oak and maple; a bounty of lakes and rivers; slats of granite in Canada turning to mounds of black dirt in Minnesota. The envelopes were carried by horseback, train, and finally, small boats that pitched on wind and wave. Those letters traveled in the deep of winter, through freezing winds and blizzards and tundra-like conditions. They traveled in late fall and early spring through fierce and blustery storms. They traveled in the relative ease of warm summer days, the smell of hot dry pine needles wafting around them, along with the black flies. No matter what, these letters always made it to their destination.

Over the years, the tale of the old Scotsman traveled also. From Ma and Pa, the story wound its way into the heart and legends their aging children told. Bernie and Gert leaned into the telling with as much feeling as the first time they had told it to me years before. Their cheeks were flushed, both pairs of blue eyes were lit up. The most important part of the story was Mama's magical, mystical, mythological faith . . . but intrinsic to the telling was the way this faith had touched someone who "had no religion."

The receiver of these letters, Pa, was already a believer, yet there was a subtext there. He himself was not known for putting these three letters on his envelopes. No, it was Mama who was famous for this, perhaps more feminine, perhaps more fervent expression of faith. He was the receptor. A successful lumberjack, he towered in his six-foot-two sturdy body, surrounded by men hardened to long days of labor and cold air. Several of them were gathered with Pa by the huge stone fireplace after eating, rows of men still finishing their homemade pie and coffee. Mixing with the pungent aroma of woodsmoke, the smell of roast beef hung in the air. With the wind rattling the few windows, none of them were in a hurry to venture outside and go back to the sleeping bunks. This was the small piece of rest in their day that began before sunrise. One of the men Pa was standing with was Matt Spang, a kindred spirit he had met in camp. Later, Matt would start his own sawmill and marry Kate's sister, forever connecting their two lives.

A dark shape formed out the window, surrounded by the sleepy gray of driving rain, and moved toward the door. Pa, his dark blue eyes sharp and keen, recognized the slant of the walk, and the shape of the bag slung over the shoulder. He cried out, "It's the mail!" and sprang to open the solid oak door.

They couldn't believe he had arrived in that weather. As the door opened and the wind rushed in, long benches of plaid wool shirts and suspenders turned to watch while the few heartily greeted the mailman, made room for him by the open fireplace, all of them anxious for words from loved ones.

As one of the men gave him a welcoming slap on the back, the old Scotsman looked at William Hoolihan and with a quiet reverence, pulled the letter from the top of his thick bag.

It was this no-religion man, in front of a group of tough and weathered lumberjacks who spoke in awe of that letter and its power to have saved his life. "What is it with this letter?" he asked.

His voice sank to a low volume, a pitch lower and softer than his usual boisterous and jovial tone. There was a quality of tenderness in his voice, a tone one might reserve for speaking to a loved one after a long absence. This quality in his voice stopped every man in the small group, caused each one to listen closely.

He paused, aware of the attention directed at him. The spark and roar of the fire he stood in front of, warming his cold bones, snapped its way into the space between his words.

Gingerly, both wanting to hold the letter in his thick, leathery hands and wanting to drop it like a hot potato from his calloused palms, he handed it to Will with all eyes watching, and added,

Kate Hoolihan (the author's grandmother, on the right) and her sister Nora, who followed Kate from Canada to Minnesota.

"Without it I would be a dead man, and all your letters would be floating to the bottom of the lake."

Silence hung for a moment among the small group of men, along with a sudden, aching realization of the closeness of death and distance of loved ones. Will took the long thick envelope. The letter looked ordinary by then. He spotted the letters, BVG. They were crystal clear, unsmudged by water, a dark clarity on off-white paper, and a smile spread across his ruddy, fair complexion.

"It's from Kate," he said simply. "All the way from Peterborough." He slid the envelope into his flannel shirt pocket, a slice of warmth beating beside his heart through another hour of conversation and beating all the way back to his bunk and small reading lamp.

Chapter Thirteen
The Bridge to Peterborough

Certain people are perfectly placed to provide bridges between generations. Furthest back in what I knew of the Hoolihan clan, the history inside of dates and names, was a woman named Bridget, mother of my grandfather Will, my great-grandmother, grandmother to Bernie, Gert, Dan, my father. Her very name contained the word "Bridge". She was born in 1841 and crossed over from Ireland at the age of three. But the person who provided the bridge between her and me, between that initial immigration and my world, was the outspoken Cousin Rosemary (my father's cousin). She was my bridge back to Peterborough. And the following story is hers as she told it to me.

Three miles out of town, the train began to slow down. Golden and flame-orange maple leaves became less of a blur against the deep green pines out her window. In spite of being only six years old, Rosemary could feel the long-awaited and equally dreaded slowdown. The kind white-haired ticket man was suddenly beside her, saying, "This is your stop, honey. Gather your bag." She heard the announcer coming through the train, as he had done before each stop. This time he was saying that name she'd been told to listen for, "Peterborough . . . next stop, Peterborough.." She clutched the soft cotton quilt her mama had made for her when she was a baby, and said the name again to herself, *Peterborough*. She liked the feel of it on her tongue, had heard the name since she could understand words. So much talk from her father and Uncle Will about "back in Peterborough." The name reminded her of sledding down a hill on a warm winter day. Peterborough, Ontario, Canada.

"Granny Bridget" she was less sure about. Her papa had told her how much she would love Granny Bridget... but Rosemary still missed her mama. Although Mama had spent so much time in bed, sick, Rosemary could still sit at the bottom of the bed and tell her stories. Then one day, she couldn't do that anymore. One day her Mama quit talking and was taken from bed to a huge box in the living room. Then a lot of people started showing up at the house, bringing food, the women crying. People came on horseback, a few in their Model A's.

Cousin Rosemary.

And then, her mama was gone.

Ever since, Papa had talked about sending her to Peterborough to live.

THE GENTLE, STEADY September sun almost disguised the hint of fall in the wisps of a cool breeze as Bridget stood on the train platform with her thirty-three-year-old son Sam beside her at the edge of Peterborough. The letter from her son Patrick had arrived ten days before, with the news that little Rosemary would be on today's train, arriving at 4:00 p.m. Although it was running a little late, that wasn't unusual.

Bridget couldn't imagine why three of her sons had to move all the way to Minnesota. There was a restless edge in the family. Bridget recognized it, knew that was part of why her father had put her on a boat when she was only three and brought the family all the way over from Ireland.

Ah well, Bridget thought, *at least Minnesota is closer than Ireland.*

She and Patrick had been writing back and forth about the possibility of Rosemary coming to live with her. Bridget's heart went out to the wee one—to lose her mama at such a young age. In spite of all the losses in Bridget's own life, her mama didn't die until Bridget was well into her forties, and it was hard enough then. Patrick had written that Rosemary was a good girl and a bit of help already. Surely she would be even more so as she grew older. Still, Bridget felt a twinge of nervousness. She'd been living alone since her youngest son Sam was married five years ago. Sam and Amelia lived just across the street and would be of some help to her with the young girl.

For the two days Rosemary had been traveling, her mama's quilt never left her hands. The nice ticket man often checked on her. And then the train's brakes were making that funny loud sound, and Rosemary's blue eyes locked onto the view out the window nearest her. She saw a white-haired lady in a long skirt and high-necked, long-sleeved blouse with a shawl over her shoulders. Rosemary thought, *That must be her.*

Rosemary was glad she hadn't eaten much all day or she might feel sick. When she put her hand over her heart, it was racing. It felt like her heart might jump right out of her. She held both hands and her quilt tight over her chest, then clamped her mouth shut to keep her heart inside.

Then she was standing on the platform with her quilt and bag. And suddenly she was meeting her very tall Uncle Sam, who shook hands with her and took her bag. Granny Bridget was kneeling down beside her, asking how her trip was, and leaning over to kiss her on the forehead. Rosemary felt, more than saw, a kindness in the deep blue eyes of both Bridget and Sam.

Then she was between them on the wagon, with the horses pulling them along. She felt sleepy as the September sun streamed through the trees and across the farms they passed and warmed the quilt, still wrapped in her arms.

Over sixty years later, for a book on family history, Rosemary wrote, "The fact that she was seventy-five when I went to live with her demonstrates that she had courage."

In the last few years of her life, Rosemary lived in the convalescent ward of the hospital in Grand Rapids, Minnesota. From her wheelchair, tubes running from her nose to the oxygen supply, Rosemary's eyes lit up when I asked her to tell the story of going to Peterborough to live.

The author's sister Cathy and their father's cousin Rosemary at a family reunion.

"Imagine that—she was seventy-five years old. Nobody asked her if she wanted me, but she didn't blink an eye. And we got on famously, except that she had some awfully old-fashioned ideas, which I could never tell her were old-fashioned. But they were. We disagreed on quite a few occasions about the length of skirts. She thought I should wear skirts to my ankles and long sleeves and high necks all the time. We had the occasional Irish spat, but other than that, we got along real well. She was one grand old lady. In the beginning she took care of me, but near the end I took care of her."

Bridget died when Rosemary was nineteen. Not too long after that, Rosemary returned to Grand Rapids, Minnesota, where her cousins, my father's family, included her for many meals and events, and where she met the man who became her husband.

Rosemary's eyes, clear as a spring-fed lake in the sun, looked at me. She said again, "I know what *I* would have said if someone sent me a child when I was seventy-five." Her voice became thoughtful and she added, "I suppose, when you're used to taking things all your life . . ." I could only surmise that she meant Bridget had a hard life and had learned to take that hardship in stride. Rosemary shook her head as she told me the story, clearly still affected by her admiration of and gratitude for Bridget.

At Bridget's knee, many times Rosemary heard firsthand the stories of her great-grandparents, back on the "olde sod." Bridget's father,

Samuel Anglesey, fell in love with and married Mary Ellen Ryan. He, perhaps a Protestant, could not inherit the title he had expected to inherit of Lord Anglesey, because he married a Catholic. I thought to myself, *Aha, a rulebreaker, a black sheep in the making*. Instead of a title, he was given the chattels (or personal articles) of the estate. He sold those to pay for their passage on a ship to Canada with enough left over to buy a farm on Young's Point, near Peterborough.

Although my family likes to claim its lineage as 100% Irish, what about this name Anglesey? It's about as Anglo-Saxon as a name can get. I wonder what connection this name, this forefather of mine, has with Anglesey Island, off the coast of Great Britain, known for being a great vacation place. My brother Dan, who has done a lot of genealogical research, has a theory. His theory is that Bridget's father was the black sheep of his English family, a black sheep perhaps for no other reason than that he fell in love with and married a red-haired Irish woman, charmed by her beauty or her lilting voice or her easy laughter or her hard-working bones. But perhaps he had a bent toward, a predisposition for, being a black sheep before he chose her as his wife. Perhaps his being a black sheep, an outsider in his homeland, impelled his journey to Canada as much as the hardship of those times in Ireland. Perhaps black sheep are the family seers—the ones who foreshadow or bring on change.

However, when I ran the black sheep theory by Rosemary, she said, "Now isn't that just like the Irish. To embellish the story a bit and make themselves sound just a bit more glamorous." She said this, in spite of being mostly Irish herself. I had to laugh—she was what one would call a straight-shooter.

By the 1840s and '50s, the potato famine was in full swing. Stories abound of men wandering the Emerald Isle with green tongues, so hungry they ate the grass they found on their walks. Many family members had begun to shrink to nothing, and were fighting over small pieces of land. Years of drought had stripped their larders empty. Conditions on the boats coming across the Atlantic were horrible, and many died en route or on the crowded, over-infected and understaffed Grosse Island landing spot in Canada.

In 1841, Bridget was three years old when her parents packed her, her one-year-old brother Richard, a few clothes and a goat onto the hold of the ship. Goat milk was the children's main form of nourishment for the six weeks it took to cross the Atlantic. Walking from their home in County Clare to the sea's edge, they boarded from the west coast of Ireland. I wondered if Rosemary's solo train ride brought back memories for Bridget of her cross-Atlantic trip at an even younger age.

I imagined the four of them—Samuel, Mary Ellen, young Bridget and Richard—huddled around one wooden berth, savoring a single daily drink of goat milk. The goat would have been kept below and I wondered if they had to protect themselves against others stealing the goat milk. They would have been wrapped in wool blankets, a small defense against the cold wind seeping in through the small cracks. Since bathing would have been impossible and conditions extremely crowded, the smells were dank, sweaty, and moist from the sea air. Samuel, who had been a breadbaker in Ireland, would step up onto the deck, smoking a pipe with the other men, trading information, stories of the land to be had ahead of them. The women sang songs to the restless bewildered children, played finger games, lost their tempers, held the small bodies close to keep them warm, sent quiet and fierce prayers out into the dark of night.

Sailing to British North America (Canada) was cheaper than sailing to the U.S. Sailors on the British/Canadian ships were less skilled, and liquor and drunkenness were allowed on board, whereas American ships prohibited liquor while sailing. An Irish historian writes, "dishonest speculators were responsible for the existence of 'coffin ships' but the Irish peasant's wild desire to escape Ireland, combined with his utter ignorance of the sea and geography made him eager to risk himself in any vessel." (from *The Great Hunger* by Cecil Woodham-Smith)

"Coffin ships" they were called—many of the passengers died on board or were so sickly upon arrival, they never recovered. The ship's main purpose was to bring timber back from Canada, but they filled the ships going over with people. Wooden berths were hastily put up between decks, and it wasn't until 1842 that a law was passed requiring "that the height between decks, where the passengers slept and lived be not less than six feet, no deck was to be laid below the waterline ... a stock of medicines must be carried though not a doctor and seven pounds of provisions were to be given out weekly and three quarts of water per person daily." (Woodham-Smith)

My great-grandmother Bridget and her family sailed before these minimal laws were passed. It must have been a combination of sheer will and strength and more than a wee bit of luck which carried them. And their faith.

Granny Bridget (as Rosemary called her), in her later years, liked to talk of crossing the Atlantic and of how hard the first few years in Canada were. They landed in Quebec and then they traveled free by barge down the St. Lawrence, because Canada was trying to encourage settlements inland. They ended up near Peterborough and found a plot of land to homestead. In her old age, Granny Bridget remembered the crossing of the ocean, the warm goat milk she and her brother shared, and the modest shelter her father put together for them when they landed. It was back-breakingly hard to clear the land, and the woods were thick with flies.

Within years, their farm included some livestock, an orchard and a huge garden. Bridget's mother, Mary Ellen, is listed in a Canadian census taken in 1871 as being sixty years old and having:

> Two acres of land—improved, two gardens/orchards
> Half an acre of potatoes equaling thirty bushels
> One milk cow
> Two sheep
> Two swine, one killed during year
> One hundred pounds of butter
> Eight pounds of wood

When Bridget was seventeen, her father was no longer alive and her mother began to arrange a marriage for her. She gave Bridget two choices. Of the two, Bridget chose Dan Hoolihan—a handsome, curly-haired redhead whose nickname was Dublin Dan, because, as Rosemary put it, the map of Ireland was written all over his face. His farm was also nearest to Bridget's family farm. He, too, remembered crossing over from Ireland as a child. He was a skilled step-dancer, and he was big, tall and handsome. The two families were pleased. These families had left so many loved ones behind and had brought with them so much hope for the new land. A new breed of Irish, Canadian Irish, was promised when these two married on October 25, 1858.

Promised and delivered. Bridget and Dublin Dan had eleven children, their last born twenty-three years after their marriage. Their children were: Thomas, John, Patrick, William, Mary, Edward, Margaret, Elizabeth, Daniel, Fanny, and Samuel. William, their fourth-born son, was my father's father. Patrick was Rosemary's father.

Because only the oldest or older sons inherited the farm, when the middle sons, Patrick, William, and Edward were in their twenties, they came to northern Minnesota to look for work and land. They arrived in 1892, found work as loggers, and found land to settle on. According to Rosemary, my grandfather William was the most successful and the most aggressive of the three brothers. Edward never married and he returned occasionally to Canada to live with his mother. He ended up dying in Peterborough, and was buried with his mother and father. Rosemary called him a bum. Patrick married, and when his wife died, he felt inadequate for the task of raising a girl child so he sent Rosemary, his daughter, back to his mother in Canada. He kept his son, and together they farmed the land. He much later remarried and adopted one more child. Rosemary stayed in Peterborough until Bridget died at the age of eighty-nine.

After Bridget was widowed, with two of her eleven children still to finish high school, she earned her way as a midwife. Even after Rosemary arrived, Bridget was still a working woman. If a baby was due, the two of them packed up and went to stay, sometimes for up to two weeks, with the family in need. Bridget not only helped deliver and care for the baby, she helped look after the other children as well.

As Rosemary told me these stories, it was clear she admired Bridget's feistiness. She told me that Bridget was a flaming redhead until her hair turned white. She had pierced her own ears, and she offered to pierce the ears of anyone else who desired it. I imagined this part of Bridget emerging after her husband died. It struck me as a wild edge breaking out of the constraints of a body covered in long skirts and long sleeves.

The familial blend of wildness and restraint asserts itself in Bridget. She wore a bustle and a headcap. Black lace for weekdays. White lace with pearls and ribbon for Sundays. According to Rosemary, she had a reason for everything she did. She wore the bustle to keep her kidneys warm. She smoked her clay pipe after fifty because her doctor told her it would be good for her digestion. Rosemary added, "I think Bridget told herself that." She also drank dandelion wine to aid her digestion. To this bit of information Rosemary added, "Guess who picked bushels of dandelions to make it? I worked like a demon in that garden. She was a tough lady."

Author's father and Great-Uncle Sam the step-dancer in Peterborough.

After dinner, sipping tea, Bridget read shapes, signs and omens in the tea leaves in both of their cups. Bridget, in a superstitious vein, warned Rosemary against ever naming a child Dan. She had lost her husband Dan at a young age, she had lost her son Dan and felt the name was bad luck. Of course I have an Uncle Dan, a brother Dan and a cousin named his son Dan!

Bridget spoke with great affection for her husband Dan. Their children loved to sit on his lap and run their fingers through his curls. Her youngest son, Sam, took up step-dancing and as the story goes, wore out a pair of shoes a month until close to the end of his long life. He and his wife lived across the street, taking care of Bridget and checking on her in her old age. Rosemary said Sam and Amelia saved her by giving her the odd nickel for spending money. Rosemary had one uniform for school, which she wore every day. The kids with money had two uniforms, she said—one wool and one cotton—but hers was a blend that had to work for cold and warm weather. When it came time for her first communion, Granny Bridget spent weeks sewing by hand a beautiful, long white dress for her.

Describing Bridget, Rosemary said, "She was as Irish as you can be without being Saint Patrick himself." Of Bridget and Catholicism she added, "She thought she brought Catholicism over here single-handedly." One of Bridget's favorite sayings was, "With the help of God and a little of me own strength."

In Rosemary's stories of Bridget I received a clear look back at our roots of faith, which clearly extended back further than I could see or hear. And those are just my grandfather's roots. My paternal grandmother's family were the Scollards and they settled in Ennismore, a small town near Peterborough. Its nickname was the Holy Land, because of the religious fervor (yes, Catholic) that abounded there.

One of the ways this religious fervor was expressed in those days was the nightly litany of saying the rosary. This extended down through the generations and into my childhood. Often Uncle Sam and Aunt Amelia, who Rosemary says were *very* religious, came over in the evenings to join Bridget and Rosemary on their knees on the floor. Yet, in Bridget's later years, unless Sam and Amelia were over, Rosemary said, "One of us could usually persuade the other to pass it by. She mellowed quite a bit in her old age."

Once Rosemary told me that "Bridget had a good Irish temper. We had a woodstove and when I provoked her, she was good at flinging a stick of wood. I learned to dodge real well."

Ah, the redheaded Irish temper. We all knew it in my father by the way he sucked in his cheek—that was the beginning, the warning sign that someone was in serious trouble. He and his siblings said that they feared their father like they feared the Lord. When one of my own children crossed me I had to struggle with my temper, the part of me that would like to fling the nearest object at hand. I parented in a world where acting on such an impulse was not only frowned upon but against the law. Bridget lived in another world. What we shared was the impulse and the struggle to manage it.

I'm intrigued with my great-grandmother, the pipe-smoker. She used a long clay pipe. When the pipe was yellowed with nicotine, Bridget put it in the coals of the coal-stove, often holding it between two long forks, until the nicotine burned off. She liked her pipe clean and white. Rosemary said she smoked it all day long and lived until she was eighty-nine—"Not such a good ad for the dangers of smoking." When Rosemary came in from school, she could see from the front door to the back room where Granny Bridget would be sitting in her rocking chair, looking out the window. When Rosemary brought a friend home, Bridget threw the apron she always wore over her pipe— as a thin wisp of smoke floated up and out of the apron, which she acted as if didn't exist. Rosemary had a vivid memory of Granny Bridget sitting in the chair, as smoke rose up and out from under the apron.

In one of the few photos we used to have of her, Bridget was sitting on her front porch in a rocking chair, reading a book, which Rosemary said was a Bible. Perhaps the picture was taken on a Sunday afternoon, Bridget's regular reading time. Somewhere in her rugged life, she had learned to read. What I noticed were her long, bony

Granny Bridget, the author's great-grandmother. Taken in Peterborough, Ontario.

fingers. The picture was black and white, and I could see the crease between the finger bones, running along the length of her hand. The fingers look huge, long, and sturdy. Not unlike my own fingers, that my father called piano hands. In a similar photo, Bridget wore a long full skirt, long sleeves, with a white collar around her shoulders. Her white hair was pulled back and up, and her cheek bones were pronounced. Her face was strong and angular—distinguished looking.

Rosemary and I admired the picture together. "She was a tough lady," she said again, and added, "She was a grand old lady." In the air there was a sense of awe mixed with admiration. I thought about the strange twist of fate that orphaned this woman, that sent her to live the remainder of her childhood with this grandmother she would never have known very well otherwise. I thought about being able to visit Rosemary in the hospital in the last days of her life, able to hear firsthand again those stories from the early 1900s of a life in Peterborough, the life my grandparents were born into and left behind. I thought of how Rosemary's life and her stories were like a bridge across the waters of history, connecting the rush and flow of many decades.

On my last visit with Rosemary she looked at me and grew suddenly wistful. "You remind me of my daughter Joanna. She had the same red curly hair you have."

A shock went through me. Never, in all my years of knowing Rosemary, did I know she had lost a daughter at the age of two. I found out later from my parents that her child drowned in Lake Pokegama.

I hugged Rosemary goodbye and kissed her cheek. When she died a month later, I imagined her close beside her long-lost daughter, her husband Hank, and Granny Bridget. I could see Bridget—ears pierced, pipe in hand, and perhaps a glass of dandelion wine, laughing with Rosemary about their fights over the length of skirts.

I fingered my own pierced ears and noticed how, especially when I'm in Canada, I enjoy a good cigar and a glass of wine. A toast to the familial blend of wildness and restraint. A toast to courage—"with the help of God and a little of me own strength."

Chapter Fourteen
The Jig Is Up—The Farm

FAMILY RUMOR says my grandfather Will left Peterborough because "he couldn't throw a stone without it landing in a relative's yard." After having driven myself the roads outside of Peterborough, Ontario, I can sense that farming, a love for that kind of living close to the land, must have been in his blood. Perhaps the desire for land was what led him to leave. None of us really knew why he chose Minnesota—it must have been the promise of land, and perhaps the land reminded him of Canada.

Will, Bridget's fourth-born son, was known for his smarts and his physical strength. I wonder how often he quoted his mother, "With the help of God and a little of me own strength." He created, built, masterminded the farm, which before *the house* was home to his huge family. The farm held a huge and important place in all of their memories.

His life on the farm came after his time as a lumberjack and county sheriff. Although the farm was dismantled by the time I was born, the land was still in the family. The land itself has always felt especially hallowed to me, rich and sacred. And so many stories were told of life on the farm, it was forever alive in my imagination. My father, even in his last months, said he could still vividly see and remember the farm.

The following is an excerpt from my father's memoirs written at the age of ninety-two, not long before he died.

> I was the first one born on the farm, with three others born after me. I thought that the farm was a wonderful place to live—about 200 acres, lots of room to run with Pal [the family's black lab] over to the sand pit where we could play in the sand pile,

down to the railroad tracks where we would pick wild strawberries and then bring them home and get cream from the walk-in cooler and have a dish of wild berries and cream and sugar. A large garden had almost everything—carrots, lettuce, cabbage, asparagus, beets, onions, new potatoes in the spring and of course sweet corn in the late summer.

Also, we had quite a large orchard with crabapples and plums in season. I did not like having to weed the garden—on hands and knees—but I guess one would call it a necessary evil. There was also a large raspberry patch and strawberry patch—there was lots of room to plant whatever.

My dad fattened and butchered his own beef and pork. Salt pork for all winter and fresh beef butchered in the fall and kept in the walk-in cooler and/or frozen in winter until used for the table. There were lots of chickens, fresh eggs every day, and nice plump hens for chicken soup or for roast chicken.

One should not fail to mention milk and cream and even our own homemade butter.

Many food items were canned in-house and stored in the home basement—canned crabapples, plum jelly, canned venison, wild and tame raspberries and blueberries picked by most of the family going out on berry picking expeditions which lasted all day, with picnic lunch having been brought along. My dad and some of us boys would go on a scouting expedition days before the picking day.

Living on a dairy farm in those days of the 1920s—there was plenty of food and drink—all you had to go to town for were salt and pepper and flour and some other herbs and of course bananas, oranges in season. I shouldn't forget peanut butter—favorite of us young boys. We ordered peanut butter from the *Montgomery Ward* catalogue by the five-pound pail. When the pail arrived and was brought home we took the top cover off and there lay about a one-inch layer of peanut oil. We boys had to stir the oil into the rest of the peanut butter before we could have our first peanut butter sandwich. On fresh-baked bread, especially when just out of the oven, it was a real treat.

North of the big house, but adjacent to it, was the well house with a walk-in cooler and ice house. The well house included well pump, legs of the windmill and the connector of pump to windmill. The windmill pumped all the water needed except during long spells of no wind, which was very seldom.

There were two large water storage tanks in the basement which held 1,000 gallons of water for household use, and one in back of and to the west of the well house, which stored many gallons and was piped to the barn for livestock in the winter. It was on a gravity feed to the barn because the barn was at a lower level than the storage tank. The tank in basement of house was pressurized to furnish running water to the house.

This farm, which bordered the village limits of Grand Rapids, had electricity, which was uncommon in any form in those days. My father offered to and did pay the special cost of a pole line and wire from the village limits to the house.

Ole Swanson was the electrician in those days and I suppose he wired the house. He used his fingers for a Volt Meter. He would wet his finger and stick it in a socket and if he felt a tingle then there was electricity there, or 'juice' as Ole said.

I point out the matter of electricity because the house and barn were wired for it.

There was another building directly west of the house called the cookhouse. It was one big room with a wood cookstove, one big long table with benches for eating and an upstairs also with bunks for sleeping. This was for feeding and sleeping extra help at threshing and haying and other pivotal times.

I should explain the cooler room which was between the ice house, and the well house—all in one building. The cooler had ice on all three sides and a dark door entry on the east side. This was where all dairy products were kept in warm weather and fresh meats and milk.

I go to all this building detail to show that this was no ordinary farm building arrangement. Pa imagined and executed the

At the farm—Uncle Dan and his younger brother Ted in front of the wagon, author's father and his brother Matt in the wagon.

Left to right: Uncle Matt, Uncle Ted, the author's father, and Uncle Dan at the farm.

The family in front of the farmhouse before it burned.

whole thing with help, of course. Other buildings included the barn, silo, pig pen, chicken coop, and machine shed—which included a single stall auto garage and also a tripod for hanging animals to be dressed out—for pork and beef.

Not to be forgotten was a large earth-covered potato warehouse with an entrance chute an one side and exit doors on the opposite side, both accessed by road.

My "big deal" was being allowed to take Nel and Del, our team of horses, and drive them and the roller down to the west field and roll the field. The "roller" was just like a tool that is used to roll the gravel smooth on a new road. You had to roll the oat-seeded field after planting, if no rain, to keep the wind from uncovering the seed. Rolling made the dirt covering the oat seed smooth so the wind would not uncover the seed. I do not know if the horses were male or female. I didn't take too much note of that—but they were certainly very gentle or my dad would not have let me take them and the "roller" to do the west field. Nel and Del pulled the sleigh for our outings but also helped haul hay and helped with lots of the heavy work.

Someone else who helped a lot was Jake, who came along one day, obviously hungry. He ended up staying with us and Pa had a small shed built for him. He was from Switzerland, according to my older brothers and sisters. He never spoke much English but he loved Pa and Pa treated him well. He was, according to Ma, "heaven-sent," as he helped with so much. He stayed with us 'til the farm burned and then ended up in the county home.

All this about the farm days is from the eyes and mind of an eight-to-ten-year-old.

The author's father wrote a note on the back of this photo: "Dan (left) and Jim [author's father] riding horses on the farm (about 1932). Pretty serious business, as you can tell by our expressions."

An unforgettable experience I must not forget to get down: Midnight Mass on Christmas Eve. Everyone went except one or two of the oldest, left to guard the farm and tend the stoves and furnaces. My dad hitched up Nel and Del, the old faithful team of horses, to the big sleigh.

There were plenty of buffalo robes and blankets and away we went to St. Joseph's for midnight Mass. We young boys would get off and hang onto the sleigh and slide along on our boots. The girls all sat with Ma and Pa, all bundled up. At this time, the mid-1920s, the Reverend Hennebry was pastor. He was famous for his very, very, very conservative views on heat and lights at church.

But on Christmas Eve Midnight Mass he would throw conservation to the birds and turn on every light in the church. You could see it from three or four blocks away and on the inside it was unbelievably bright. We didn't know the church even had all those lights. It not only brightened the church but also everyone's spirits.

My dad stopped at the church and we all got off the sleigh and tromped into church while my dad took the horses to the livery barn, which was just across the street, where the U.S. Post Office is today. The horses were kept warm while we were in church.

Back home, a couple of hours later, was the big feast: fresh pork roast and potatoes and gravy, vegetable and mustard pickles and dill pickles and lots of fresh butter and bread and homemade doughnuts (twisted), hot tea and hot cocoa. Our mother always made a big batch of doughnuts—both the round ones and the twist type (the younger boys' favorite). She would make a full crock of these donuts. I think the crock was ten-gallon size.

Midnight Mass, the big 2:00 a.m. meal and the big crock of donuts were Christmas traditions. Milking the cows in the a.m. was usually a little late on Christmas day—but in the spirit of the day was done even though a little late.

It was my Dad's dream to be a gentleman farmer after his years of being a lumberjack and the sheriff. In one day the dream was gone up in fire and smoke.

I was a ten-year-old boy at that time and I do not remember him crying or even raising his voice but I do remember my mother saying it was the Lord's will. I would hear that many times over the years from my mother, pertaining to anything not planned for. FAITH? Yes, and with capital letters.

–From the journal of James S. Hoolihan

It was March of 1929. The descent of the dollar was like a huge stone on a gentle hill—just beginning to roll, slowly, about to pick up incredible speed, to crash in a million pieces at the bottom. On a farm outside of a small northwoods town, a mother, father, twelve children and the hired hand, Jake, lived. The farmhouse was sprawling and roomy. The huge living room floor, made of white pine, was where on celebratory evenings the braided rugs were pulled up and Ma got out her fiddle and neighbors came and danced until the wee hours of the morning. Several men in the group took turns calling out the dance moves. The piano was played by the oldest daughter, Mary, and Dan. Dan and Jim, and the older brothers, Jerry and Bill, all played drums. Often, they played in town for three dollars a night, turning the money over to Ma and Pa.

In one day everything changed. Much was lost. It was a story told often, mentioned at most home Masses, referred to regularly. But the real story, the sustaining story was about what survived.

A teenaged Gert and her sister Marg stepped off the school bus and walked the long road leading to the farmhouse. The surprisingly warm March sun flowed over the rolling hills of the farm, lit up the soft beige of winter-crisp weeds sticking up out of several feet of snow. Here and there the long-frozen snow was running in rivulets and small, muddy streams. Everyone remembered how sunny the day was, the promised hopefulness of spring in the air near the end of a harsh Midwestern winter, and how the sun's gentle warmth contrasted with the actual events of the day.

Inside, Gert paused for a moment at the large living room window, admiring the sun's touch across the rolling hills, feeling for a few moments almost dreamy with its promise of easier times to come. It had been a cold, cold winter. Tired of wearing her long underwear, she couldn't wait to be done with them. She felt lulled by the sun streaming in the large window, splashing its way across her freckled arms and the pine wood floor at her feet.

Aware of her father, quietly reading in the chair behind her, a flicker of worry flitted through her body. It was unlike him to not be down in the barn at this time, helping Dan, Jim, and Bill milk the cows. He must not be feeling well. He was involved in all the daily chores of the farm, and worked especially hard during planting and harvesting season. Gert, too, knew the whole farm operation was her father's dream come true. He had been involved in the creation and building of it every step of the way. From his sheriff days, he had connections with law enforcement, and several prisoners had been brought out every day under the care of a deputy to work on several of the buildings. A construction family from town built the huge barn that housed livestock and a large hay loft. The farmhouse itself had been moved from a different location, and then a spacious screened-in porch was added on two sides.

Gert turned away from the window and admired her father's handsome, weathered face. Despite his years on the farm, he still dressed like the lumberjack he once was—flannel shirt and wool pants with suspenders over them. For haying and other chores, he put on his farmer overalls, but most days this simple costume covered his huge, strong body. His sheer physical strength, although sometimes intimidating, was always a comfort to Gert. She felt he could take care of anything.

"Pa, can I bring you a cup of tea?"

"No, thanks, Gert," he answered. "Your ma just fixed me one before she left."

Gert climbed up to the room on second floor she shared with two of her sisters and removed her stockings, as she did every day. She slid into her hand-knit green slippers and padded across the hall to the bathroom. She filled a small basin with cold water—they only had heated water in the kitchen—and rubbed the stockings with a bar of soap, then hung them over a towel rack. A junior in high school, she had only one pair and liked them clean every morning. When she returned to her room, Marg was no longer in sight, so Gert hurried down to the kitchen to help with peeling potatoes for dinner.

Ma had greeted them at the door with a hello and instructions to mind the pork roast in the oven, to peel and boil potatoes, and pick a vegetable from the root cellar. She then got in the truck with Jerry, one of the drivers in the family, to go pick up her sister, Aunt Nora (Spang), and go to Stations of the Cross. It was Lent, and she was faithful about the weekly Thursday service. After the Stations, they would pick up Eleanor from her job at the county commissioner's office and cousin Rosemary from her job, as she was also invited to dinner. *A full crew,* Gert thought happily as she counted out potatoes: "one for each person and one for the pot."

When Marg walked into the kitchen and mentioned that she smelled smoke, Gert's first reaction was that Marg just wanted to get out of peeling potatoes. Gert rolled her eyes as Marg left the kitchen to tell Pa. "That's odd," she heard her father say, "The only stove lit today is the one in the kitchen." The two of them began poking their heads into the dining room, front porch, bathroom, and then up the stairs.

On the second floor, in the boys' room, a barely visible plume of smoke curled near the window sill, along where the wires ran for the one light in their room. Pa got his hatchet from outside the front door. By now, Gert was beside him as well as Marg. He told them both to stand back and he chopped through the wood beside the window. A single huge, golden flame shot up in the air.

There was a split second where no one moved, so shocking was the sight, both of the small curl of smoke and then the flame, which quickly leapt bright and clear. It was a blazing trail lighting up the path right behind Pa's hatchet and arm.

The girls sucked in their breath, adrenaline rushing in their bodies, and yet they stood frozen, as if their feet were rooted to the moment forever.

Out of Pa's mouth came the words, "The jig is up."

These four words vibrated, as if each were an electrical conduit. What reached Gert was the full power of that surge. The words entered her body, careened around inside of her, creating a current of energy, a raw jagged lightning bolt powerful enough to provide a memory charge for the rest of her life.

Then Pa said to Gert, "Go get the boys from the barn."

Gert flew down the stairs, flung open the front door and ran, her pigtails flying in the wind she created. Down the slope to the barn she flew, losing one slipper on the way, running past her two youngest brothers, Teddy and Matt, playing in the wet snow. Out of breath, near tears, she flung the barn door open and ran in, crying loudly, "The house is on fire, Pa needs your help!"

Bill was closest to her, seated on a low stool with a pail beneath the cow. "Ah, Gert," he said a smile playing at the edge of his lips, "now that's a good story." Dan and Jim (my father), a couple of cows down, looked up from their stools, hands busily squeezing udders, and looked at her with mild curiosity.

Just then Bill's cow kicked the pail over, unheard-of behavior. Bill looked at the spilled milk, felt the alarm in the cow's body, and looked back up at the fear on Gert's face. He said to his younger brothers, "She's not kidding. Let's go."

All of them felt it now, the current of alarm running between them in the barn, in the air itself, in the agitated animals.

Gert ran back to the door and the boys followed. Gert retraced her steps, the green mound of her lost slipper appearing on the trail before her. She reached down and plucked it out of the snow, suddenly aware of how cold her left foot was.

Once out of the barn, the house was in sight, a small lick of flame visible above its north side.

"Oh my Lord," Bill cried. With their feet slipping on the path, the four of them raced to the house. Gert tore in the front door and heard Pa yelling from second floor, "Bring up any water! Any water you can find!"

Marg had gotten on the party line and put in a call to the fire department, but it would be awhile before they arrived to help.

Pa had locked the door to the basement where the windmill-generated container of water was because, beside the fact that it wasn't full at the time, he didn't want anyone trapped in the basement unable to escape the fire. In the kitchen, water pressure was low. Marg and Gert and Jim filled a few pans, but the water ran achingly slow. Outside, Bill and Dan wildly pumped out by the cistern a hundred feet away from the house. As many buckets and pans as could be found were carried by brothers—and before long, neighbors—to the pump. But pumping, even by the strongest of arms, is slow, especially in contrast to leaping flames, fanned by the open air and light March breeze.

Impatient and desparate, Gert grabbed the huge pan of water from the stove filled with peeled potatoes and ran it up to her father, potatoes and all. But the small buckets of water could do little to douse the growing flames. Even as the volunteer firemen poured into the house, there was little anyone could do without more water.

Suddenly remembering her two youngest brothers playing outside in the snow, Gert ran back downstairs and outside. Just as she did, she saw the truck pulling up the drive with Jerome at the wheel and Mama, Eleanor, and Rosemary inside. They all piled out. Out of the corner of her eye, Gert caught sight of Mama standing still, as if unable to quite believe what she saw. Looking around, Gert saw Matt and Teddy still playing in the small ditch along the road, just beginning to look at the house, just beginning to notice something going on. Their clothes were wet and she told them to stay right beside Mama. She ran back to the house and up to their room, and grabbed some dry clothes and shoes. As she did, she noticed Jerome in her sister's room, pushing Mary's hope chest out the second floor window. There was the sound of shattering glass, the rumble of firemen and neighbors, moving in a mad frenzy to remove belongings, to save what they could.

In the living room, she heard Rosemary organizing a few men in her usual bossy manner, "Get the piano. It's on wheels . . . there's four of us, we can roll it right out the front door."

Gert felt a momentary and intense gratefulness for her cousin's bossy nature and whipped out the door ahead of the piano. She felt a need to focus now on the little boys and ushered them down to the barn, thinking it safe and warm and far enough away from the house. She helped them change clothes. They were wide-eyed now and full of questions, "Is the house going to burn down to the ground? Where will we sleep? Can we see the fire?"

She had just gotten them into dry clothes when a neighbor, Walt, walked in and told her the barn was not a safe place. They were afraid the hay might catch some flying sparks. Walt walked Gert and the boys out, and another neighbor drove them to Aunt Nora's house.

After Gert and the boys left, the firemen and gathered men stretched a wire from the fire truck across the north side of the house and pulled it down, right through the roof and wall, sheering off a slice of the house and separating it from the burning house. They were able to pull it far enough over to cover the cookshed that was next to the house. This in the end drew the fire line. It was separate enough and separated by enough snow and melting snow to keep it from igniting.

The rest of the house, however, burned down to the ground. Despite the snowballs being thrown, the vain attempts with small buckets of water and melted snow, all stood helplessly by as the flames ate four bedrooms, a large living room, dining room and kitchen. The basement root cellar, full of home-canned tomatoes, corn, pickles, raspberry, strawberry and peach preserves became piles of black soot, molten mounds of melted glass amid unrecognizable substances.

Scattered in the snow on all sides of the house were piles of clothes, the piano, the huge dining room table, an assorted jumble of chairs, dresser drawers full of clothes, and Mary's hope chest.

As the flames died down, members of the family left with various neighbors and friends. Mama and Papa headed to Aunt Nora's with Dan and Jim; the two little boys were already there. A neighbor with a teenage girl took Marg, and they picked up Gert from Nora's.

That night with everyone safely distributed, the only family member who didn't know what had happened was Bernie. On duty as a nurse at the hospital in town, she was wiping a feverish brow when she first heard the fire alarms. As she went off duty, she wondered aloud where the fire was. One of her co-workers had just heard and came up to her, saying, "Bernie, I have terrible news. The fire was at your family's farm. I have my car. Get your coat and I'll drive you there."

By the time they arrived, the farm was clear of people. An eerie emptiness floated across the fields. A half-moon lit up the hills and the smell of smoke hung thick in the air, its dark underside clinging to every breath Bernie took. Where the farmhouse once stood there was only a pile of black soot and ashes. Off to one side, the entire north wall of the house stood collapsed against the cook shed. Nearby, the piano stood, covered and protected until it could be moved the next day. Strewn in the snow were various belongings. Bernie caught sight of an old gray raincoat of hers—it looked like someone had reached into the kitchen closet and pulled out everything inside of it. Her only belonging that escaped the fire was that old gray raincoat.

When I imagined that day, the image I was drawn to was that of Bernie, alone but for her co-worker in the blue light of dusk, surveying the ruins of a home they had all lived in for ten years. Odd piles of clothing scattered around on top of clumps of blackened snow. Moonlight glistened over mounds of ice, where thrown water had refrozen. Strangely beautiful ice formations hung from the part of the house that lay exposed and hanging over, near the cookshed. The piano, covered, was waiting for its new home. The inside wall of a home, a remaining slice of what used to be whole was lying wide open, vulnerable to the forces of nature. The sight cut a naked, gaping fire line across what Bernie had known—the north wall of the house. And now, the empty space in front of her. A wide-open emptiness which once held family dinners around a large table. The living room where her oldest brother Sherman died of a burst appendix. Where her mother gave birth to the last four children, all boys. The front door was gone, part of the rubble at her feet . . . the door where she had entered the house so many times. The space itself had a palpable presence and she stood in front of it, trying to absorb what had happened, what it could mean for all of them.

The gray raincoat caught her eye: not a favorite, it was one she kept on hand for rainy days at the farm. It was old, but long and sturdy and had served her well over the years. Although she had some of her favorite clothes and things with her at the hospital, there were numerous items she had left behind: her high school scrapbook, a few favorite letters from her cousin, Rosemary, when she lived in Canada. She wondered where they were in the dark, iced-over piles in front of her.

After a long time just standing and taking it all in, Bernie walked over and picked up the raincoat. She ran her fingers down the length of its cold dampness. Her fingers caressing the material comforted her somehow. Her entire body was spinning. She felt herself—as perhaps her father did when he uttered those prophetic words—buffeted with images of the past ten years, all the life that farmhouse had held in contrast to a suspended blank slate about the future. A painfully uneven balance. There were so many of them in this family, some still so young. Bernie turned slowly away from the scene and asked her friend if she minded driving her to Nora's house. Even though she had heard no one was hurt, she wanted to know for sure.

At Nora's, she found her parents and Nora and Uncle Matt sitting at the kitchen table drinking tea, the young children asleep, two and three to a bed. At the sound of a car, Matt looked out the window and seeing her, announced, "It's Bernie." She entered the kitchen, embraced her mother and greeted her father, noting his worried and weary expression. She sat down to hear the story of the day.

I was also drawn to images of Gert that day, so frighteningly jolted out of the normalcy of imagining her sister to be sniffing smoke in order to get out of the day's work. The innocence of that sibling rivalry stands out in contrast to the heartbreak of the steady stream of action set off by Marg's report of smelling smoke. The power of Gert's fear entered her spine at its base and rode up every vertebra—from the moment the flame leapt out of the wall. It was days before her back relaxed enough to begin to soothe the ache out of it. The strangely philosophical reaction on the part of their father echoed over and over again inside her mind—"The jig is up." It was as if at that moment he saw not only the flame leaping in front of him, but the future of this family he was in charge of and their past as well. In that leaping flame, he saw all the days they had cherished on this beautiful piece of land, all the sweat and hard work and satisfying good times. He saw his expanding family, riding on the horse-drawn sleigh over the hills of the farm, on their way to midnight Mass every Christmas for so many years. He heard the songs sung from the back of the sleigh and from inside his home. He saw that the future would be different—that the moment the flame leapt up his life and the lives of all those in his care would never be the same again.

I wonder how many times the scene played out in front of my grandfather's eyes. How many times did he question his decision to lock the basement, to make inaccessible the in-house water supply. That day, when the flames began to leap, his primary concern was for all the lives around him, even the neighbors and firefighters who arrived to help. The steps to the basement were narrow, and there was only one entrance. If fire blocked it, if part of the house above that entrance collapsed, there would be no way out—anyone down there would spend long moments trapped before being suffocated by the dark smoke, the collapsing structure. He must have decided that would be the worst thing that could happen, to lose a life in the basement while he fought the flames above it. He shut the door. He locked away the largest water supply on the farm, locked away the possibility of spending the rest of his life imagining a loved one's death trapped in a burning, collapsing basement.

One of the enduring stories of the farm burning, as often told by Bernie and Gert, was how nothing broke in Mary's hope chest. Mary, the oldest sister and engaged, was planning a summer wedding. I sat at Bernie and Gert's kitchen table and heard the story many times over the years. They were incredulous every single time they got to the part about the hope chest. Bernie would say, "There were picture frames inside and dishes and do you know, nothing broke!"

Gert emphatically continued, "And you know, it was pushed out from the second floor window. Imagine, glass falling and landing two stories down and not breaking. Nothing broke!"

They didn't actually call it a miracle, but the emphatic way they repeated the words, "And you know, nothing broke!" conveyed that it was one of the memorable, miraculous moments in their shared history. They would go on to tell me that the dishes and glass frames were swaddled in layers of homemade quilts, but this was secondary information. The primary information was the unbelievable—what remained intact in spite of a harrowing descent.

The piano that was saved graced the foyer in *the house* for seventy-five years. Every time I stopped to visit, I played it. If I raved about what a beautiful piano it was and how I loved its touch and tone, both Bernie and Gert would say, "You know this piano survived the fire." Or, "Pa bought this piano for Ma for their second wedding anniversary. 1902. It is still a great sounding piano, isn't it?"

I like to think of the piano as a quiet witness to this family's life. The piano was an integral part of a century's worth of love, loss, happiness, and mourning. Since 1902, the piano was there as each of the twelve children were born . . . and as family members died off over the years. The piano was the center of celebratory moments on the farm. When this family moved into town, the music bridged their old life and their new life. The first night Dan sat down at the piano and Mama got out her fiddle, everyone, from youngest to oldest, knew they were going to be okay.

When I asked Bernie and Gert, during one of our storytelling fiestas, what they learned from the farm burning, they pondered for just a moment. Then Bernie piped up, "Well, we learned that you shouldn't wait to eat the raspberry preserves."

Gert nodded and laughed, rubbing her arms as she looked back in time, as if to hold herself in this world as she stepped back into an earlier one. "The night before the fire, we girls were sitting around the kitchen visiting. Mama was over at Nora's. Eleanor suggested we crack open some raspberry preserves. Warm bread was coming out of the oven, and our mouths watered at the thought of those fresh berry preserves on top of warm bread. But one of us, I can't remember who, said 'No, we better not open a jar without Mama's permission.'"

Months before, those five sisters had been in the kitchen sweating as they canned fruit alongside Mama, and even though three of them were then out of high school and working on their own, and two left in high school, they all deferred.

In the days and months to come all five girls regretted not having tasted those sweet berries on the evening they had felt the impulse. The day after the fire the berries were crushed under mounds of melted glass and debris amid piles of crusted snow and mud, and would never be tasted by anyone.

My father, Jim, was milking cows in the barn, and was one of the four younger boys who ended up at Nora's later that night. Over the years when I asked him about the fire, he described Gert's pigtails flying when she ran into the barn. He described how wide her eyes were—huge and frightened. He was a man of few words, but his words often went straight to the heart. Once, I sat across from him at the dinner table and told him I'd had a cup of tea with Bernie and Gert, and they had told me the farm-burning story again. He shook his head slowly. He put his fork down, and said, "It was a terrible day. A terrible day."

The raw truth of what he said entered me. Goosebumps appeared on my skin and I watched his face turn inward, where I could only imagine what pictures were going through his mind. He was only ten years old at the time.

Pa rented a house in town where they lived, crowded, for many months until he bought what became *the house*. At the age of sixty-two, Pa dismantled his beloved farm, sold the cattle, and kept the land. He learned to drive a car and reinvented himself one more time; he became the road foreman for the county and settled into a life in town. Rosemary used to say about him, "He wasn't one to let the land stand still beneath him." This ability to keep moving forward, to keep recreating a life is something I deeply admire. It is a kind of ancestral energy I have tried to tap into when I need to reinvent some part of myself.

From my father's memoirs:

> There were thirteen of us at the time. Mary, the oldest girl, was married while we were in that house [the rental house]. Jerry, the oldest son, went away to school. Bill, the next oldest boy, was working for a road contractor and was away from home most of the time. Bernadette, the next oldest girl, was a nurse at the hospital and worked nights most of the time. Eleanor, next oldest, worked at the courthouse. Marg and Gert, the two youngest girls, found work when and where they could get it. We younger four boys took our duties up at the rental house. Milking the cow in the a.m. and p.m., feeding the few chickens and taking care of the house garden and yard. It is the big Depression now and with the loss of the farmhouse, this big family has to pull together and make a go of it—there will be at least one family rosary every day. The motto of our mother and father is 'the family that prays together stays together'.
>
> I don't know now how that big family made it in that rental for what must have been two years at least.

My father, in some way, was able to get money for the purchase of the "house" at 835 Second Avenue Northwest. What a house—five bedrooms and a big kitchen, dining room and middle sitting room and front parlor. A big front porch and room for a big garden. Beautiful hot water radiators for heat in winter. "Paradise." And a miracle. The house went up for sale in 1932 and my father was able to organize the purchase in those hard times. Price—$4,000.00.

So with the move from the "rental" house to the newly purchased big house there was great family 'joy' even in those bad economic times, the Depression. Our father found a job as a road foreman for the county. He had never driven a car and didn't know how so the older boys, Jerry and Bill, had to teach him how to drive. Our family owned a Model A coupe.

After learning to drive, when leaving for work in the early morning he woke up the household and neighbors with his very heavy use of the throttle. He said he had to warm the car up before taking it to work. Pa apparently had it die on him after starting it so I assume he felt the best way to prevent that from happening again was to 'put the gas pedal to the floor.' And that could be heard far and wide. I estimate he was sixty-five to seventy years old at this time.

In the early years 1932-1934, both Jerry and Bill played drums for different orchestras. Depression or not, people wanted to dance and have a good time. The next drummers coming up were Dan and Jim (myself).

We had at one time three complete sets of drums in the house: the pay for one night was about three dollars, maybe five dollars on New Years Eve or the Fourth of July. That was a lot of money then, for three or four hours work, from 9:00 p.m. 'til 12:00 or 1:00 a.m.

Jerry, the oldest, used his influence to get the local artist Ted Tinquist to paint a scene on one base drum. It was a lake scene, with the moon shining on the water and of course it drew some "oohs" and "ahs" from the dancers.

We even had the base drum with the painted scene fitted with a light inside that would turn on and off automatically, to draw more attention to it.

I do believe that we were known somewhat famously up and down the Iron Range as the Hoolihan drummers. Anyway, if not famous, we did bring needed cash home to the big house and big family.

Both my father and Gert would say they didn't really mind moving into town. In spite of all the fond memories everyone had, it had been a hard life in many ways on the farm. But they knew it was a sadness and a disappointment—the loss of a dream—for their father.

The farm lived on in the stories told by my father and his siblings. The land also stayed in the family. Some of my siblings and I and our families, annually, the day after Thanksgiving when many of us used to be in town, would go out and walk the farm. Or, on snowy years, we built bonfires and brought sleds. There were years when my parents joined us, as did Bernie, Gert and Dan. Sadly, no longer.

The barn at the farm, before it burned down.

The farm path winds through exposed hills to a pine forest and eventually abuts the cemetery. On the years of little or no snow, we walked from the farm to visit the graves of those who had passed on. It was and still is beautiful land. The farm buildings are all gone and the land has been used by neighbors as an ATV trail and, when there's snow, as a snowmobile playground. Into my early twenties I could hang out in the barn and immerse myself in ancient Hoolihan ancestry. The barn lasted the longest, but fell to its demise one year; we think it was the late 1970s. Since no one in the family used the property, my cousins who are executors for my aunts and uncle have put the land up for sale.

Nothing lasts forever.

THAT FARM WAS WHERE I first felt and indulged my writing impulse, somewhere in my high school years. I bought my first writing notebook at the local Ben Franklin and rode my bike the several miles to the farm, where I sat on the hillside and began to write. My notebook was lined, with a beige cardboard cover. I opened it and inscribed my

Thanksgiving weekend at the farm. Seated: the author's father, the author's mother, Aunt Gert. Standing: Uncle Dan, the author, a family friend, and nephew Sam.

Top left: the author's parents hiking at the farm. Top right: Aunt Gert, during her last visit to the farm. Bottom: the author and Uncle Dan at the farm during the 1999 family reunion.

favorite quote of the time from *Siddhartha*: "Within you there is a stillness and sanctuary to which you can retreat at any time and be yourself." Even then I imagined the rolling hills in front of me as a working farm, my father and aunts and uncles as children, running the paths, the barn full of hay and cows. I admired the peaceful pastoral beauty of the land with its rolling hills and pine trees. I felt the pull of my history and wanted to respond to it with words.

WHEN I THINK about what survived that terrible day, I see a love of music in the image of the piano we have all gathered around so many times (which graces my living room today), a hope chest, and a metaphorical, almost mythological encouragement to taste life's simple treats today. I also see the ability to reinvent oneself, in spite of age, and the graceful (faithful?) acceptance of fate.

These were the gifts that rose from a day of flames in 1929 and were given wings with which to travel across time.

Chapter Fifteen

Storm Prayers

THE PRACTICE OF SAYING storm prayers had its roots in Canada and the farm. But it was a practice I might have missed if it weren't for my Aunt Alice. This was another story that was served to me on her story-idea hors d'oeurves platter. Aunt Alice was there that day at the lake cabin on Pokegama, Bernie and Gert's place, and I wasn't. But she made a point of telling me about it the following day. "You have to write about this," she said. So the following is how I imagined that day and what I gleaned from both Alices (my aunt and my mom), and Bernie and Gert as well.

A HOT GUST of wind rattled the leaves and bushes around the screened-in porch along the front of the log cabin. Bernie and Gert were busy hosting a bridal shower in their cabin high on a hill, its front windows overlooking Lake Pokegama in northern Minnesota.

On that particular day, damp with sweat, they were serving iced tea, lemonade, bowls of nuts and platters of homemade raisin oatmeal cookies and gingersnaps to the ten ladies gathered for the occasion. Ham and tuna sandwich loaves had already been served, raved about, and eaten, along with a simple fruit salad. The Pyrex plates with lavender lilies were cleared and stacked in the kitchen, to be washed later.

Dark clouds had been steadily closing in since the festivities began, providing, along with the heat, a continuous stream of conversational focus. Bernie looked up from the pile of gifts waiting to be opened, and out the front window. Then she stood up and gasped.

In the porch at the cabin on Pokegama. Left to right: Father John, Aunt Gert, Aunt Eleanor, Sister El Ann, Aunt Mary, Aunt Bernie.

All heads rose from their glasses of tea and freshly bitten-into cookies in time to watch a wide sheet of gray rain moving in across the lake, in a steady powerful advance. The lake surface in front of the rain was smooth, but as soon as the rain fell, the lake turned dark, roiled up by the force of the huge drops falling. It was heading straight for the cabin. A dark, forceful rain pounded loudly as it reached the roof over their heads. The torrents fell straight down so there was no need to close the windows, and a quick blast of cooler air blew in through the screens. Right behind the onslaught of rain came a huge, jagged, piercing, iridescent green bolt of lightning followed by deep thunder. Bernie and Gert exchanged glances and then Bernie cleared her throat.

She announced, "We'll be putting the party on hold for a moment while we all say storm prayers."

In a room full of women, all of whom considered themselves to be religious, cousin Rosemary asked the question for the rest of them: "Storm prayers?"

Bernie replied quickly, "Mama always had us say storm prayers, even in the middle of the night." A slight impatience permeated her words, just a hint of irritation at the need to ask such a question. The Alices exchanged a knowing, here-we-go again glance. Rosemary, ever the outspoken one, was incredulous, "You mean, right now, we're going to say prayers?"

"Oh yes," Gert added gently. "Whenever there's thunder in the air, we pray."

"I'm not getting on my knees on this hardwood floor," protested Rosemary. "I'm too old for that."

Gert, always the peacemaker, gave a quiet laugh. She was quite used to her cousin's opinions. Gert assured her, "We think the Good Lord understands that. No need to kneel, we can pray from our chairs."

The twelve ladies sat, a few still at the table, the others in the chairs on the other side of the room. They were dressed for lunch in various shades of well-ironed pastel plaid or flowered skirts and matching sleeveless button-down cotton blouses. The nucleus of the group were the five white-haired sisters: Mary, Bernie, Eleanor, Margaret, and Gert, the youngest at seventy-five. Rosemary, ample-bodied, was there along with the two sisters-in-law, the Alices, and the other sisters-in-law, Aunt Theresa and Aunt Peg.

One young brunette stood out in the crowd, since the bridal shower was in her honor. She was the daughter of the family who had been so good to Father Bill, Marg's son and cherished nephew of Bernie and Gert. The bride's family, very active in Father Bill's parish, had fed him many dinners over the last fifteen years. Her mother, the youngest of the older women, sat near her. Over the years they had come to know Father Bill's family well. Bernie and Gert's bridal shower was a way of expressing thanks to this family.

Gathered around the Mary statue at the lake cabin. Kneeling: Uncle Dan and Aunt Gert. Standing, left to right: Aunt Marg, Aunt Eleanor, Aunt Mary, and Aunt Bernie.

Just out the window from the festivities on the west side, rising up out of her shrine, was the statue of the Virgin Mary, in a small grove surrounded by pine trees and the thick, luscious summer scent of pine needles. Earlier that day, Gert had arranged fresh purple irises in a vase at Mary's feet and brushed dirt from the silver rosary draped over her praying hands.

Out of a center drawer of the old wooden buffet edged between the side wall of the cabin and the long wooden table, Bernie pulled out a small, tattered black leather prayerbook, a long white candle—its wick black from previous burnings—matches and a vial of holy water. Handing the prayer book to Gert, she set the candle in its crystal shamrock-shaped container. Then she sprinkled holy water all around the edges of the porch, a few drops landing on the shoulders of the well-ironed blouses as Gert's soft, soothing voice entered the expectant hush.

> "Jesus Christ King of Glory came in peace
> God was made man—the Word was made Flesh
> Christ was born of the Virgin Mary
> Christ walked in peace through the midst of them.
> Christ was crucified; Christ died; Christ rose from the dead.
> Christ ascended into heaven.
> Christ reigns; Christ conquers; Christ commands.
> May Christ defend us from all lightning.
> Jesus is with us!"

She then launched into, "Our Father, who art in heaven . . ." and everyone joined in for this familiar prayer. Bernie and Gert's praying created a powerful current, the force of it pulling them all along. No one in the crowd—not even Rosemary—wanted to be seen as not religious. True piety was so honored in this group that the most pious earned a certain kind of prestige, even power. Once the prayers started, it was automatic for all of them to respond, to give up any resistance to the force of Bernie and Gert's matter-of-fact drive, their air of "this is simply what we do. Since you're here you get to do it with us."

The "Our Father "was immediately followed by a "Hail Mary." Their voices, although differing in pitch and volume, created a lilting rise and fall against the backdrop of thunder and pounding rain. Occasionally Rosemary sighed, making it clear she thought the prayers were going on too long.

Then Gert continued by reading from a yellowed sheet of paper in front of her,

"Oh God, be appeased by the supplication we address to thee and through the intercession of the Blessed Virgin Mary, Good Saint Joseph, all the angels and saints defend us from all dangers, through Jesus Christ Our Lord and Saviour."

Everyone answered "Amen," ready for this to be the *final* amen.

Gert inserted the sheet of storm prayers inside her prayer book, closed it and handed it to Bernie to put away. The rain became a light tapping against the roof. The candle remained lit. Bernie and Gert breathed a visible sigh of relief.

For Mary, Eleanor, and Marg, these prayers were a pleasant reminder of prayers said together when their mother, Mama, was alive. For the rest of them, it was one more example of Bernie and Gert and their tendency to take religion a step too far. Rosemary was clearly glad to get on with the party and anxious to get home for her afternoon nap. Aunt Alice was amused enough to bring the story to my attention, but both Alices were used to this. Since the death of Jerry, Aunt Alice was included more often for dinners, and even trips to Uncle Dan's camp, with Bernie and Gert. But there was no getting fully inside the circle of sisters, which the two Alices called the Inner Sanctum. They shook their heads over the un-challengeable level of piety and yet they admired it.

Marg handed the bride-to-be a gift. My mother, known for her neat penmanship, was in charge of writing down gifts and givers. She picked up her pen and notepad. The bride's first present was a mother-of-pearl rosary that Bernie and Gert ordered from Fatima, home of miracles and a shrine to those miracles. The beads were passed around the room, reverentially appreciated, "Aren't they beautiful? And they come specially blessed!" The next gift opened was a set of powder blue bath towels.

With a renewed passing of the cookie plate and refilling of iced tea glasses, the shower was in full swing.

"MAMA ALWAYS HAD US say storm prayers." This was the line that stayed with me long after my Aunt Alice told me the story of the bridal shower. Before long I found myself at Bernie and Gert's kitchen table, drinking green tea and enjoying a homemade walnut peanut butter oatmeal cookie, and asking them about storm prayers. They told me that storm prayers were said in their youth—even in the middle of the night.

"Did your mother get you up to pray?" I asked, unable to imagine why a mother of twelve children would ever want to wake any one of the sleeping children.

Gert's blue eyes were large and round as she answered, vehemently, "She didn't have to. When the thunder started rolling, we all piled out of our beds and down the hall to their room. Mama and Papa had a big room on the farm with two huge double beds on each side and a woodstove in the middle. We called it the incubator room, because there were always babies or younger children on the other side of the room."

Mention of the incubator room reminded me that Bernie once said she found her mother's pregnancies embarrassing when she was in high school. To the older children in the family, it seemed there were always new babies arriving. New babies, young toddlers, kept warm all night long, all winter long in the large and sprawling master bedroom, the incubator room.

Both of them looked thoughtful. Bernie spoke up, "Mama had great fear of storms. I think it came from living in Canada where the storms were so bad. And the storms could be really fierce on the farm. We were up on a hill out in the middle of the country. Papa wasn't afraid. He would walk down to the barn to calm the animals, and then Mama would really pray. In the green flash of lightning, there would be Pa, his hat on, halfway to the barn. Inside, we were gathered all over the room, on our knees or on the bed, rosary beads in hand, following Mama's lead. On chilly nights, it was always warm in there because Pa kept the woodstove going."

Gert piped up, "Pa would sometimes stand in the window, looking out on the farm as if he could protect it by watching it, and Mama would say, 'Will, please get away from the window.' A friend of Mama's had been struck by lightning. He moved out from under a tree on his farm in Ontario, thinking the lightning was over when a bolt flashed into the air and killed him. On the spot. She never forgot it."

In their big old house on Second Avenue or their log cabin at the lake, Bernie and Gert had copies of the storm prayers typed and ready in a drawer in a central location. As the storms rolled in, they gathered their rosary beads, prayer books, holy water, and special written prayers in hand. Whether alone with each other or in a room of ten women, they prayed. They were carrying on Mama's tradition, its electric current of fear running alongside, but always subservient to, their faith, in the incubator room of their lives.

Note: In a conversation with my two priest cousins about storm prayers, they both remembered their mothers saying a prayer that included warding off pestilence. Father Bill sent me the following prayer and said his mother ended every rosary with it. When I researched storm prayers with Bernie and Gert, they gave me a simpler version but I am certain they were well-acquainted with the following prayer, which covers all bases, across time.

O Holy Virgin Mary, conceived without sin, I choose you this day to be the Lady and Mistress of our home, and I pray that you, in the name of the Most Precious Blood of Jesus, your Divine Son, and of your Immaculate Conception, will preserve it from fire and lightning, from tempests and thieves, from cholera, influenza, diptheria, malaria, and all other pestilential diseases. Bless and protect every member of this family, preserve us from sin, from sudden and unprovided death, and from all other evils and accidents, in the name and through the merits of the Most Precious Blood of Our Lord Jesus Christ. Amen.

Part Three

Faith Takes:
Reorienting Faith In My World

An aeiral view of the author's cottage in Canada.

Chapter Sixteen

Storms & Sanctuaries

When I was just getting to know my future husband and found out his family owned an island in Ontario, something deep inside me clicked. From the beginning, we traveled to the island every summer, although at first we came for only ten days or two weeks. One or the other of us was in graduate school; I worked for years when I only had two weeks vacation per year; and my stepson played baseball. Then as we both moved into the teaching profession, we started expanding our summer time in Canada. Also, at first, Chris's mom, our dearly beloved Deenie, spent most of the summer there, and we were, to a huge extent, her guests. In those early days, Chris's sister and children came often and so we juggled schedules. Over decades, things shifted. In the last few years of Deenie's life, the only way she made it to the island was through our efforts. We drove seven hours to Cleveland from the island, picked her up and brought her to the island, where she mostly stayed in the cottage or spent time on sun-warmed decks, and we all got to be together. She was with us there in the ninety-fifth year of her life and died at ninety-six. Our attachment to that island was deep, and she knew we loved the place as she always had. After Chris's mother died, we bought out his sister's half. I am proud to say that the name Hoolihan is on another deed for Canadian land, and it is mine.

When I was a kid and we drove to Atikokan to fly into Dan's, we loved crossing the border into Canada. We always sang the whole song, "O Canada," as we left Minnesota behind and entered Ontario. My dad knew all the words and helped us along. This is a tradition I have carried on. From when our kids were young we would break into "O Canada" as we drove across the border. When my son was a toddler he announced, "We're in Canada now. I *wuv* Canada!" As a teenager, he rolled his eyeballs as his father and I sang but he couldn't help but join in on the chorus. One summer, when he was a slightly older teenager, it was just he and I driving across the border. At his suggestion he called his sister's cell phone and I called Chris's cell and together we sang the full anthem to them. Now he sings the whole thing with us and between us, we know all the words. We all love Canada and especially so the moment we first arrive.

One summer, when my kids were young and we had been painting windows on the cottage all day, we decided to go into town for dinner. Our friends from Minneapolis were visiting—Caitlin's friend Jessi and her mom Christine. Christine had been helping me with the paintbrush all day, and we felt too tired to cook. As we pulled up at the restaurant dock, we heard a rumble of thunder in the distance which, in retrospect, should have sent us hightailing it back home immediately. But we were tired and hungry, and still lulled by a canopy of blue skies and sunshine above us.

By the time our food was served, it was pouring rain, and thunder and lightning were crashing around us. "Can't go out in this," my husband said. Then he told us a story of watching, from that very place, that on-the-water restaurant, a fellow teenager take his boat out in lightning. From the window we were sitting in front of, he watched the lightning strike and the kid was thrown in an arc out of his boat. He died when he hit the water. We all digested, along with our food, this image of a young boy flying out of his boat and into the waters of his death.

For a few minutes, as we were finishing our main meal, it looked like it might clear. But then a second wave of wind, rain and lightning moved in. Our plates were cleared, and dessert was served. Then it was closing time, and though we weren't the only ones marooned, we began to wonder how far we could stretch the generosity of the staff who were ready to get in their cars and drive home.

As the second wave receded, almost an hour past closing time, my husband said, "I think we can make a go for it now." I questioned the choice but felt, too, like we had long outworn our welcome at the restaurant. No one was saying, "No, don't you dare go out on that water yet."

I was nervous from the outset, the lightning moving south of us but still visible, the knowledge that nothing is a stronger draw than an object on the water. Once Chris made the decision, he was in a hurry to act on it. This was no time for weighing the pros and cons, for discussing other options. Besides, his ability to maneuver the boat through any kind of wind and weather was an ability I deeply trusted.

We piled in, life jackets on all the kids, and headed north. The dark air was thick all around us. We had about a twenty-minute boat ride between us and home. The first few minutes seemed fine. But then, although I didn't fully realize it at the time, what appeared in front of us was the third wave of the storm. In the final minutes on that boat, I couldn't bear to look ahead or behind us. I held onto both of my children, and Caitlin and I began to recite, "Hail Mary, full of grace." It surprised me the way the words just started coming out of me, and the way Caitlin joined in right away, like she'd been waiting for me to throw her a lifeline. She had recently learned the prayer in Sunday school, which my son was still too young for. We said the prayer loudly, to hear ourselves over the screaming wind. We fiercely concentrated on it. Kelly, wide-eyed, only four-years-old, listened and clung to my arms and lap. The darkness around us felt safest, but then it kept being lit up in such a way, I couldn't determine where the bolts were coming from. I had the sense that lightning surrounded us, but my entire focus became looking into the eyes of my children and Caitlin's friend Jessi. I used the words, repeated over and over again, as a way to hold us steady, in a boat buffeted by wind beneath a sky on fire with lightning. The repeated words were an anchor we could wrap our fear around.

The image of that boy flying out of his boat tried to work its way across the screen of my mind. It was too easy to imagine us being catapulted in a bolt of lightning to our deaths. I chased it away by saying the prayer louder and slower. I was an adult in a boat with six people, three of whom were children. With every flash of light I saw—but didn't want to see—in my peripheral vision, I knew we were in trouble. Then I saw a particularly bright flash, and a particularly stricken look on Caitlin's face. Above the roaring scream of the wind and the racing of the engine, I heard Chris yell something about going to shore, and I felt the boat take a sharp right. I looked up and saw a dock and lights further up a hill. He pulled in expertly at a much higher speed than he ever used to dock, and shouted for us to get out of the boat. As the boat rocked against the dock, Christine and I held it and pulled the children out. By now, Chris yelled, "I'll take care of the boat, get the kids off the dock." They were all in tears.

We pulled and carried the crying children off the dock and began climbing stairs. Above us, on the deck, more lights were being turned on. The children were wailing, and above the children and the wind I heard what came to me like the voice of angels, an older man and woman, saying "Come on up." The woman was talking directly to the kids, saying, "You're okay now, honey, you're okay. Come on up." We climbed at least fifty stairs and then, suddenly, we were inside. We were in a protected, well-lit place, and this kind woman was still murmuring to the sniffling children, "You're okay now, dears." Waves of gratefulness moved through me with as much force as the weather we had just left behind, and even more so as Chris joined us a long couple of moments later. It was much later that night that he described to me the third wave of the storm bearing down, the bolt of lightning that jagged across the entire sky in front of our boat and the moment he decided we had to get off the water, immediately.

We spent about an hour with this wonderful, kind couple. After the children settled down, softened by our gentle hosts and the comfort of being inside, my daughter sat at their electric piano and played a few songs. When she finished, I went over and played "Dr. Zhivago" and "Song of the Soul," as well as a few of my then-current favorites. The music helped calm us all down, and our hosts enthusiastically appreciated it. Before too long, we stepped out onto the deck and looked up to see a clear sky full of stars. The lightning flashes were so far past us we could hardly see them. We thanked our angels of the night profusely, and rode home quietly, pulled into the boathouse, and breathed a huge sigh of relief. When the phone rang in the cottage, it was our worried neighbor across the way, who had been watching the storm and our empty boathouse. She wanted to be sure we were all okay.

My dreams that night were full of electric images, and our children twitched in their sleep more than usual. I felt the delicate and sturdy net of people who had caught us that night: the older couple we had never met before, the neighbor who was looking out for us. I thought about the way the prayers had buoyed us up and given us courage through the dangerous part of that trip.

The next day we brought a fresh bakery pie to the older couple and thanked them again. The man thanked my daughter and me for the music. Another wave of gratefulness blew through me for this ability to connect with people through music.

A couple weeks later, my son said to me, "Will you teach me the Mary prayer? The one you and Caitlin said in the boat on the lightning night?"

And so, on a small island in Canada, when the going gets wild, we said our own very modified version of storm prayers, two hours as the crow flies away from the place where my grandmother first said them herself. She traveled to Minnesota to live, taking with her her Irish Canadian ways and fears and solaces. I still travel back to Canada in the summers from my home in Minnesota, back to the roots of wild storms. Back to sanctuaries of faith and beauty in a land of wind, water, rock, and sky, where the call of the loon floats into dreams and daily conversations.

Chapter Seventeen

Faith for the Roadblock

"There is yet faith.
But the faith and the love and the hope are all in the waiting.
Wait without thought, for you are not ready for thought.
So the darkness shall be the light and the stillness the dancing."
–T.S. Eliot

AS I EXPLORED my history more, my beloved "spiritual" teachers and their stories, all of it shone with the subtle sheen of moonlight upon the uncut diamond of my own faith. My deathbed scene had opened me in many ways, shed a new light on the religion and faith of my childhood. Still, there were a series of openings, of circumstances, needed to draw me back to anything formal, such as attending church. That road had been circuitous, multi-layered, yet interwoven with the deeper, more all-encompassing quest: how does one have faith? Acquire it? Live it?

Rolling into my forties, I began to turn around in my mind and heart the idea of faith. Was this raw need, the occasional but recurring anguish a factor of age, parenthood, circumstance? The concept—perhaps I should say *ideal*—of faith shimmered in front of me like an uncut gem. I admired its lucid beauty but struggled with cutting it to fit the shape of my life. My relatives, whose faith I was coming to deeply admire, believed in God, Jesus Christ. I didn't feel the need to believe in the same vision but what I, desperately at times, envied was the way their belief gave them a steadfast way to accept life's difficulties and have hope about what was ahead. In my Al-Anon meetings I was slowly moving from wanting to close my ears when I heard the word "God" to learning new ways to think about and envision God. A God of my understanding... this was not a given for me but something I wrestled to both shape and name.

What was the shape of faith in my life? I had made it through my teens and twenties and even early thirties on some sort of loose, all-encompassing notion of a positive attitude. No need to define a shape, to choose a tool for sculpting the gem, nor an angle to begin the cutting. Things simply happened and, heavily influenced by the sixties and seventies, I concentrated on "going with the flow". I was resistant to the old, familiar forms.

The going-with-the-flow positive attitude began to feel a bit thin and in desperate moments, when Bernie and Gert, or my Mom and Dad offered their prayers, I believed in them—their love and their prayers. They were there for me as I was inching my way back.

"Despair" would describe the period of time when my husband and I were emerging from several years of limping our way through guiding his son, my stepson, through adolescence—a difficult, ego-disintegrating experience that created harrowing passages for our marriage. There were years of dealing with issues like his failing grades, his skipping school, his coming home hours after his curfew, or not coming home at all until sometime the next day. There were 4:00 a.m. drunk arrivals, with him stumbling across the basement, throwing up, or puking under the tree just outside of our bedroom window. As upset as we both were and scrambling for help—I'm convinced we put our therapist's children through college during this phase—it divided us. I never felt my husband was tough enough on his son, and I was always only a stepparent. I had stepped outside the moral code of my family by marrying a divorced man with a child from a previous marriage, and I was alone, an explorer in an untamed wilderness. I was grappling with my own moral code. Part of my marriage vows was to care for my husband's son, who came with him into my life. Caring for him, although genuinely a pleasure for the first few years, became, for a time, a dark and unlit thickly-wooded forest. The tangled roots of seen and unseen trees kept tripping me.

At this same time, our daughter was toddling her way to young girlhood, demanding our attention every inch of the way. One night, in the midst of a long wait in an urgent care doctor's office (a neighborhood cat had lunged for her face, gouging her), she climbed up on a chair to look at herself in the mirror. From that perch, in a split second, she saw and reached for the wall-mounted plastic box of discarded syringes, and in spite of the fact that these boxes are supposed to be impenetrable, she poked her finger on a stray syringe sticking up at just the right angle. Her father and I were both inches away, but tired and stressed out, and sharing a momentary lapse of real attention. "That's how all accidents happen," my older sister said, trying to assuage my guilt. For the next six months, we faced the spectre of AIDS, for no one knew whose body fluids were on that discarded syringe. At three-month intervals, I took my young daughter in for the blood test and attempted my own modified version of prayer: "please, please, please." Terrified, I enlisted the prayers of Bernie and Gert and Dan and my parents during those six months, not trusting the strength of my own. I imagined Uncle Dan sending his prayers straight up from the cockpit, small wishes ascending directly up through cloudless skies.

When the test was negative at six months, the doctor said it would have shown up by now. For my own piece of mind, we did two more tests—one at nine months and then again at a year. We were lucky, which didn't erase the hours I spent reliving that night in the urgent care office.

During my stepson's rocky high school years, it was clear to us that there was too much turbulence in our family life to expose an infant to. But after my stepson left for college, after months of wondering whether or not to have another child, we decided yes. That road, however, was fraught with peril—months without conception and then a miscarriage, then more months of trying unsuccessfully to conceive. Coming from a family of eight, with my Irish Catholic heritage of large families, the last thing I expected was to have difficulty conceiving. Disbelief slowly gave way to depression. As the months wore on, so did my melancholy. It lifted briefly, when I became pregnant, but the ensuing loss of miscarriage left me bereft again, back to the monthly cycles of hope, and the dark days of disappointment.

Simultaneously, our finances became tighter and tighter. I was having a hard time finding teaching jobs, and no book contract was imminent.

With little breathing space in our lives, and shadows of loss and potential loss looming around us, I found myself envying the faith of my mother and father—a faith that kept them alive through more than thirty years of raising eight babies, young children, then teenagers on a shoestring budget. How did they do it, I wondered, and so gracefully? What kind of inner strength sustained them, a strength they both credit to their relationship with God, faith, and religion? I knew that my father, Uncle Dan, and Uncle Ted had survived the trenches of World War II and all gave credit to their faith and the rosaries being said back home for helping them survive. I found myself envying the faith of Bernie and Gert, whose lives surely took twists and turns they hadn't counted on. Yet they adapted, gracefully and with great spirit. And I always admired Dan, who seemed able to lift off at a moment's notice. Burdens and worries often kept me mired, earthbound.

I kept wanting to swim out into the sea of my career, into the sea of another conception and child, into the sea of success, but life kept sending me back to shore with tidal waves of disappointment, failure, grief, and sadness. I needed something to keep me going. Al-Anon was helping me in slow and steady ways to accept the things I couldn't change, reminding me to have the courage to change what I could and encouraging the wisdom to know the difference. This strength was building slowly in me, so slowly (and deeply) that sometimes I couldn't see it.

I was aware that, unlike my parents, and Bernie, Gert, and Dan, for whom the form of their

A newspaper clipping about the three Hoolihan brothers in the military: Uncle Ted, the author's father, and Uncle Dan.

faith had always been absolute, wholehearted, and defined, I flailed at the edge of uncertain waters.

My most basic question was: how do I acquire faith? Or, how do I believe my life is worth living, that my struggles will lead to more verdant pastures? How could faith help me live my life, especially in this difficult period? How might I reclaim the baby of faith, after years of having thrown it out with the bathwater of my discontent, disdain and disillusionment?

In bed at night, I turned to poetry. I meditated on the lines from T.S. Eliot, trying to absorb them, to believe them, as I murmured the words to myself, over and over again:

> "There is yet faith.
> But the faith and the love and the hope are all in the waiting.
> Wait without thought, for you are not ready for thought.
> So the darkness shall be the light and the stillness the dancing."

The idea that faith could be in the waiting held me fast. I was definitely in a period of waiting. I ached with the waiting. I longed for the tide to turn. To wait without thought... The idea of it felt freeing. In each area of my life, I had done what I could do and now I needed to let go. To let go is to wait without thought, to give up on exerting personal control, to honor the limits of personal control. When you really want something, this is very difficult to do.

"The darkness shall be the light." The darkness that closed in around me often haunted me, yet these words gave me hope, sustained me toward the image of eventual light, of transformed darkness. It's a concept easy to comprehend from a distance, but much more difficult to grasp when the darkness feels so all-enveloping. Yet the words surrounded my soul, fed me in the vast lonely places.

"The stillness shall be the dancing." Because the outer world kept turning me away, I was forced into a long period of inner reflection. The stillness inside me was a place where no wind roared, no leaves fell from trees, no branches caressed other branches. Stillness, unearthly stillness, was my inner space. Some days fear lined my body, grew in my consciousness a deep thicket of woods, blocked out the sun, cut off my ability to move. Other days, I fell into the deep silence and found there a murmur of utter peacefulness.

Around this time my parents were visiting me and some of my siblings in the Minneapolis area. They told me they wanted to go to Sunday Mass at the Basilica of St. Mary, which was only a mile from our home. It was around Christmas time and the Basilica, America's first, was decorated for the season with a pine wreath suspended from the ceiling in the middle of the church and poinsettias on the altar. It was beautiful. The building is architecturally stunning: it is huge and the paintings on the ceiling above the altar are reminiscent of all the famous chapels in the world. The statue of Mary rises high above the altar, looking beneficently down on us all. Her arms are wide open at her sides, with open palms, the same pose as Bernie and Gert's Miraculous Medal statue above their kitchen sink. The wide open arms always spoke to me of acceptance, openness. As I gazed up at Mary, I felt soothed. The music was comforting and uplifting—old familiar hymns sung by the full choir. I was surprised at how good it felt to be there with my parents.

I went with my daughter, off and on for the next few weeks and months, always feeling a bit tentative and shy. Always I was greeted by the ushers with a friendly and welcoming smile, which meant a lot to me. One day, announced from the altar, was that evening's Vespers service. I was intrigued and decided to check it out.

That late afternoon I drove by myself the mile from our house down the hill to the huge, beautiful Basilica. I entered the church alone that Sunday evening as dusk deepened the blue light sweeping across the windless winter street. I felt nervous. The church was dimly lit in soft candlelight that caught the waning light of day as it shone through the stained glass scenes around me. It was Lent, the weeks before Easter. A purple cloth was draped across the altar. Candles flickered on the walls. A small group of people sat in the front pews, scattered about, sitting quietly. I slid into an empty pew. Self-consciousness fluttered around me. Could anyone tell I didn't really belong here? Was I doing everything right so I wouldn't stand out? The quiet reverence in the air, the soft light, the beauty of stained glass, marble, and sculptures of saints surrounded me, soothed me. So did looking up at Mary, shining in a kind of half-light from above.

A thin film of light splashed across the marble floor of the altar, then drifted into shadow in front of me. An expectant hush settled in the air. Two musicians walked out onto the altar on the right side of its center. One sat at the organ, the other stood with her flute by a music stand, just next to the organ. Organ and flute.

I gazed at them, but also at the intricate designs of the huge, round stained glass windows in front of me. The swirls of color floated around my tired brain as the flute began to move like wind through my bones. When the woman's breath blew through her instrument, the flute whistled, sang, and flowed like a river, touching every cell of my body. I was transported to a land of sheer beauty. On earth I may feel stuck, but here in this sacred space I could feel wind and water rushing, unimpeded, through my skin, my blood, my bones.

Organ and flute. An incredible combination, and in the weeks to come there were other incredible combinations—organ and oboe, piano and violin, harp and organ. The human breath blown through a flute reached deep inside me, sending a sensuous shudder up and down the river of my bones and shivers rippling across my skin. The high notes of a violin, held the length of the bow crossing, drew the breath from my body, begged for release as the notes plunged back down, tumbling, dancing again. I had never felt so strongly the exquisite sensual pleasure of the breath withheld and then released. In the deep dark mystery of music, there was a stillness and an acceptance of grief that soothed me. There I could begin to feel the dancing in the stillness, the music in the mystery, the dim light in the darkness.

At the end of a half hour of receiving this gift of music, I followed the small crowd. We left our pews and walked up the few stairs and along the passageway on either side of the altar. Behind the altar in the huge church were choir stalls, built into the wall in a semi-circle. We filed into those seats and into chairs set up on the floor directly behind the altar.

When we were all settled, a few moments passed in silence. Then about ten choir members, all dressed in long off-white robes, processed in from one side of the altar. At the center of the altar, they filed through the open grate of door that surrounds the altar, each taking his or her place in a semi-circle on the altar, their backs to the center of the altar itself. An air of solemnity accompanied their quiet movements.

The director raised her hands, mouths opened and out came exquisitely sung prayers. Prayers written many centuries earlier, ancient evening prayers, sung in monasteries since the twelfth century. I was astounded by the purity of the human voice—how ten people could create such a clean and deep beauty. All these years I had never fully considered the human voice as an instrument. These were voices in song, but voices who had practiced so often and so deeply that it was as if a power moved through their bodies. Bodies and air—nothing else—created this amazing sensation that lifted me up and out of my heaviness and allowed me to float.

I wept. For the beauty in the music, for the grief inside the beauty, for the light in the darkness. I wept for the long tradition of Catholicism and all the best it had to offer—in its study and practice of contemplation, its creation of worship through music. Waves of gratitude rippled through me for those men and women and their incredible voices. How many hours of practice, of devotion, did it take to know their parts so well? Their voices entered me, stilled me, attuned my body and blood to reverence, through the profoundly simple vehicle of the human voice in song.

I thought of a line from the Catholic Mass where the priest holds his hands high and says, "Only say the word and I shall be healed."

I shall be healed. Only sing the songs and I shall be healed. Healed of all the splinters and fragments of the day. Healed of small and large heartaches. Healed, healing.

Months went by, almost another half year. The healing came and went, but deepened in me each time. My husband and I were walking our way through the grief of a miscarriage. The following fall I got a teaching job. Ah, movement forward! A dream realized, a desire granted. We were still trying to conceive, and the movement forward in one area of my life made me feel wildly optimistic in the other area. Perhaps for that reason, the arrival of my period that January made me feel heartbroken. I reached a new low. The old Catholic images of a punitive God reared up in me with an intensity I hadn't felt in years. Despite years of working to dismantle that male judgmental image, of creating kinder images for myself, I was shocked that the old image lived so deeply within me. At a fundamental level, I still felt punished, abandoned, and judged by a male god. I was convinced I was being punished for the previous sins or sexual dalliances I'd had years earlier.

The very idea of faith seemed a personal mockery. I didn't have it, didn't deserve it. This concept of deserving things—love, happiness, faith, fortitude—based on following very prescribed actions was one of the roots of this struggle of mine with the church. Because of course the flip side is being undeserving (shame?) and that feeling of (or fear of) not deserving is a painful way to live. So, in spite of my years in Al-Anon, of gently re-envisioning my concept of God toward a God of understanding and acceptance, this old way of thinking asserted itself into my emotional crisis. In all those years of *Baltimore Catechism*, of grueling confessions, was the message that we had to earn God's love and that God's wrath had to be feared. My image of God had a lot to do with an all-powerful being doling out rewards and punishments—especially punishments—in direct response to all of our actions. (Busy guy.) Although forgiveness of sins and redemption was always there, so much of the focus was on sin. Shame, a hue of not-deserving, was connected to sin, especially any sin that corresponded to sexuality. Because of how religious my family was, my family system backed up and supported this way of thinking, so intertwined I can't tell which had the most impact. Together it was truly a double-whammy. Sinfulness and shame were heavy weights to carry through life.

So much focus on what wrongs we have committed or might be likely to commit left little space for self-love or self-acceptance. No wonder so many in my generation walked away. We had lived into a time where we needed daily to honor faith over fear, gentle encouragement over shame-filled punishments. This old way, of using fear as a prodding iron to get people to behave, falls apart once one starts to question the rules and the rulemakers. For sometimes the people in charge, we were discovering, broke the rules, in egregious ways. And sometimes the rules changed. Matthew Fox's book *Original Blessing* offered another voice probing this question of worth, another way to view our humanness (and God) outside of the strictures and structures of sin.

As I sat in contemplation and let the Vespers music wash over me, a line from the Easter vigil kept recurring inside my head. It's Christ's line, as he hangs from his cross, asking, "My God, my God, why have you forsaken me?" I felt forsaken. I felt forsaken, alone, bereft, betrayed by my body and who and what else? Fate? God? The universe? A question for me was, could I shed this way of thinking about being punished, about not (ever) being good enough and still find comfort in a church? Although I was contemplating a return to (Catholic) prayer I was not willing to return to feeling always so undeserving, so close to my shame.

The two lines, "My God, my God, why have you forsaken me?" and "Only say the word and I shall be healed" could form the cornerstones of my year of obstacles—the cyclical feelings of abandonment and the moments of healing. Vespers never failed to heal me, to reach deep inside me and replace all fear with a deep, flowing river of trust. And, simultaneously, as I had been doing for years, I was rebuilding in weekly twelve-step meetings an image of God to be one who could listen to all the bereft stories I heard of family neglect and abuse and alcoholism—a God of each person's understanding who would accept pain and offer healing. Instead of sin we studied shortcomings; we looked at how we fell short of what we could be. Instead of rules we looked at who we had harmed and worked on making amends. We worked on forgiving and accepting ourselves. We talked about and explored prayer and meditation. Those meetings were an integral part of a deep spiritual growth for me.

Could the combination of what I found at Vespers, at church on Sunday as certain music moved and transformed me, and the deep river of spirituality I found in Al-Anon be called faith? Could these be added to my lifelong love of nature to form an expansive sense of worship and spirit? Perhaps I was carving out ways to illuminate my previously uncut diamond. Perhaps, just perhaps, I was beginning to find a shape of faith that fit my life.

Five days into that January tailspin, my husband called me from work and said, "Why don't you and Caitlin meet me at the skating rink?"

It was early evening, a weekday. Dusk was settling on the lake, sweeping across this beautiful outdoor rink in the middle of Minneapolis, just blocks from our home. Lake of the Isles has been an incredible source of comfort to me in all seasons; it is one of Minneapolis's chain of city lakes preserved by prescient forefathers. In the winter the city clears a large oval rink and keeps it flooded for skaters. As we entered the warming house, the blue light of dusk lit the surrounding pine trees and the ice shone with shades of a darkening rose and indigo. The western sky swirled those same colors. Tufts of cloud above us opened up and sent down large, gentle snowflakes. They brushed against my cheeks, eyelids, my plaid wool coat. I skated beside my husband, lover, and friend of thirteen years. We watched our daughter zoom joyously back and forth across the ice, throwing herself with delight into the edge of a snowbank.

Suddenly, with no effort on my part, the darkness inside me shifted. As snowflakes melted on my skin, the punitive God image melted. Into my heart poured the utter beauty of a winter day turning to the blue light of dusk, and a deep gratitude for the loved ones beside me. Into my heart returned a God of kindness, sensuality, beauty, and family. It was a moment of grace.

A month later I was pregnant with our son.

Into the stillness came his dancing, into the darkness came his light. A time of waiting without thought was behind me and now, forever, a part of me.

Chapter Eighteen
Five Takes on Faith

Take One:
Are Ye of the Faith?

A FRIEND OF MINE told me a story of traveling in Ireland and stopping to buy a rosary for his wife. Someone in the shop asked him brightly, "Are ye of the faith?" He answered, "No, but my wife is."

For days, that question threw a haunting, humor-tinged echo across my inner dialogue. Could I wholeheartedly say yes? I wouldn't want saying yes to mean that people would make assumptions about me or about my beliefs. I resisted having what felt important to me as an individual be subsumed into an "in-group"—the spiritual social club.

And yet, as someone who was exploring my history and deep roots in this faith, how could I possibly say no? I swear there was Catholic DNA bouncing in all of my cells. "Once a Catholic, always a Catholic" was a saying a few of us threw around but it spoke, I believe, to how deeply formative those years of rituals were. Separating from what we disagreed with about Catholicism did not erase the deep reverberations of memory, and perhaps identity.

Many people I know who grew up Catholic but don't go to Catholic church will say, "I still feel like a Catholic" or consider themselves Catholic. One friend explained it to me, saying, "It's almost like being part of an ethnic group. " Many of us struggle with what we call "Catholic guilt," which surfaces in myriad and multiple ways. (But that's a whole other book.) It was and is a cultural sense of identity, one encoded in our cellular memory.

My aunts, in their prime, regularly polished the chalice, cleaned the altar, and could be counted on to light candles for Lenten vigils. My parents traveled to Europe and around our country in their early retirement, sending postcards home about the churches and services in each place that they visited. Back home, my mother, up until walking became more difficult for her at the age of ninety, was a regular reader of the gospel and distributor of communion at Mass. In our family, we knew that when the old ones in the family didn't go to church, they were not feeling well.

Crucifixes graced the walls of most rooms in my childhood home, and for sure at Bernie, Gert, and Dan's as well. If an item was lost, St. Anthony (patron saint of lost items) was prayed to and thanked when the item was found. God and/or the saints were responsible for every good that happened in our lives, and the source of comfort and solace in hard or frightening times.

The phrase, "Jesus, Mary and Joseph" was heard often and in varied ways. In a bad temper it was my father's first curse. Scary. In a time of need, it was said plaintively. In my father's late years, in his nineties, if he was having a bad day—in pain or anxious—I could hear him saying quietly, repeatedly, to himself, "Jesus Mary and Joseph," almost like a mantra.

When my brother Matt successfully landed his first solo flight at the Grand Rapids airport I was there with my parents and Bernie and Gert. He came in smoothly and as soon as the wheels settled on the runway, Bernie and Gert broke out into a chorus of "Praise the Lord"—with great enthusiasm.

On Good Fridays of my childhood we spent three hours in church, following the stations of the cross, singing the haunting melodies, those reverberating metaphors of sorrow entered my bones.

The news about JFK's death reached me in church—the school was gathered for a pre-Thanksgiving Mass and Sister Mary, the principal, came to the podium to make the announcement. I still remember the collective gasp of horror. JFK was our Catholic hero.

Then there were those nightly rituals of my early childhood, a practice dropped by the time I was a teenager, of saying the rosary on our knees, scattered around the living room. In the closing prayers for the rosary, which my parents recited from memory, there was a line about "in this vale [pronounced "valley"] of tears." It was a line I always waited to hear, in part because it signaled the near end of this time on our knees but also because it sparked poetic images in my mind and appealed to my sense of drama. "Valley" is what I heard and I pictured a gentle green slope between two mountains, lush and green, but hemmed in somehow, afloat in tears, a valley of human tears. I could see the green of the valley floor, the blue of the running water of tears. I was not untouched by my mother's fervency when she recited this line.

Yet even my need for poetic images in prayer slipped beneath my rebellious response to the form and its overriding presence in my life. It is still mysterious to me why I felt such a strong need to throw this all away for so many years. How did I, considering the immersion of my childhood, become so estranged from the concept of God? (And yet, in a strange, paradoxical way, it was because of the immersion of my childhood that I felt the need to.) My anger with the church's position, with having been indoctrinated at such a young age to see myself as a sinner, created the estrangement. But what I was unable to do for so long was separate God from the church. Why would I (or so many others) want to worship a God who saw me as "less than" for being female, or as a sinner until I repented. I had to thoroughly leave that old version behind before I could create a more loving version of God for myself.

WHEN I STEPPED OUT of the circle of organized religion, my spiritual needs did not die. Instead they led me to explore other paths: philosophy classes, women's spirituality groups, meditation, nature, yoga, therapy and body work, the twelve steps of Al-Anon, vegetarianism. I read books on shame, trying to decipher how to let that go.

What I began to see over a long period of time was that any spiritual path, at its deepest and truest, connects to every other spiritual path. We're all struggling to make sense of this great mystery. Struggling to find ways to keep clearing the path between us and what is most spirited within and around us in this amazing universe, its vastness and power beyond full comprehension. I began to wonder why I held the Catholic church to such high standards of perfection that when I bumped into its imperfections and its imperfect practitioners, I was so willing to throw it all out.

The morning I almost died radically opened up and redirected the angle of my questioning. Perhaps I had spread my wings long and hard enough after decades of searching that I could, without fear of being swallowed up, explore, examine, taste, study and reclaim the roots which were the gift and burden of my birth. The morning my family gathered around my hospital bed, I felt a hint of how rich and deep the soil around those roots must be.

I had a friend who was a Buddhist, a friend who was into mindfulness, another friend who was a serious practitioner of yoga. These practices shared the purpose of quieting the mind, finding one's soul, and finding peace in one's soul. A friend, born and raised Catholic, said to me, "I don't know how to pray anymore." She told me this with a sense of longing, wistful longing, in her voice, perhaps even plaintive loss. I found it sad, even tragic the way the church lost so many of us; some individuals actually pushed us away and some still do today. Every time I hear of the church lacking in compassion or judging or pointing a finger of shame I feel that tug inside me . . . and I remind myself that I can take what works for me and leave the rest.

Still, a form of prayer that touched me was my parents, in their nineties, saying the rosary together every afternoon. Indeed, they knew how to pray. If they were concerned about one of their children, grandchildren, or their own health issues they did what they could about it and then they prayed. My mother, a widow now, centers her day around the rosary in the morning at her assisted living place and the Mass on EWTN from 6:00 to 7:00 p.m. I know not to call her until it's over and then I ask which priest was on because when my dad was alive they nicknamed the priests. "Oh," she might say, "It was Mumbles tonight. So hard to hear his sermons. Last night it was Smiley and I can almost always hear him!"

But I have come to believe that prayer can take many forms. Its common denominator is stilling the mind, calming the soul, accepting what is, breathing in and out, honoring life by paying attention to it.
From Mary Oliver:

"I don't know exactly what a prayer is.
I do know how to pay attention . . ."

I began to think of God as a Great Spirit, so vibrant and all-encompassing that if each of us took a slightly different path toward Him/Her/It, that would be okay. It would be way more than okay. It would be a celebration, a painting on a grand scale, intricately etched and designed, swirled in breathtaking colors and quiet spaces.

Take Two:
So Many, Such Faith

It began to be important to me in an unexpected and quietly fierce way to impart to my children the spiritual tradition (without a suffocating strictness) that had been carried on in my family as far back as I could trace my lineage—back to Granny Bridget and her parents in Peterborough, Ontario, and even further back than that. I needed to pass some semblance of the tradition on; I could not bear to be the one who cut it off. I wouldn't want my children to be at my deathbed in the future and not be able to join in these prayers with others around me. Or, if they were to be suddenly sick themselves, and these prayers were invoked by me or aunts or uncles or cousins, I couldn't bear it if they sounded foreign or meaningless to them.

Even my husband (non-Catholic to this day) came home one day from the inner city school where he taught and said he was noticing that many of the kids who were in the best shape came from families who had a church affiliation—any denomination, but definitely a community.

I enrolled Caitlin in the children's program at the Basilica when she was five, and one day soon after it felt right to sign myself up as a member. Still, I did so hesitantly. I did not want to feel suffocated in any way—I needed a lot of space around me. I was growing to love the place, the sense of serenity as I settled into my pew Sunday mornings or during the special Vespers services. Often I felt moved to tears as the choir filled the building with its beautiful, majestic music on my way up to communion. Yet I didn't want to feel swallowed up by old rules, shame, or fear-based images.

Always, Mary reigned above the altar, welcoming and accepting me. When our son was six months old, Kelly was baptized in the back of this church around the fount. Sun streamed through the stained glass and as Father Dale poured the water over his beautiful head, I felt at home—at home in spite of the struggles I still had with "the church." I put my faith in the many efforts being made within the church to heal and reconcile these wounds and inequities.

Several years after our son's baptism, our daughter made her first communion along with almost thirty other second-graders. They walked down the long aisle in pairs, the girls in white dresses, the boys in their white shirts and small dark suits, and took their place on the altar for the moment they'd been preparing for all year. The place was infused with a special heightened sense of innocence that morning.

My parents and several of my siblings came for the event. Bernie, Gert, and Dan, no longer traveling much, were unable to make it but had sent a rosary specially blessed by the pope as a gift for Caitlin. The church, which is huge, was particularly crowded that morning and as the parade of members to communion streamed on, we watched from our third-row pew. My mother, obviously touched by what she was watching, leaned over at one point and said to me, "So many people coming to communion, such a sign of faith."

In a world where we read daily of murders and rapes and genocide in different parts of the world, where our human darkness is splayed nightly across our TV screens, I wanted to hold close this image of a Sunday morning, my mother leaning over to say, "So many, such faith," of the children in their white dresses and white shirts and this stream of people moving forward for consecrated bread and wine, wrapped inside of beautiful choral music, like waves rolling into shore.

So many, such faith.

Take Three:
9/11

THE MORNING OF 9/11, both of my children were home sick. My daughter was in eighth grade, my son in third, and both of them had felt a little under the weather when I woke them. I could have pushed them to go to school but decided not to; I was home and not teaching that day. It was my daughter who called to me as I was putting away dishes. They were watching TV and those shocking and frightening images had interrupted their morning program. I entered the room and watched in shock and fear. We watched it together and shared the horror. I think in some ways it was beyond comprehension for my son, as he was so young. But not so my daughter. As the morning went on, I realized my son did not need to watch this any more. I made a few phone calls to loved ones. We were all shaken.

But I did feel an exquisite comfort in having my children with me that day. I knew they were safe. I could touch them, be with them.

After a while my daughter said, "I would like to go down to church and light a candle for all those people."

I felt in that moment that I had done something right—that she would, at that age, think of her church as a place to go for sanctuary and comfort on such an awful day.

"Yes," I said.

And so the three of us went down to the church, which was quiet and hushed and peaceful. We were the only ones there. We brought our dollar bills and stuffed them in the small slot. Each of us took the long wooden stick and lit candles in front of the Mary statue in the back of the church. In quiet whispers we said, "Please help all those who died and all their family members."

A counterpoint to the raw horror of that day was the simple shared activity of lighting candles, together, in the gentle light of midday in our church.

The next day my neighbor and friend Marti called and asked if I wanted to go to the memorial Mass being held in honor of 9/11. I felt grateful to have a friend who would call me and we could go together. The place was packed and we slid into the pew. That day, that whole week, was full of tears. To share the sorrow was a palpable solace. I fell in love that day with the hymn "How Can We Keep from Singing." The Basilica choir (which obviously I am a big fan of) sang so many verses as the waves of people moved up for communion. Verse after verse followed by the chorus of "How Can we Keep From Singing." It was haunting and comforting and deeply soothing. And I thought, *I need this kind of ritual in my life.* This ability for a group of human beings to join in sorrow and share it through the beauty of music and the comfort of prayer would be difficult to find elsewhere.

Take Four:
The Heart Attack

A FEW YEARS BACK my oldest brother had a heart attack. Out of the blue on a week night I received a phone call from his friend, about ten-thirty at night. He had been playing racquetball with a group of guys he had been friends with since college.

The ER he had been taken to was about a twenty-minute drive from my house and I said I would be right there. My brother's ex (or almost ex) had been phoned first, and she was on her way but had a longer drive. She had given the friend my number. I called one of my sisters, said I was on my way, and would she call all the other siblings?

I drove, worriedly, the twenty miles to the Fairview Southdale ER. I walked in, found the waiting room and there were my brother's friends. "It's pretty serious," one of them told me. "He is in the cath lab—they're putting a stent in his heart. They couldn't wait. The doctor said for us to wait in the lobby outside the cath lab, and when he's done operating, he will come talk to us there."

I knew my almost-ex-sister-in-law was on her way, and I knew some of my siblings were on their way. But for the time being, I was the only family member there. The friendship between my brother and these guys went way back to college at St. John's University. One of them who was usually in that group is a priest, and so when I said, "We could use a priest," they replied that Marty hadn't been with them that night—he couldn't make it.

I felt fearful that my brother might not make it. I wished for the comfort of a priest and prayers, and as we gathered up and headed through the main lobby to find our way to the cath lab lobby, I ran into a family friend. "Sue," I gasped. "What are you doing here?"

"I brought Father Michael in," she told me. "He had a nose bleed that wouldn't stop and called me."

At that time, Father Michael was my beloved parish priest. Again, I gasped, "You mean he's here? My brother is in with a heart attack and I just said we need a priest."

She understood immediately, and said, "When Father is done with the doctor, he'll come find you. Where will you be?"

In the lobby outside the cath lab, we waited and talked. I enjoyed being with the friends, the "Johnnies" who I hadn't seen in a long time. When I told them the Father Michael story, a couple of them said they knew him well. I thought, *Of course, I'm immersed in the moment in what could be seen as the Irish mafia.* There we were—Hoolihan, Linehan, Cassidy, waiting for O'Connell. In the midst of tension and apprehension and fear, some humor and definitely some serendipity were going on.

My siblings started to show up. Then the doctor came out and showed us on an x-ray where he put the stents. He told us we could see our brother up on the fourth floor in about fifteen minutes. Father Michael found us, and after a round of greetings among old friends, my brother's friends left. Father came along with me and my siblings as we all gathered around my brother's bed. He was completely out of it, hooked up to many machines, and he did not look good.

We joined hands, and Father said his healing prayers. I forget if he had a prayer book with him or if he did it by memory. His nose was taped up and I had a moment of concern for him and yes, guilt. He probably just needed to go home and rest but here he was, giving all of us the comfort of prayer as we anxiously looked at our brother, hovering between life and death.

It was very comforting, and as I walked him down the hall afterward, I thanked him profusely. Days after the event and my brother's initial recovery, my mother sent Father Michael a hand-written note thanking him from the extended family.

Through most of the following day, my brother's situation was precarious. His children were called, but all lived out of state and needed to make flight arrangements. A few of us stayed all night. I left in the morning to shower and check in on my kids and grab some of my students' papers so I could sit in the waiting room and read them. Some of my siblings showed up in the morning. We gave my next oldest brother the task of calling Mom and Dad in the morning so they knew what was going on. It was clear to all of us that they should stay up north.

Sometime about mid-morning we were all allowed in again to see Jim. He was still completely under, and plugged into machine-land. His skin looked gray. He was breathing through a respirator. The oldest in the family, he was always so competent and capable. Now he looked vulnerable, helpless.

We all took that in quietly, uncertainly. Them my older sister, Cathy, tentatively said, "Would everyone be okay with saying a decade of the rosary?" I loved her for her courage and for being so right on.

Everyone nodded.

So we stood around Jim, held hands, and prayed the "Our Father," ten "Hail Mary's" and a 'Glory Be'—a decade of the rosary. Soon after, the nurse shooed us away, back to our waiting room where we had set up camp.

There was a lot going on that day. My brother's three grown children arrived and his ex left. Then the new woman in his life arrived and it was all pretty intense. But after about twenty-four hours, they removed the respirator. My brother was able to breathe on his own, and his recovery began. He is, to this day, quite healthy.

One of my brothers, who at the time was somewhat estranged from the family, told me later that saying the rosary around Jim's bed was what felt most authentic, genuine, and caring to him—not all the talk in the waiting room.

I was struck by that. There is something powerful embedded in ritual, in joining together to pray the prayers of our youth. There was a deep resonance and an ability to express care. None of us knew what to do or what to say. And it became a vehicle, a way to join together and send Jim what the new-age people would call good energy, white light, healing energy. We all felt it—whether angry at the church or not, whether actively participating in the church or not.

Take Five

A FEW YEARS AGO I felt drawn to the 10:00 a.m. service on New Year's Day at the Basilica. It was a year when I needed that extra spiritual sense for beginning the new year ahead.

It was cold, and I went alone. I sat near the back, as I usually do. The lights were gentle and soft. A few people were there but it was by no means packed. As soon as I sat, I felt soothed. My breathing evened out as my bones and muscles relaxed against the hard wood of the pew.

The priest spoke from the center of the altar. He opened the service, quite simply, by saying, "We gather together today, the first day of the New Year, as men and women of prayer."

I rolled the words around inside my brain, and a small light went on. I realized, in a surprised way, it was a community I could comfortably belong to—the community of men and women of prayer. It had taken me years to get to this place. But that morning, that first day of the year, I knew I had arrived at a destination that had mystified and eluded me for a long time.

Part Four

Lifting Off & Leavetakings

Top: The extended family at the 1999 reunion.
Bottom: The older Hoolihan relatives at the 1999 reunion. Standing: Uncle Dan, Dorothy Spang, Aunt Margaret, Mickey Spang, and the author's father and mother. Seated: Aunt Gert, Aunt Bernie, Aunt Eleanor, Uncle Milt.

Chapter Nineteen
Lift-Off & Eagle's Wings

"If you would indeed behold the spirit of death, open your heart wide unto the body of life.
For life and death are one, even as the river and the sea are one."

–Gibran

My experience with nearly dying very much tuned me into the dying process of others.

Back in August of 1999, some of my cousins and siblings organized a family reunion, knowing that the remaining six siblings of the original twelve were on borrowed time.

My cousin said, "This will be the last big reunion where we'll have so many of the older generation still alive." And although we all said it to each other, what happened in the following months still came as a shock.

The reunion opened as every event in this family does, with a Mass said by the two priest cousins, Father John and Father Bill. Afterwards, a professional photographer took pictures of all of us. We gathered in front of the altar of our hometown church, of course. There were 150 of us and we spilled off the edges of the photo. The two oldest—Bernie was ninety-three, Eleanor ninety-two—both made it to the reunion. Although both could still walk, it was decided that the day's activities would wear them out so they were in wheelchairs, clad in their white hair and broad smiles and green clover pins. Flanking them were Gert and Dan, their sister Marg and her husband

Left: fun on the beach at Uncle Dan's camp. Right: Uncle Dan with his haul in front of the fish house.

Milt, my parents, some of the older Spang cousins. and the multitudes of descendants from the two original couples—Kate and Will Hoolihan and Nora (Kate's sister) and Matt Spang.

As Bernie said, "We all had a jolly time."

The day after the reunion, my sister and her son, my oldest brother and his wife, and my two kids and I embarked on a trip to Uncle Dan's fishing camp. Uncle Dan picked us up on Perch Lake just outside of Atikokan, Ontario, and flew us into camp in two loads. We spent three beautiful sunny days with early morning fishing, mid-day swimming, nighttime bonfires on the beach, complete with many renditions of "O Canada!" and Uncle Dan's moose-hunting stories, one after another. It was my first trip there in twenty years, my last time there with Uncle Dan, and my children's first visit. The whole trip felt like a waterfall of joy—flying out that time was when I felt wildly lucky and had the premonitory sense it would be the last time I would be a passenger in that plane with Dan as the pilot. I still remember that long, slow taxi ride out to where he had a stretch of water in front of him, the slow meditative sweep, the take-off, flight,

1999 visit to camp. Left to right: the author's former sister-in-law Mary Lou, brother Jim, nephew Tom, daughter Caitlin, son Kelly, sister Jane, and Uncle Dan.

and landing all steeped in natural, wild beauty. Then we were dropped off on Perch Lake. Uncle Dan taxied out from shore, where we watched him lift off again, alone, back to camp.

I drove and floated back to my city life.

Six weeks later I was back in the northwoods attending Aunt Eleanor's funeral, supporting my father, uncle, and aunts in the loss of their sister. Sitting beside my father at Eleanor's funeral, I felt his sadness and I absorbed into my bones the comfort of his beautiful tenor voice singing that sadness, especially the song "On Eagle's Wings." Two weeks after we buried Eleanor, Bernie sat down in the living room after eating a light lunch and sweeping the kitchen floor. Dan was reading in the chair beside her when she started speaking in a garbled voice. Then she slumped in her chair. Dan called Gert from the kitchen and then dialed 911. Bernie had had a stroke. She ended up in the hospital, where she stayed for the next ten days.

While Bernie was in the hospital, she turned ninety-four, and Gert turned eighty-seven. Their November birthdays were only days apart. Days after Bernie's stroke, I called home and found out that in order to have someone with her twenty-four hours a day, Uncle Dan was doing the night shifts at the hospital from ten o'clock at night until five o'clock in the morning, when my father came in. The day was split up among them, with my mother helping a lot along with Father John and Sister Eleanor Ann, who were able to leave their religious duties for a time to help out. They had just lost their mother. Bernie was dying, and no one wanted her to die alone.

My mom was worried about my dad and his increasing level of exhaustion. I felt worried for all of them. As I hung up the phone an urgent need to both help out and see Bernie before she died swept through me. I spent the afternoon making arrangements for my young children, and my husband was willing and able to take over on the weekend. By 8:00 a.m. Friday I was driving north. By noon I was at the hospital, looking at a much thinner version of Bernie. The left side of her body was paralyzed. She didn't know me at first, until I was around for a while.

I spent a lot of the day there. At first I felt awkward. What use would I be if she didn't know who I was? But I watched how Gert, Sister El Ann, and my mother held Bernie's hand and talked to her. I watched how the nurses talked loudly so she could hear them, and I saw how interested she was when the nurses rotated her body from side to side every two hours. They always told her what they were doing. Her right eye opened and she'd say, "Which one are you?" or a simple but clear, "Okay."

The first day I was there, she kept asking for water. "I want four glasses of cold, clean water." She said it slowly and clearly. With her left side paralyzed, speech took great effort and swallowing was even harder. The medical staff deemed it unsafe to give her water. It would travel with too much speed down her throat and choke her. So they gave her water thickened with food starch and we could rinse and wet her mouth with a swab dipped in cold water. She took the thickened water but let us know she was less than satisfied. Usually a swallow or two of the thick stuff was followed by the phrase, "I want clean water."

"Doesn't it break your heart not to be able to give her water?" Gert asked me.

"Yes, " I replied. Those days in the hospital, I made sure I drank outside of the line of Bernie's vision. I felt grateful every time I was thirsty and could drink water.

Father John said Mass every day for Bernie. She sat, raised up on her hospital bed, took a small piece of communion dipped in wine and mumbled the prayers along with the others in the room. The home Mass became a hospital Mass. After the Friday afternoon Mass, my mom and I stayed with Bernie while Gert, Dan, Father John, Sister El Ann and my father went home for dinner.

Out of the blue, Bernie announced, "I'd like to bake today, if only I can find the recipe."

My mom and I humored her and responded. Mom suggested she make those good oatmeal muffins and I started talking about my favorite cookies she and Gert had made over the years. Into this chatter, Bernie added, "The recipe calls for four glasses of cold, clean water."

She often made us smile or laugh. The farm days were on her mind. More than once, when she was talking of water, she added, "Cold, clean water from the well on the farm." It must have been her favorite water from her long life.

By Friday evening she was beginning to remember me as her niece, Patty. I was beginning to feel comfortable holding her hand and talking to her, swabbing her mouth with cold water when she wanted it. I could understand her pretty well. It was harder for Gert, Dan, or my parents because they were all in various stages of hearing loss. We worked it out that I would cover the night shift from 1:00 a.m. until 7:00 a.m., making it possible for both Uncle Dan and my dad to catch up on their sleep.

My mom and I were on the dinner shift until Gert and Sister El Ann relieved us. After dinner I retired to the bedroom of my childhood and slept from nine o'clock until midnight. Forty-five minutes later, I walked in the door of the hospital room. Uncle Dan was in the corner chair, reading. Bernie was dozing peacefully. Dan asked if I had ever been at the bedside of a dying person, and I answered that I hadn't. He spoke of the dying ones he had tended to: Ma, Pa, his brothers Matthew and Ted, his cousin Rosemary. He told me he had just said the rosary to Bernie; the ruby-red rosary beads still lay draped across her right hand. On the table beside her was a small prayer book with prayers for healing, prayers for the sick, and prayers for the dying. Two small plastic bottles of holy water stood on the night stand, one specially blessed from Lourdes. Next to them was lavender healing oil, blessed also, which Sister El Ann had brought.

When my father was on duty, he was less comfortable with words but faithful with the holy water. Every fifteen minutes or so he would rub some on Bernie's forehead and anyone else's forehead who was in the room. I loved my father's hand moving across my forehead, lightly and gently anointing me. Uncle Dan did the same to me and Bernie and himself before he said goodnight.

And then I was alone in a quietly lit hospital room with a dying woman, a dear aunt of mine, who had made me laugh, made me think, and whose stories and spirit had been a living link all my life to my past.

When her right arm and hand started reaching up and around, almost fluttering, I got up from the chair and stood beside her. My two fingers fit right inside of her small, shrinking hand. Her bony fingers gripped me tight and she started moving my fingers inside of her hand, around in circles. I remembered her at the stove, stirring peaches, and I asked her if that was what she was doing. "No," she replied. "I'm milking cows."

I laughed and said, " I thought only the boys had to milk the cows."

"Oh no," she reassured me in her slow-talking way. "We girls milked too. And this is how you do it."

There she was on her deathbed, teaching me how to milk cows.

Once she turned to me and asked, "Can I quit now? I'd like to quit and go to my grave."

I rubbed my hand across her forehead and said into her ear, " You can quit anytime, my dear."

But still, she hung on. My dad said he felt that she often had a look on her face as if to say, "I'll go when I'm ready."

Dylan Thomas's poem lived inside of me those days:

"Do not go gentle into that good night
Old age should burn and rave at close of day
Rage, rage against the dying of the light.

Grave men near death who see with blind sight
Blind eyes which blaze like meteors and be gay
Rage, rage against the dying of the light."

Her Pretty Weasel eyes did burn bright and her sharp and humored ways occasionally emerged from her primarily sleeping self. When I was on night duty, I sang her the chorus from "Eagle's Wings." Earlier in the day my dad and I had gone over the words, helping each other remember them. The song and my father's singing of it was my most poignant memory of my Aunt Eleanor's funeral, and Dad said he remembered singing it at Uncle Jerry's funeral many years before. The song easily moved me to tears, so I could just barely sing it to Bernie. And I was sure it was conjuring heartfelt memories in Bernie's head.

The chorus goes, "And he will lift you up on eagle's wings, hold you in the breath of dawn, and teach you to shine like the sun, and hold you in the palm of his hands." The melody is both beautiful and haunting.

I choked my way through it, holding Bernie's hand as I sang. At the end I was quiet and she was quiet but she looked up at me with her one good eye. Then she said, "Can we all go to bed now?"

"Oh, yes," I said, holding back my sudden desire to laugh.

In the morning. my parents relieved me and I told them a few of the stories of the night; they especially liked the cow-milking story. I went home and fell into bed, got up four hours later, went for a run, showered, ate something and returned to the hospital for the 4:00 p.m. Mass. One of the things I learned is that a deathwatch is all-consuming. If you have time to eat and sleep and renew yourself just a bit for your next shift, you are lucky.

For the Saturday afternoon Mass said by Father John, Bernie really perked up. She asked for her glasses for the first time since she'd landed in the hospital. Before the Mass began, she took a couple of sips of cold, thickened water from the nurse. We raised her up to a sitting position and she opened both eyes, which must have taken great effort. We were a small group but we filled the room: Mom, Dad, Sister El Ann, Father John, Gert, and me. When Father John opened the Mass with the sign of the cross, I watched Bernie's right arm move methodically with great effort and determination as she moved it up to her forehead, down to her chest, and across to both shoulders making the sign of the cross. How many times in her lifetime had she completed that gesture? She murmured all the prayers, took the small piece of communion dipped in wine, and at the kiss of peace everyone kissed everyone else in the room, and one by one, kissed Bernie. I slipped my two fingers inside of her hand, bent down and kissed the weathered and deeply veined top of her right hand. She held on tight to my two fingers, then slowly raised my hand inside of hers up to her lips and kissed it. It was a moving moment for all of us in the room.

That night I returned again at 1:00 a.m. Uncle Dan and I visited again for a while. Back in September, as a way of thanking him for flying me and my children into camp, I had sent him the chapter of my book that was about him. Months had gone by. I'd seen him at Eleanor's funeral, and he hadn't mentioned it. But on my second night shift, in the hospital's quiet light, he thanked me, said he found it inspiring. "You've got a way with words," he told me. "Why, as a wordsmith, you're right up there with Pat Buchanan." This statement was followed by a hearty laugh—a rub at our political differences. We both laughed. I was happy to think my words had inspired him. Then he added, "You got it ninety-nine percent right." Of course I had to ask about the one percent that was not right, and he waved his hand and said, "We're not going to worry about that." It felt as if he had given my writing his benediction, even including the Pat Buchanan comment.

When he left, I noticed that Bernie was more restless than the previous evening. I had a chance to ask her if she remembered when she and Gert and Dan prayed around my bed when I was so sick. "Oh, yes," she murmured, "Long time ago."

"Twenty years ago." I added, "You have been very special to me ever since."

We were holding hands, and she said, "You are very special to me, too."

Earlier in the day, one of the nurses asked her if she was having good dreams, since she was sleeping so much. "Oh, yes," she said. There was something about the way she said, "Oh, yes," those days in the hospital that was incredibly sweet and engaging. I could have listened to her say those two words for a long time. The nurse then asked, "What are you dreaming about?"

She was quick to reply, "Heaven."

So in the middle of the night I asked her, "Is the sun shining in heaven? What is heaven like?"

"Oh, yes, it's sunny and pretty."

"When you get there, will you look out for me?"

"Oh, yes."

I was standing close to her, right in her line of vision—a few quiet moments passed when she mumbled something I had to ask her to repeat. It came through clearly the second time, "Pretty hair. You have pretty hair."

"Thank you," I murmured, touched that she would muster the energy to give me a simple compliment, to acknowledge an aesthetic pleasure she could still feel and absorb—the sight of red, curly hair. In her youth, all of her life, she had known and loved people with red, curly hair.

Sometimes she would grasp my fingers inside of her hand and rub herself: across her chest, sometimes moving up to her forehead or along her cheekbones over and over again. I was struck by her need to comfort herself and the way she led me to help her. No words were exchanged and often her eyes were closed. No longer eating, taking less and less of the thickened water, she still reached that hand out. The need to be touched, to have one's hand held in the warmth of another's, outlasted by far her need for food or water.

At 7:00 a.m. my parents arrived, and I went home and slept for four hours. Awake by noon, I ate breakfast and hugged my parents, who were just off-duty and back home, goodbye. When I stopped by the hospital, Gert and Sister El Ann were in attendance. I spent a last few minutes holding Bernie's hand and rubbing her forehead; I kissed her goodbye, told her I loved her and would be praying for her, and walked down the corridor, knowing I would never see her alive again. It was time to return to my life, to my six- and twelve-year-old kids, my husband, and my teaching.

My sister Jane drove up from the cities and took the night shift for the next two nights. Bernie was talking less and taking in less liquid. When Jane left, my dad and uncle split one more night shift. Then Bernie died on Wednesday, late morning, November 17, 1999. The morning she died, the sun was shining into her hospital room, all over the northwoods, and across my city home as well. It was an unseasonably warm November day and I was outside in the sun, reading student papers, when I received the phone call. Tears fell down my sun-warmed cheeks. Even when you know death is coming there is no way to prepare for its finality. It made me happy to know that when the final moments arrived, Sister El Ann and Gert were beside Bernie. Prayers for the dying had been said numerous times already, but they were said again. Father John, Uncle Dan, and my parents arrived within minutes for a final round of prayers together.

There were rows and rows of us at the funeral—so many nephews and nieces that she had touched. So many of us wanted to support the remaining ones in the front pews: Gert, Dan, Aunt Marg and Uncle Milt, and my parents. There were six of the original tribe of twelve alive for the reunion in August of 1999. On November 20, 1999, at the funeral, only four remained.

THE EVENING BEFORE the funeral, the Carmelites (the lay order Bernie and Gert had been involved in most of their lives) led the rosary. They wore what looked like giant scapulars around their necks. The huge brown squares lay in front and in back against their clothes—almost like an apron but with white insignia across the front. At first I was sort of mystified by their presence and their outfits.

I hung around with Gert and Dan and my parents throughout the entire three hours of people coming in to pay their respects, two small prayer services, and all of us talking and reminiscing, occasionally wiping our eyes. When it was time to go, the place almost emptied out, I, along with my cousin David, followed my dad and Uncle Dan up to the casket. We were the last ones in the room. After a moment, Uncle Dan said, "Good night, Bernie."

My dad echoed, "Good night, Bernie."

My cousin and I looked at each other and then followed suit. "Good night, Bernie." There was something oddly and powerfully comforting to be able to say to her that simple phrase one last time and be able to see her face, waxen and frozen in time as it was.

In the morning, the huge extended family gathered at the funeral home for final prayers and a final viewing of the casket. For the prayers, Gert asked if she could stand by Bernie's casket, and so she did, joined by her sister Marg and Uncle Dan. My father sat in the front row, flanked by his wife and children. It was clear that in these final moments, before Bernie's physical presence would be locked away, Gert wanted to be as physically close to her as she possibly could. All of us cousins watched those siblings kneel on the cushioned kneeler in front of the casket to say goodbye. I watched my father take his turn saying goodbye to this sister, almost twelve years his senior. She had been present for his entire life. I took my turn, as did all my siblings and cousins. Then, we filed out to our cars that were lined up outside the funeral home. And we drove, in procession, with our headlights on, behind the hearse the block and a half to church. We filed into church solemnly, slowly, in procession behind the casket, and paused in the entry area before entering the larger, more public church. My father and Uncle Dan were asked to spread the beautiful woven cloth over the casket. We watched these two brothers unfold and gently spread this cloth that would now cover their sister throughout the service.

I was asked to speak at Bernie's funeral, a deep honor. I so wanted to get it right—especially for her remaining siblings. Both of my priest cousins told a few special Bernie stories as well. The soloist, who lived near my aunts and knew them both well, sang a beautiful "Ave Maria." At the end of the funeral, the rows of Carmelite women filed out first. For a moment, I could not figure out why. Next, the casket was wheeled out. The pallbearers were my brothers and male cousins. Pew by pew we followed, singing "Eagle's Wings," flanked on both sides of the long hallway by the Carmelites, those women of prayer with their brown squares with a huge white insignia. It was then that I understood and felt a passage of comfort in their presence on either side of us, the grieving family members. Wiping our eyes with Kleenex or our sleeves, we filed out to our cars. Gert, Dan, Sister El Ann, and Father John were in the lead car, followed by Aunt Marg and Uncle Milt and their son Father Bill in the next car, my parents in the next one, and then a line-up of my siblings and cousins. Lights on, a police car leading us, we processed out to the cemetery and buried Bernie, eleven days after her ninety-fourth birthday. Bernie was buried between her mother and her sister Mary. I knew as I stood there that one day my parents would be buried there as well.

IN THE WEEKS following Bernie's death I began to think of her leaving us as her own form of lift-off. The long, slow, almost meditative running of the engines. Her aging, her days in the hospital, the left side of her body unable to move, the effort it took for her to speak or swallow. And then, on the last day, the labored breaths, the propellers beginning to spin. It was hard for her to leave her loved ones here, to leave the love of life she had always resonated to. But at some point she began to feel a stronger pull from the other side, where plenty of other loved ones had gone before her. A place where she would no longer be weighed down by gravity or the body's burdens.

And then, at the moment of lift-off, her soul, the essence of her spiritedness, leaving her body, lifting off—riding currents of air and mystery and light we can barely imagine.

Perhaps all of us around her bed in those final days helped her lift off as well.

Chapter Twenty
Uncle Dan's Final Flight

"The summer's gone and all the flowers are dying..."
–From "Danny Boy"

WHEN UNCLE DAN'S heart trouble first showed up, he leaned over to me in the quiet moments before a home Mass was about to be celebrated and said, "Patty, the mighty oak has swayed a bit in the breeze."

One of my siblings said, "Nothing wrong with his ego." But more than that, the statement captured the essence of his incredible physical strength. In his later years that strength did ebb and "sway in the breeze."

My mother had told me that the last time he came home from camp he looked ashen and went straight to bed. She and my dad happened to be over visiting at *the house* when he came in from the airport. That was the summer after my last flight with him.

He slept a lot in the next few days, and then began a fall season of tests. Medical tests. What exactly was wrong, and could it be fixed? After a series of tests in Grand Rapids and Duluth, Uncle Dan put his foot down. "I want the best," he said. "Mayo Clinic." He was referring to the nationally renowned clinic in Rochester, Minnesota.

So my parents and Gert drove him to Rochester, checked into a nearby hotel, and kept him company through days of tests. I took a day off of work and drove to Rochester to be with them. When I arrived, Dan was alone in his room, sleeping. I slid into a nearby chair with my book and waited. When he woke up, he was happy to see me. "I was just taking a nipper-napper," he said (always one to have fun with words). Then he added, "I was dreaming about being at camp. Going for a swim, loading the woodstove."

He laid there for a while and we chatted quietly. Then out of the blue he sighed and said, "It's been a long, rugged life." I was surprised and asked him what he meant. "Well, there was Omaha Beach. I was in the first wave of infantrymen. We went in after dark to get set up before the Germans came at dawn. But they were ready for us, and started coming at us. I saw a lot of guys not make it. I must have been charmed to have come out of that alive."

He shook his head, as if still trying to comprehend the experience. He was eighty-three years old with at least sixty years of life experience between that moment and Omaha Beach. Yet the event reached across his memory, called to him and to some extent, defined his time on earth. He was awarded a Purple Heart after being wounded in action at St. Lô in France. Over the years, he had talked only occasionally about hiding in foxholes and knowing survival was in his own hands. He told us about how he hid socks in his helmet because he hated having wet feet.

My parents and Gert kept Dan company as he lay in bed, resting between a battery of tests. One day the conversation began with a commentary on how good the Rochester water tasted, but it easily and quickly traveled to the well water that was pumped at the kitchen sink, at the Canadian camp, which was known for having great water. Their brother, my Uncle Bill, when he was alive, worked for Culligan—a water and heating company. One time he brought back a sample of water from camp to get tested. It was returned with this comment: "Nothing can be done to improve this water." There we all were, decades later, in the Mayo clinic with this story of Dan's well and pump, Dan's place in Canada—a thread of familial pride and nostalgia woven through the story.

After several days of Dan's medical tests, my sister Jane and I returned for the diagnosis. We all knew Dan's heart was compromised. We wondered if they would they do surgery. Jane, the nurse, is always good to have around because she can translate medical information for the rest of us. But the primary info came through loud and clear—

surgery was not an option. There was nothing Mayo could do for him except to let him try a new experimental drug called Tikosyn. My father heard the part that there was very little Mayo could do for Dan, and he choked up. Jane and I and our mother stood close to him and Gert. I flashed on stories of their childhood, how my dad and Dan were always together on the farm. Uncle Dan was the ringleader and his favorite phrase, according to Gert, was "Me and Jim are going to . . ." Here was my father, in his eighties, facing the knowledge that this brother he had shared so much of his life with wouldn't be around a lot longer. Now, of course, that might seem obvious at his age. But that moment around Dan's bed with the doctors talking quietly to us, the awareness hit deep.

And so the next day the four of them caravanned north. There was a flurry of phone calls to the cousins in Grand Rapids. I called my cousin Mary to say, "They're on their way. They're all so tired. Can you buy some basic food supplies? Start the fire for them?" "

"Yes, of course," she said. "We'll get the house warmed up and ready for them."

They stopped at my sister Cathy's, which was about a third of the way, where she had homemade soup waiting for them.

They made it home safely and settled in.

And thus began the Tikosyn Era.

Tikosyn Era

> "But come you back when summer's in the meadow
> Or when the valley's hushed and white with snow
> 'Tis I'll be there in sunshine or in shadow . . ."
> –From "Danny Boy"

WE WERE AFRAID Dan might last only a couple of months. But we underestimated Gert's loving care and Dan's love of even a sedentary life. The Tikosyn was to be administered twice a day, twelve hours apart. They agreed on 9:00 a.m. and 9:00 p.m. As a new drug, it was strictly regulated. It could not be purchased even with a prescription from the local drugstore. Instead, it came in the mail. Instructions for administering this drug were precise. If a dose wasn't given within a half-hour of the prescribed time, then it was to be skipped. In three years, I think Gert forgot a dose about a total of three times. Although each time sent her into a paroxysm of guilt and worry, it didn't seem to have an obvious effect. Dan lasted for three years, never returning to camp, although numerous offers to get him there were made. He never flew his plane again, although he did get in it as a passenger with Steve, a good family friend and the one who took over flying the Stinson.

ONE DAY, my dad and I wandered over to the house. Uncle Dan was in his spot by the woodstove in the kitchen, and we sat there for a while before I asked where Gert was. "She's upstairs, go on up and check on her," Dan said. I walked up the stairs, calling to Gert. I didn't want to startle her or catch her in a stage of undress.

"Oh, Patty," she called out. "I'm just getting organized to put curlers in my hair. The angels must have sent you. It's getting harder and harder to do this by myself."

I appreciated and savored being thought of as angel-sent. Gert was sitting in front of her small wooden vanity and mirror. Her curlers and bobby pins filled a small shoebox. I spent the next ten minutes putting curlers in her freshly washed hair. The fine-toothed plastic comb slid easily through her thin, silver-gray hair. She had a specific order and gave me clear instructions: three curlers on the top, two on each side, and as many as I could use on the back (free form!). The last little bit of hair on each side was curled and clasped with a bobby pin. She really appreciated not having to raise her arms and do it all herself. I'm sure her curlers were fifty years old—pink plastic, with plastic picks to hold them in place. The curlers led us into a conversation about Tip Top Lodge in Canada, owned so long ago by Dan's friend who made a fortune making and selling Tip Top curlers and many other products. The conversation took me back to my ten-year-old self and a memory of walking into Tip Top Lodge and being completely blown away by its exoticness, its woodsy beauty. But the whispered knowledge that Uncle Dan's good friend and fellow pilot was a "millionaire" was almost beyond comprehension to my "peasant" life and soul at that time.

As I finished up and Gert gave me one of the infamous (BVG) hairnets to put over the curlers, my eye was caught by the sight of a small alarm clock on the nearby tall dresser. It was clicking and set for an hour ahead. Puzzled, I asked about it. "Oh," she said, "that's set to Tikosyn time. I get confused with daylight savings, so this is the clock I go by for giving Dan his Tikosyn."

"Tikosyn time." A clock on an upstairs dresser set to Tikosyn time. Although the Tikosyn era lasted much longer than expected or predicted, it still seemed too short. During those three years, Dan was occasionally hospitalized to have the fluid drained from his lungs. With the heart pumping at about a quarter capacity, a lot of fluid can build up. One of the things Gert made him do every day was weigh himself. When he gained more than ten pounds it meant it was time for him to go in again. The last time he did this he said to her, "No more. I don't want to spend any more time in the hospital."

When I went to visit him during his last stay at the hospital, I came in and gave him a kiss on the forehead. I was wearing lipstick, a muted purple, and without realizing it I left a mark. When Gert arrived a few minutes later she hugged us both and then stared at the purple mark. Looking concerned, she asked, "What happened to you there? Did you bump yourself?"

Puzzled, he put his fingers to his forehead. I was puzzled too, at first, until I realized and then laughed, saying, "It's my fault. It's from where I kissed him. It's my lipstick."

Then he grinned too, saying, "I could use more bumps on the head like this one."

A few moments later, Gert walked out in the hall to ask the nurse a question. In a moment of quiet appreciation, Dan turned to me and said, "That Gert. She is true blue."

I nodded. *Indeed she is. True blue.*

Uncle Dan had always been a man of great personal strength. So it surprised us all that he handled his physical demise with such emotional grace. He never complained, he always lit up when people came to visit, and he never lost his sense of humor. He held court by the woodstove, usually in the kitchen but sometimes in the living room. Friends, nephews, nieces—everybody dropped in, and he was happy to see every one of us. Tea, coffee or a beer were offered and shared.

My cousin Jim's son (another Dan) interviewed him about a month before he died. One of the questions Dan asked, which later became part of the eulogy Jim (my cousin) delivered, was, "What has been your happiest moment?"

"Right now," he answered. That ability to be fully present in the moment, in spite of the huge physical changes for him, is what is often practiced these days in mindfulness workshops.

I could always get Uncle Dan to play the piano when I visited. First, I played my regulars for him, and then I would beg him to play. He had a jazz number that I loved and tried to emulate, but I could never play it like he did. His jazz always made Gert jig. Such a joyful, lively song. It made me feel happy just to hear it. I still miss it.

Uncle Dan playing piano, with the author on the bench beside him.

He died between Thanksgiving and Christmas of 2003, a little over three years from his diagnosis at Mayo Clinic. That fall I had gone north to help celebrate Gert's birthday in mid-November. Then my kids, husband, and I went north for Thanksgiving. It was to be my last Thanksgiving at *the house*, though I didn't know it at the time. Gert, Dan, and I shared a glass of wine, and toasted to being together, being at *the house*, all of us gathered around the woodstove. I came back again on Friday and played the piano as I did on Thanksgiving. Dan played me his favorite tunes—a little slow and rusty at first, and then it all came back to him. Gert and I smiled at each other. My kids and husband got in on the Friday visit. After Kelly filled up the woodbox, Uncle Dan found an old checkbook box filled with change and gave it to him.

Saturday I came by *the house* to say goodbye. He was asleep on the couch in the living room. I walked in and watched him, his breath rising and falling, his face as handsome as ever. I could see that he had gained weight again, but his face was peaceful. I blew him a kiss. If I'd known it was the last time I would see him alive, I might have kissed him directly on the cheek, even woken him. But we'd had a couple days' worth of wonderful time together. I hugged Gert goodbye.

The following weekend he fell near the woodstove and knocked a part of it loose. Gert had to get him up and shove the stovepipe back into place. It must have been adrenaline, because at the time she was eighty-nine. In retrospect I should have seen it as the sign it was, that the end was imminent.

I was in close touch with *the house*. I had spoken to both Gert and Dan in the aftermath of Dan's fall—both were a bit shaken but fine. Regrettably, I neglected to call that Tuesday morning. I had gone for my morning run, got my son off to school, and shoveled our walk. A few fresh inches of snow had fallen in the early morning hours. Then it was time to go to work. I planned to call when I got home from work, about 2:30 p.m. That was post-naptime for them.

There was more shoveling to be done when I returned from work and it was about three o'clock when I placed my call. Mary answered the phone. She was their wonderful friend who came once a week to help with housecleaning. They were very fond of her. She had heard a lot about me, and though we had met only once, we felt like we knew each other. "Oh, Patty, " she said, her voice catching. "I didn't want to be the one to tell you, but Dan just passed away. Your dad and Gert got him in the car to go to the clinic and he died in the car."

My first thought was, *Oh no, not today, already?* My second thought was that he got his wish to not return to the hospital. My third thought was how perfect it was that he was with his brother and sister when his final moment came.

He hadn't been feeling well that morning, and Gert decided he needed to be seen at the clinic. My dad came to help with the trip to the doctor. It took great effort for Dan to dress that day in his khaki pants, flannel shirt, and leather boots. "He died with his boots on," Dad told me, a note of triumph in his voice.

Gert, in retrospect, wished she had just let him stay home. But I pointed out that perhaps my dad wouldn't have been there. He died practically in mid-sentence, in the car, a few blocks from *the house* with his brother and sister surrounding him. "I should have known," she said for months afterward, carrying her own regrets.

I called my mom, who had tears in her voice as she answered the phone. "Listen, Mom," I said, "I'll make arrangements to come tomorrow. Gert is going to need somebody to answer the phone and the door."

Later in the evening, I called Gert and told her I would be there the next day and would be happy to stay with her. "That will be good, Patty. That will be real good. You can sleep in Bernie's room," she told me. My brother Matt came for those days also, and though he stayed at a hotel, he and I kept each other and Gert company through those first hard days.

Death Dreams

"You'll come and find the place where I am lying . . ."
—From "Danny Boy"

I REMEMBER UNCLE DAN telling me that his father, the lumberjack sheriff, would dream of white horses when there was a death in the family back in Canada. He had dreamed of white horses the night before news reached him that his mother had passed away. This was the time before telephones. Pa was in northern Minnesota and his mother was back near Peterborough, Canada. When the telegram arrived, he was saddened but not surprised.

On one of my last visits with Uncle Dan before he died, he told me he had dreamt that Bob Moffatt—his best Canadian friend and longtime business partner—brought so many chickens, still clothed in their white feathers, that he couldn't find room to store them all. He filled the freezers and fridge but there were still some left over.

I didn't see it as a death-is-coming dream until after he died.

It didn't really hit me until I opened the side door of *the house* on the morning of Uncle Dan's funeral. Bob Moffatt was standing there with his fur hat on and a chicken in hand. "I thought I might find you here, " he said to me. We hugged. I invited him in but he said no, he would see me at the funeral. I thanked him for the chicken, closed the door, and flashed on Uncle Dan sitting at the kitchen table just two weeks before, telling me of his dream.

Farewell Flight—Funeral

"And kneel and say an *ave* there for me."
–From "Danny Boy"

A COUPLE MONTHS before Dan's death, I had published a short essay about him in *Flight Training* magazine. It was about him, his flying, how much I loved flying with him, and the last flight we took together. Dan had said the story made him feel proud.

At his funeral, many of his pilot friends had read the story. I was pleased to know it had been read and enjoyed by his many fans.

Bob Moffat came; the pilot friends, Canadian and American; many, many of Dan's nieces and nephews; and our children. My cousin Jim gave a eulogy that captured Dan perfectly.

The funeral was packed, and there were full military honors at the cemetery. It was a cold, blustery December day. At one point out at the cemetery a small plane flew overhead. Many of us caught each other's eyes and smiled upward, feeling his presence in that flight.

Afterward, some friends and relatives gathered at *the house*. Before long we gravitated to the piano, the one that has been in the family all these years. I played, and a group of siblings and cousins sang around me, which was a deep comfort. "Danny Boy" brought tears to all of our eyes. It was also played as the funeral service ended. But many songs were sung, and we knew that such a gathering would garner Dan's enthusiastic approval.

As aware as we all were that we were going to achingly miss this man, there also was joy in the air, and in the camaraderie, the shared love and joyful and humorous memories among us.

Of course we sang numerous times "O Canada!" The Canadian pilots were driving home and we had to give them an appropriate send-off!

An aerial view of Uncle Dan's camp in Canada.

Chapter Twenty-One
Gert's Surgery

AFTER DAN'S DEATH, and during Gert's year of slowly moving out of *the house*, her health issues began to emerge. She had grown a "goiter" in her neck area, making it difficult for her to swallow and affecting her voice. It was connected to her thyroid. She told me that she had had this "goiter" surgery in her twenties. She had begun to move her medical needs from Grand Rapids to Duluth, taking her sister Marg's recommendation about a good doctor.

Marg's two children in Duluth (Betty and Father Bill) took Gert under their wings, and enfolded her in the love and daily care they had always given their mother. Father John and Sister El Ann had just recently moved into the monastery in Duluth, from Father's parish home in Wisconsin. These loved ones and other cousins who lived in Duluth all formed an important network for Gert. The doctor told Gert her heart was stronger and she was in better shape than some fifty-year-olds he had seen. He felt she could handle surgery.

So, with a little bit of nervousness on all of our parts, we gathered. I met my mom and dad in Duluth, and we checked into the same hotel. We met with Betty, and arrangements were made.

Betty would do the early morning pick-up of Gert and my parents and I would meet her at the hospital. It was to be an early morning surgery. Every one of us was worried; after all, Gert was ninety. There was quite a gathering in the waiting room as cousins came in: Father Bill, Sister Eleanor Ann, Father John, and more. When the doctor came out he told us the surgery had gone well and we could go see Gert in about an hour.

I watched my dad, eighty-six, tall and frail, go in and kiss her on the cheek. "Jim," she said. "It's so good to lay eyes on you." Her voice was scratchy, rough. It was hard for her to talk.

During the day, she slept. We took turns being with her, taking a break, calling Marg and letting them talk. Marg was back at St. Ann's, where everyone was asking about Gert.

Recovery from surgery is rough at any age and it wasn't easy for Gert. We decided she shouldn't be alone that first night, and Sister El Ann and I offered to stay with her, splitting the shift. There was a small waiting area down the hall and whoever was off-duty could catch a few winks there. Gert slept a lot, but when she woke up she was happy to see a familiar face nearby.

This wasn't the first time Sister El Ann and I tag-teamed in our caring for Gert. Earlier in the winter, when Gert was back at *the house* by herself, she went through a bad bout with the flu. Sister El Ann tuned into this and showed up at the front door, ready to stay for a few days. Gert said then and later, "I was never so happy to see someone in my life. I'd been feeling 'punk' for days but I didn't want to bother anyone."

When I asked El Ann how she knew, she said it was Father John's pastoral sense. They had spoken with Gert on the phone, could tell she wasn't feeling well, so John said to El Ann, "Why don't you go? She needs you more than I do right now." Without further ado, she got into her car and showed up a couple hours later at Gert's front door. It took almost ten days to nurse Gert back to full health. El Ann stayed for five nights and then I came and stayed another four nights.

During the day after Gert's surgery, my parents and I, on a break from hospital duty, went for lunch. We ate outside, looking over the beautiful, uplifting expanse of Lake Superior. "You're a great daughter, Patty." My dad said to me. "Thanks for taking such good care of Gertie."

It was a moment to hold close. I had only rarely heard him use that name for her, but I knew it took him back to days on the farm when she was pigtailed and young. The special connection I felt for her and with her was intricately connected to the web of love between my father and I. Betty and Father Bill's devotion to Gert, Father John and Sister El Ann's care, and the care of so many other cousins, too numerous to name them all, were intricately connected to the love their mothers and fathers had for Gert. Their interwoven hearts reminded me of an intricate lace pattern, where all the threads are separate, but woven together to create a distinctive and beautiful design.

Gert recovered, but had to take thyroid medicine from then on.

Chapter Twenty-Two
The Rescue Mary Mission

"The breezes blowing over the sea from Ireland
are perfumed by the heather as they blow."
–From "Galway Bay"

My dad had been almost superstitious about his questionable ability to live past the age that the oldest men in his immediate family had lived. His father died at the age of eighty-seven and Dan died just a couple months short of his eighty-seventh birthday. The other males had died at younger ages. There were more emergency trips to the hospital with Dad's heart condition the year preceding his eighty-eighth birthday than before or after (until his last year, four years later). So I decided to come back to Minnesota from our summer home in Canada for my Dad's eighty-eighth birthday.

This trip back to my hometown for this special birthday lunch coincided with obvious changes at 835 Second Avenue. The house had sold a couple months before. Gert had moved to Duluth. In the spirit of new ownership and new vision, changes were already visible. A couple of trees had been taken down—the tall pines that once sheltered Mary. There were signs of construction on the house.

I had hitched a ride from the Twin Cities area up north with my brother Dan, sister-in-law Rosie, and niece Bridget. After the wonderful celebratory birthday lunch, the four of us drove by *the house*, like foreign spies, circling the block, driving slowly through the neighborhood.

"What happened to the Mary statue?" I wondered out loud. She was no longer on her throne of cement and brick so lovingly constructed by Uncle Dan. As we crept through the alley, I spied Mary leaning up against the garage. We stopped and got out to examine her. She was intact, but separated from her throne, which obviously had to be broken open to release the statue. Hmmm. What to do? Bridget and I thought we should collect her on the spot. But Dan deferred, saying, "We better see what Dad thinks."

Off we drove to visit my parents after their post-luncheon nap. I got on the phone to Gert in Duluth, who was upset by the news that Mary had been dethroned, especially without her knowledge. Part of the agreement with the new owner, she told me, was that he would leave Mary until someone came to get her. "Do you want us to bring her to Duluth?" I asked Gert and added, "We could easily do that on our way back to Minneapolis today."

"Oh, could you?" she asked. And then, "I suppose we should check with Father Bill. I want it to go in his backyard at the parish in Duluth. That way I can go visit her, at least from time to time."

Next I called Father Bill, who said it would be great if we brought Mary to Duluth. We could just drop her off at St. Ann's Assisted Living in the care of Marg and Gert. He would pick it up from them the next day and get Mary to her next resting place in the rectory garden.

The next step was clear. We deemed it the Rescue Mary Mission; I have always thought we should have t-shirts made up. My brother had a blanket in the trunk of his car. We pulled up in the alley again behind 835 Second Avenue. We parked and looked around, feeling furtive. The four of us lifted Mary into the blanket, swaddled her and laid her gently in the trunk. Even though we had permission from the owner of the Mary statue, something about the whole mission felt like we could get busted any minute. Perhaps it was just the overriding knowledge that this land no longer belonged to our family. After seventy-five years, it no longer was ours.

We managed to traverse the roads from Grand Rapids to Duluth without cracking or injuring Mary. We brought her in, wrapped, and knocked at Marg and Gert's door. Gert, as always, lit up to see our

The three on the left were participants in the Rescue Mary Mission. From left, sister-in-law Rosemary, brother Dan, niece Bridget, niece Erin, author's father, then-sister-in-law Laura, author's mother, niece Courtney, nephew Conor, and author.

faces, hugged and greeted us, and then led us to her single room, with its single bed and a table filled with her paperwork. Marg's room had two twin beds and Gert slept there, so that Marg and she didn't worry about each other at night. Gert would trot down to her own room to shower, do paperwork, or nap. In the morning, she would don what she called her "traveling clothes" and walk two doors down. The home had a rule that residents had to be dressed, not in robes or PJs, when they were out in the hall. So we laid Mary on Gert's single bed, and Gert fussed with her a bit.

"Thank you," she said. "I'm upset to think about that shrine coming down without me knowing. I am so glad you came along and found Mary."

I CAST A BACKWARD glance as we filed out of the small room. Mary, peacefully wrapped in a blanket, was settled comfortably on the narrow twin bed.

Father Bill arrived the next day, and soon set Mary up in his yard. On many Sundays he had Gert and Marg over for dinner—they said he was a pretty good cook—and so they were able to enjoy Mary in Duluth.

The Rescue Mary Mission was accomplished! Recently, Father Bill gave the Mary statue to my younger brother Matt, who has her settled in a nook by a giant pine outside his cabin, overlooking water and trees.

Mary's current place at Matt's cabin.

Chapter Twenty-Three

Goodbye to Gert

*"But they might as well go chasing after moonbeams
or light a penny candle from a star."*

–From "Galway Bay"

MARG AND GERT were so close, sharing such a small space. They loved being together. Gert moved fluidly from a tight, daily partnership with Bernie, to one with Dan, and then with Marg. The two of them were truly inseparable and led quiet lives together, side by side, with lots of family visiting and get-togethers. Marg died a quiet and peaceful death a couple of years later, from pneumonia. I went and stayed with Gert for two nights before that funeral and we caravanned to Grand Rapids with Sister El Ann and Father John. We all stayed in the same hotel, along with a lot of other cousins.

At that point we were down to two left of the original tribe of twelve—Gert and my dad. Their sadness at the loss of Marg was palpable. Gert broke down standing in front of the casket and many of us surrounded her, trying to ease the sadness. My dad, also sad, was very protective of Gert.

Back at St. Ann's, Gert gave up her single room and moved into Marg's larger room. My parents visited as often as possible, and were able to drive themselves (at the ages of eighty-nine and ninety) to Gert's ninety-sixth birthday party, which was a "jolly" gathering of cousins and good friends. I think those next months and years were lonely for Gert. She often spoke of missing Marg in particular, but often the others as well. She outlived Marg by a couple of years.

The family at Aunt Gert's ninety-sixth birthday party. Left to right: Cousin Mary Louise, sister Jane, the author's mother, cousin Mary, author (behind Aunt Gert), cousin Betty, and the author's father.

In the end, Gert surprised us by dying quickly. Or at least, it seemed quick to us. She went into the hospital on a snowy Christmas morning with pneumonia. Sister El Ann called me. The roads were bad all over the state, and especially in the Duluth area. Sister El Ann was with her the entire twenty-four hours in the hospital. Father Bill and Father John both came and went, and Father Bill was there most of the night. But El Ann never left. I called and wished Gert a Merry Christmas and told her I loved her, not guessing of course it would be my last conversation with her. She had had pneumonia before, had close calls before. Always her strength had won out.

Sister El Ann stayed by her bedside, in spite of her own cancer causing her much back pain. I so wish I could have been there with them, and El Ann was kind enough to tell me the next day that I was with them in spirit. Gert's two priest nephews were there early in the morning, blessing her again. The two of them stepped down the hall to get a cup of coffee. Sister El Ann was holding Gert's hand when she quietly took her last breaths and slipped away.

Father John, Aunt Gert, and the author's parents at Gert's ninety-sixth birthday.

I wondered as she lay dying that Christmas Eve night if she remembered horse-drawn sleigh rides of past Christmas Eves. I wondered if she felt Nel and Del pulling her into the next world, felt all those siblings beside her on the sleigh calling to her from the next world.

THAT NEXT MORNING, as I was throwing a bag in the car to head to Duluth, I called Betty to let her know I was on my way. She was the one to tell me Gert had just passed away. When Betty told me the news, it was hard to grasp. I had so wanted to see her again, so wanted to be with her, wanted to say goodbye. When I put the phone down my twenty-one-year-old daughter looked at me and when I told her that Gert had just died, she put her arms around me and held me while I wept.

Then I called my cousin Mary Louise, who was in Gert's room by then with Father John, Sister El Ann, and Father Bill. Mary Louise arrived moments after Gert took her last breaths. They were all praying around her body when I called. We spoke briefly of letting my dad know and the decisions he would need to be part of.

Later that day, I met Betty at Gert's room, and together we picked out clothes for her to be buried in. We put our arms around each other and one of us said, "I can't believe she didn't wait for us." Betty had been a daily touchstone for Gert for those years she lived in Duluth. We both felt the sudden shock of not being able to say goodbye. We both felt regret at not being there for her final moments.

The author's father, Aunt Gert, Sister Eleanor Ann and Father John.

Gert's body had already been sent to the funeral home in Grand Rapids. I drove the clothes to Grand Rapids and dropped them off at the funeral home. Then my parents and cousin Jim (co-executor for Gert) and I met with the funeral people to finalize decisions about the funeral. When the funeral director took us into the room full of coffins, he started explaining prices and all the trappings of funerals. He said he would give us time alone—that it could be hard sometimes to come to an agreement. We all headed over to the more economical side of the room. All four of us were drawn to a beautiful blue coffin— simple, one of the least expensive choices. But the color blue would fit Gert; it was a Virgin Mary shade of blue. And she wouldn't want any extra money spent unnecessarily. The decision was made unanimously and easily.

THE FUNERAL WAS FILLED with her nephews and nieces. As one of my brothers said, "She had such a loving aura. I don't think she was ever judgmental. She exuded empathy." She had loved us all with the kind of open heart that is symbolized in my favorite Mary statues, above the Basilica altar and in my backyard.

Again, another cousin approached me beside the casket. We talked quietly of Gert, her kindness and her faith. My cousin asked me if I went to church and I said that yes, after taking a break, I had gone back to it, trying to approach it in a new way. She said, wistfully, "I feel like I threw the baby out with the bath water and I don't know how to get it back."

"Baby steps," I murmured, thinking of all the small steps I had taken along the way. Our conversation was wedged in between our comments of how peaceful Gert looked.

She looked beautiful in her blue coffin, a blue sweater matching her blue eyes and the blue rosary beads laced through her fingers. It was sad watching everyone say goodbye to her, especially my parents.

My Dad, with my mom beside him, was now the only one left out of the original twelve siblings.

The author and Aunt Gert outside her assisted living facility in Duluth, MN.

Chapter Twenty-Four

Leavetaking of the Last of the Tribe (Goodbye to Dad)

> "If you ever go across the sea to Ireland then maybe at the closing of your day, you will sit and watch the moonrise over Claddagh and see the sun go down on Galway Bay."
> –From "Galway Bay"

MY FATHER was the last of this original group of twelve to die. Sister El Ann beat him by about nine months. He had a strong, steady, protective instinct, shepherd energy. It was important for him to see them all off to the next world, one by one, and he attended faithfully to each of his siblings all along the way. I know it was hard for him to know he would probably go before my mom, hard to leave her behind. Once when I reassured him we would take good care of her, he said, "You kids are my consolation."

At his funeral, everyone—family, friends, cousins—talked about how he was the last one of that remarkable group of human beings. Truly the end of an era.

A few months before he died, for Thanksgiving of 2010, my family and I headed north for our annual celebration at my brother's home. For many years we had been having wonderful, warm Thanksgiving celebrations hosted by my brother and my sister-in-law with sometimes over twenty of us there. That year, Mom and Dad were still living independently in the senior citizen's condominium unit we had helped move them into about eight years before. Although my dad still drove occasionally, one of us picked them up and drove them back and forth for all our festivities. We sang around the piano at Bill and Laura's house, and we sang around the piano where Mom and Dad lived. Although Dad seemed more tired than usual, he really perked up for the singing. He sang a couple of the favorite songs, and then everyone was worried it might be too much for him—mainly for his heart. It was a very special Thanksgiving: the last with both Mom and Dad, the last with so many of us gathered around that particular table.

In early December, close to Uncle Dan's death anniversary, December 9, Dad began a downward spiral. My siblings and I spent much of December driving north, staying north. He had, along with his congestive heart failure, pneumonia, a couple of bladder stones (not diagnosed or dealt with for way too many weeks), and he was talking about being ready to die. He was in and out of the ER, the hospital, and rehab, then back at home for periods with much medical help set up. After my teaching semester ended in mid-December, I spent the latter half of the month in the northwoods, helping my parents through this difficult time. Since I didn't feel right leaving my parents over the holiday, my husband and kids came north for Christmas. It was a difficult Christmas because we had to move him from the hospital to rehab, a place where it was difficult to celebrate anything, let alone a major holiday. On Christmas day, his grandchildren came—my kids and Bill and Laura's kids—and sang Christmas carols to him. When he started to sing along, all our hearts were lightened. At his suggestion we moved out into the commons area, and several other residents and family members joined in. In spite of the pain and loss swirling around us, we treasured those moments of much-needed and cherished consolation.

He wanted to live at least through December 31, which would be my parents sixty-ninth wedding anniversary. This was his goal, and he talked openly to the nurses and doctors about wanting to get there, about having fallen in love with my mom when he was six years old. It really is an amazing love story, and he was so cute the way he talked about it. Aunt Gert's death anniversary, December 26, came and went. The bladder stones became more and more painful and between Christmas and New Year's, my brother Dan and sister-in-law Rosemary brought Dad to Mercy Hospital in Coon Rapids, where my sister Jane and her husband both work as nurses. Surgery for removal of the bladder stones was set up, postponed, rearranged and ended up being on New Year's Day. The anniversary was quietly and gratefully celebrated with a cake at Mercy Hospital; two of my siblings and their spouses (Jane and Dave and Jim and Brenda) were able to make it. Everyone else called. The roads were snowy and bad, or I would have been there as well.

But most of us were there the next day for the surgery, to help my mom through this waiting. Talking with the surgeon ahead of time, he noted that this was his first surgery of 2011 and it was scheduled for 11:00 a.m. He jokingly said to the nurse, "Could we begin at 11:11? After all, today is 1/1/11."

During this interim period my mom lived with Jane and Dave, only a few miles from the hospital.

Two bladder stones were successfully removed and my dad stayed in the hospital recovering for a few more days. However, it became clear that there were further problems with his bladder, and he soon reached a point where he decided to go no further with medical interventions, except basic pain relief. He called his children around his bed, and we came. He explained, we listened, understood, accepted. Around the room, there were many tears. We held hands and prayed with him. It was decided to say a decade of the rosary, which is ten "Hail Mary's". We took turns "leading" around the circle, and when it came to his turn he kept going. Not one of us was inclined to stop him. So we probably said a decade and a half. Several of us were smiling—there was humor there, even as we were gathered on the evening when our father told us he was giving up medical help and ready to go.

He said he was done eating too, but a day or two later he wanted a pretzel. The small curlicue kind. At first it was like he was sneaking them: after all, he had said he was done eating. But we and the staff kept offering him food. Then he decided a bowl of oatmeal sounded good with brown sugar and raisins. For many days he lived on pretzels and oatmeal. I can't eat a pretzel without remembering how they were used for consolation and celebration in the last weeks of his life. Occasionally he also had ice cream or a cheese and cracker, which previously had been one of his favorite nighttime snacks. And tea, he always said yes to green tea.

From the hospital he went to a rehab/nursing home where the cumulative power of pretzels and oatmeal and his will to live a bit longer made it possible for us to move him and my mother into an assisted living facility. The hospice program we had signed on with at the hospital moved with him to rehab and then to assisted living, where we hoped he could die peacefully under their and our care.

All of these changes happened with a dizzying speed. Places had to be checked out, and my mother needed to see them and oversee the move and decisions. I started to feel empathy for only children because it took all of us working together, dividing forces, taking turns, to make it all happen. On January 14, 2011, we moved them in to Epiphany Assisted Living in Coon Rapids. They were happy to be living together in the same place again, sharing a bed again, able to hold each other's hands as they drifted off to sleep. And the staff was great—always upbeat and helpful.

It was hard for my dad to no longer be in the northwoods, in Grand Rapids, where he had spent all of his ninety-two years except for his war years. Yet, in Coon Rapids, my parents were so much closer to all of their children. This had become imperative because they needed our help almost daily then. Dad had a brief resurgence of energy; he and Mom together settled into life in assisted living.

During that period of time, my son was competing in high school Nordic ski races—February marked the height of the season and my dad loved to hear about the races and see the photos. We all dropped in on them often, Jane in particular, as she worked and lived so nearby. She, being a nurse, was also their health care director.

For me it was a twenty to twenty-five minute drive depending on weather, roads, traffic. I usually went three or four times a week, working around my teaching and my son's ski schedule. On a Monday afternoon, Febuary 14, both of my sisters and I met with the incredible, helpful hospice team and the equally wonderful staff at Epiphany to go over his needs. We hoped we would not have to move him back to a hospital. But that Monday afternoon it was clear he was retreating from us, needing oxygen more, sleeping more.

From my journal of that day:

> "I love holding my father's hands—they are still warm, even if they are cool at the fingertips, his heart is working hard to circulate blood. One of these days his hands will be cold and lifeless. His energy drained from his body. It is draining out of him as I sit here and write. We are, collectively, watching him slip away. He is shrinking. Quieter and quieter."

But then he would rouse himself to greet someone, to hug my son, hear about his race, and look at his pictures. Then he would retreat again. After our meeting with the hospice group, I left to drive to my Monday night class. On the way, I stopped at a Starbucks to pick up coffee. A song that I hadn't heard in twenty years, but which I had previously loved, was playing. I sat down with my coffee and began to write down the words. The song was a perfectly timed gift from the universe. It became my "my father is dying" song. That evening after class my son burned it on a CD for me and as I listened to it in the weeks to come it always gave me an opening for the tears that were building up in me. When I drove north to the funeral, that three and a half-hour drive I knew so well, I drove it alone as my family members were coming later. I listened to that song over and over again, weeping all the way. It had been such an intense and busy few months, I had barely had time to process what I was witnessing and living through.

The song is called "Love Song," written by Leslie Duncan but sung initially and often by Elton John. The lyrics are: "Love is what we came here for, love is the open-end door, If you know what I mean, Have your eyes really seen?"

My father so loved us all. He made his mistakes but there was no doubting his love for all of us.

A week after that meeting was another snowy day, a Monday. It was so snowy that the place where I teach on Monday nights cancelled class. It had been my pattern to go visit my folks on Monday afternoon, then drive to my class. So I headed out about two o'clock. The roads were so bad, they made me nervous. I considered turning around, but had decided that I was going every day now that I possibly could. I drove slowly, cautiously. I entered the apartment to find my dad sitting in the living room. My parents were awaiting the arrival of the chaplain in about a half-hour. I asked Dad how he was, and he answered, "About the same."

"Mom and I are having tea," I told him. "Would you like some?"

"Yes," he nodded. He mumbled something—he was weaker and it was harder to understand him. Mom and I both listened, and heard "Cracker and cheese, please." I sat and held his hand while Mom busied herself fixing the tea and cheese and crackers. She presented us with a plate and he took a small bite off one end of cheese and cracker and then needed my assistance to hold the cup of tea to his lips to help wash it down.

He was congested, coughing up stuff. I put my arm around his thin bony shoulders. He said, "Who would think it would be so hard to die?" I told him I was sorry it was so hard, and asked him if he needed to talk to anybody, if there was anything he wanted to say or do before he died. I had one brother out in California who hadn't made it home during his sickness, and I wondered if Dad's concern about him or his family was something he felt unresolved about. But he shook his head no.

When the chaplain arrived we all held hands and prayed together. There was a quiet peacefulness in the air. After the chaplain left, we called the nurse aid to help me move him back to his bed. It was clear that his effort to sit up, to eat, and pray aloud, if weakly, had really tired him.

Once lying down, his congestion became immediately worse. The nurse aid said she would get the nurse. I called Jane, who said, "I can hear his breathing over the phone. You need to call hospice and tell them to come right away and I will be there ASAP."

There was a phone conversation between me, the hospice nurse, and the assisted living nurse in which it was decided to administer morphine. Dad's breathing was very labored and he was restless, although his eyes were closed.

The next period of time is such a blur, it is difficult for me to clearly track what happened when. The wonderful male hospice nurse arrived; the assisted living nurse gave my dad morphine. I kept holding my dad's hand, and once in a while he would open his eyes, but mostly they were closed.

Jane arrived as we were trying to help Dad sit up more on his pillows. She lifted him from the front, and he collapsed into her arms, saying, "Hold me, hold me."

Jane held him close, saying, "I've got you, Dad." I was behind on the bed and had my arms wrapped around his shoulders. It was such an achingly tender moment.

There was our silver star-earning military father who had instilled fear in us during our younger years, now completely vulnerable. I will forever be grateful to him for how open he was with us and to us as he was dying.

We all swirled around him—the nurses, my mom, my sister, and I. But at one point it was just me and the hospice nurse. I was holding Dad's hand and the nurse was checking his breathing, his oxygen levels, and his pulse. The first thing this gentle man said to me was, "I am so glad you and your sister are here."

It didn't quite register with me yet. I said, "Yes, it's a lot for my mother to handle alone."

A moment later, after checking the pulse, the hospice nurse looked at me directly and quietly said, "He is dying."

A moment I will always remember.

I nodded my head, thanked him for telling me, and asked if he had any idea how much time Dad had left, to which he shrugged. At that point my father took a loud breath and then briefly paused in his breathing. I shouted out to my mom and sister, "Jane, Mom, get in here!" Whatever they were doing in the kitchen they dropped.

Then, we all knew. It was here. This moment we had been waiting for, preparing for, for so long. My mom wrapped her arms around him, weeping, saying, "You've been such a wonderful partner all these years."

Jane and I held his hands. We were all close to him, on the bed. Jane kept saying, "I love you Dad."

I babbled," We love you so much. We know you need to go. We are here with you, your girls. We understand you need to go. Give a hug to Bernie, Gert, and Dan for us."

The hospice nurse stayed in the background. Once he quietly said, "The hearing is the last to go. You can keep talking to him."

My dad was breathing hard, then not breathing, then taking another gasp of breath, then not.

Somewhere in there the priest arrived. My sister had phoned him. Early on, I had sent a text to my sister Cathy. Jane had called a few siblings in case anyone wanted to try to come. But several of them were out of town, Cathy was way across the city, and there was a snowstorm going on.

When the priest arrived I moved away from my dad's good ear, the right ear, and over to the other side of the bed. I held my dad's left hand now, which I continued to hold for a long time after his last breath. The priest said some prayers but what I mostly remember him saying is, "It is time now that we meet death without fear."

Perfect words. They entered me, caught in my throat. Meet death without fear. We. Meet death. Without fear. I wanted to slow the words down, ingest them fully.

Somewhere in that swirl I also called my brother in California and put the phone to Dad's ear so he could say goodbye.

And then, after a few more labored, spaced-out breaths, his face fell to the side on his pillow and this incredible, peaceful countenance took over his entire body, especially his face. He looked beautiful. Jane and my mother say it was as if his soul floated away and wherever he went, it was peaceful. His face took on a porcelain quality, translucent. He was so beautiful I couldn't take my eyes off him. And I still held his left hand; I stayed on that bed holding his hand and tried to take it all in. I asked the nurse if we needed a coroner to pronounce time of death. This man emerged from the background to say, "No, since this is the expected outcome of hospice. And I am here to note it."

One of us looked at the time. It was just after 5:30 p.m. I had arrived at 2:30, and it wasn't clear then that this would be *the* day—the day my father would leave us. There I was, holding my father's hand as the heat slowly slipped out of it. I didn't want to let go as the heat from my hand kept his warm. By then, my brother-in-law David had arrived. My mom and sister and I were there—we were all there, together. Some phone calls and texts were made to let family members know. I called my husband with my cell phone in one hand while still holding my father's hand with the other. I called my daughter. My son then called me for an unrelated reason and I told him. We called my other siblings. We called the undertaker.

My brother Matt, a pilot for Delta, was flying that night. He said that when he went off duty and saw three messages in his inbox, one from each of his sisters, he knew his father had died. It was the day before Matt's birthday.

The undertaker didn't come for a few hours. I was happy to have the presence of Dad's body for as long as we did. Although I eventually let go of his hand, I kept returning to look at him. Dave, Jane, Mom, and I said a few prayers together around him.

When the undertaker came we helped move Dad's body into the bag. I said I would walk him down, and as I left the apartment, I watched my sister and brother-in-law enfold my mother in their arms. The undertaker, my father's body, and I took the elevator from the second to the first floor. I held the door open for the undertaker. He wheeled the gurney to his van and moved my father's body inside. I stood and watched them drive away. The snow had stopped, the sky had cleared, and it was crystal clear. Stars burned in the heavens, and the snow caught starlight and reflected it. My breath steamed out of me as I watched the van turn the corner. Just as he drove out of sight I thought to lift my arm in a salute.

The funeral was a few days later, and my father's body was then back where he longed to be—in Grand Rapids, Minnesota. He was buried with full military honors. He had died on February 21, and on his burial day, February 26, the temperatures dipped to five below zero. The last time I had been at the cemetery in conditions that cold was at Uncle Dan's funeral, eight years before.

The day of my father's funeral, the military men were standing in the cold, one with only one leg, leaning on a crutch. Advanced in age but resolute in their honor, six of them held flags and stood ready to play "Taps." My dad always loved the playing of "Taps." We gathered around my mom in front of the coffin, in front of the hole in the ground. And after the guns were shot and "Taps" was played, two young soldiers began folding the flag that was draped over his coffin with incredible ceremony and reverence. The cold and the silence added layers of respect. I was beside my mother as the young soldier, folded flag in hand, marched solemnly toward her. Gently placing the flag in her arms, he said, "From the President of the United States of America, we thank you for your husband's service during our country's time of need. Our sincerest condolences."

Tears were streaming down my mother's face, all of our faces. She looked him steadily in the eye and said, so sadly, "Thank you."

The flag moved to her living room at Epiphany.

My father shepherded his entire family off to the next world.

My mother, sister and I were there in the final moments to shepherd him to the other side. The long, drawn-out affair that Bernie spoke of back in the eighties drew to a close on a cold February day in 2011. I wanted to say to Bernie, "Not long and drawn-out enough, Bernie, not long and drawn-out enough."

One of my father's favorite songs he requested at his funeral contains the following words: "Friendship that has lasted through fortune, failure, and through tears." He was a deep and true friend to all of his brothers and sisters and to his children, their spouses and his grandchildren.

I realized that I had learned from my teachers how to be one who is there at the side of the sick and the dying. And although Bernie and Gert were known to say, "Mary guides us. We just do what Mary tells us to do," and although I cherish Mary-energy in my life, what I would say is that love leads you, love tells you what to do and what to say at the bedside of a sick or dying loved one.

That night after the funeral, there was a shared meal with fifty of us, all descended from my parents, along with spouses and children. We did this in the hotel in Grand Rapids, the Sawmill. After the meal, we tracked down the piano (which the hotel staff gave us permission to use) and trooped down the long, deserted hallway toward it. I passed out the song sheets, and we sang all my Dad's favorite songs: "Galway Bay," "Danny Boy," "O Canada," "When Irish eyes are Smiling." We sang rousingly and happily.

After all, in the fine tradition of this family, musical lyrics came to comfort me in my time of need, and I draw wisdom from them still.

In the words of Elton John, "Love is what we came here for, if you know what I mean. Have your eyes truly seen? Love is the open-end door. Truth is the flame we must burn, freedom the lesson we must learn if you know what I mean. Have your eyes truly seen?"

Singing around the piano at the author's parents' fiftieth wedding anniversary. Left to right: cousin Mary Louise, sister Cathy, brother Dan, Uncle Dan, and the author at the piano.

Part Five

Landings

The author and her husband's cottage in Canada.

Chapter Twenty-Five
Canadian Retreats

"With glowing hearts we see thee rise, the true north strong and free..."

–From "O Canada"

SUMMERTIME. The summer after my father's death I needed our Canadian retreat even more than usual. It is my version of "camp," only we are in cottage country and it isn't anywhere as isolated as Uncle Dan's place. Still, it is wild in its own way and I love being surrounded by water, wind, rock and sky.

Most mornings I rise early and sit on the northern rock to watch the sun rise. I call it Sunrise Point and I think of it as mine. No one else, in the history of this island, has so faithfully sat on that point like I have to greet the morning sun. I am sure it is the most beautiful and peaceful place on earth (except perhaps Uncle Dan's beach).

From where I sit, two bays open in front of me, both north-facing, one more easterly, the other more westerly. These bays give me a sense of expansiveness; they are openings toward the sheer size of the body of water I am on, Georgian Bay of Lake Huron. Gazing out, I watch the sun rise above pine trees and light up the western shore—treetops first, then moving down the long length of deep-green pine needles to the granite, which sets off reflections dancing on the water. Such incredible beauty, a new painting every time you look. This sunrise ritual opens me daily to the mysteries of the universe, to God's amazing and expansive presence. It also heals and soothes me at deep levels. How can heartbreak stand up against the force of such beauty?

Many days, I canoe over to the neighboring national park, Beausoleil, French for "beautiful sun", and run the trails. I am grateful for this love of running, for it has allowed me to learn these trails, and to discover, some years, patches of abundant blueberries. I keep my ears and eyes alert for bears and rattlesnakes, both of which I have encountered from time to time. I thank my lumberjack grandfather and bush pilot uncle because wilderness trails feel like home to me.

Here, we leave twelve hundred miles behind our busy Minneapolis lives. When we arrive in Honey Harbour, the small town closest to our cottage, we also leave behind our car. The rest of the summer, we travel everywhere by boat. Something deep in our consciousness changes when water is beneath us every time we move. Water laps around us all day, peacefully or wildly. Sunlight shimmers across water, the tips of pine trees, warms the granite beneath our feet. One of the reasons I so immediately took to this place is because of how the love of Uncle Dan's camp resides in me. Another draw is its proximity to my ancestral roots. Weavings of past and present are braided together as I breathe Canadian air: this was especially cinched when my ninety-something mother told me, blushingly, that I had been conceived in Canada on one of their trips to Uncle Dan's camp.

IN THE SUMMER after my father's death, there was a reunion in Peterborough, Ontario, of a wide range of Hoolihan cousins. A distant cousin of my mine had contacted us many months before and the event had been in the planning for close to a year. In honor of the reunion, four of my siblings flew to Canada, with three of them coming to stay at the island with us either before or after the reunion. I felt like Uncle Dan, hosting family at the cottage. No exotic float-plane flight in, but truly a sense of a getaway in a setting of wild beauty.

In Peterborough, a friendly Canadian town of about 120,000, we gathered with cousins from far and wide, mostly Canadians with a few of us Americans. We toured the old family homesteads and farm lands in the outlying areas of this town; we saw the land and what remained of the farmhouse where our great-grandparents had farmed. I could see that farm that my grandfather, as the fourth-born son,

A close-up of the author's great-great-grandfather's gravestone.

would not inherit and its rolling hills reminded me of the farm back in Grand Rapids, Minnesota. After turning off the main road and driving down smaller lanes (called "concessions"), we arrived at a small white church surrounded by gravestones. We entered through the wrought-iron gate. This small church and cemetery rested at the top of a gentle hill and the grass led down to a river. It was beautiful, peaceful, serene. We discovered that our great-grandfather, Dublin Dan, had helped to build the church.

We all wandered around until we found the gravestone for our great-great-grandfather. The gravestone was tall—about six feet—and was a beautiful shade of orange-gray granite. Standing atop the marker was a foot-high cross. "JAMES HOOLAHAN" (one of the many spellings of this name) was engraved in the stone, and beneath it the simple information: "Died 1863, Aged 75 Years." He fathered four children—among them Dublin Dan, who was married to Granny Bridget.

One of the cousins said, "Today marks the first time that descendants of this man, James Hoolahan, are together, face to face in almost 150 years." When he spoke I felt my arms ripple with goosebumps. We paused, moved slowly, let the summer breeze blow through our hearts, and took lots of pictures.

But here was what I was most struck by: Above the engraved name was a beautiful, flowing carving of the letter "H" in Celtic design, surrounded on one side by carved Canadian maple leaves and on the other by an abundance of clovers. I almost gasped when I saw this; clovers and maple leaves have been strong symbols for me all of my life. I have clover images and the maple leaf all over my house. I wear bracelets with maple leaves engraved between sections of abelone. To

Left: the author's great-great-grandfather's grave outside Peterborough. He brought his family from Ireland to Canada. Top: the author at the cemetery at Young's Point, outside Peterborough.

see these symbols, engraved in granite on the marker of my great-great-grandfather, buried in 1863, moved me. I felt fiercely connected to the images as well as to the name. This man, who traveled from Ireland to Canada, was buried almost 150 years before I stood in front of his gravesite. Yet the imagery he chose (or a loved one chose for him) to mark his place in history, his record of life and death, resonated completely with me all those years later.

One of the stories told at this reunion was about the "Cavan-Blazers." The family farms we had toured were located in Cavan Township and during the time when my great-grandparents were farming, the Catholics would gather in one of the farmhouses for Mass on Sunday mornings. The anti-Catholics, the Orange Protestant Cavan-Blazers, sometimes surrounded the farmhouse and set it on fire with the Catholics—men, women and children—praying inside. I pondered how in just four generations we could go from the kind of fierceness that made those Catholics continue to celebrate Mass on Sunday mornings in spite of such high risks of persecution, to a generation where many of us walk away, angry and disillusioned. Surely part of the failure is on the part of the church and those running it. Our culture is changing so fast you could say change has gone viral. The church—huge, mired in the old ways—is way behind in its response to some human needs and yet, paradoxically, in some ways provides for timeless needs.

Our great-great-grandfather chose a wonderful pastoral place for his burial grounds. The small white church has kept good company with the hillside full of grave markers. The river at the bottom of the hill, choppy and unsettled, blew about in the lush summer breeze. The green grass was blowing. It all felt quiet and serene, full with the simple order of the old world.

Another striking connection happened for me about a week later. I had told Chris that one of the things I wanted to do during the summer was go by boat to Parry Sound, which is about a two-hour boat ride north. It's a harbour town and has a small seaplane base. I wanted to go flying... from the water. In my current life, I have to pay to fly, unlike the Uncle Dan days. Every once in a while I really get the urge.

Our good friends Fred and Darlene joined us, and the boat ride north was spectacularly beautiful and uneventful, cruising through the Georgian Bay islands, going marker to marker, reading the charts, checking out cottages and granite and trees all the way.

At the seaplane base, we checked in and found out our pilot could take us as soon as we were ready. He and I were chatting, and when I mentioned flying out of Atikokan in the past, he said, "Oh, I grew up flying in Ignace." Ignace! I knew my uncle flew in there often for supplies. It was closer to camp than Atikokan but farther north.

I said, "Well, my uncle has a fishing camp between Atikokan and Ignace." (Even though Uncle Dan was several years gone on to the next world, I still thought of and called it his place.)

"Really," he said. "What lake?"

I threw the name out although Dan's place is the only one on the lake and it's a small lake, much lesser known than some of the lakes surrounding it. So I said the name, not expecting him to recognize it.

"Mabel Lake."

"Mabel Lake!" the pilot exclaimed. "I know Dan Hoolihan! He used to fly into Ignace on Sunday mornings and go to church. I've been to that camp—I used to fly in supplies that didn't fit on his plane. That's a sweet place, Mabel Lake. I've seen a lot of camps. It's a special one."

As soon as he said Dan's name, I felt that magical presence of my magical uncle. My jaw almost dropped; my friends were impressed! (Fred is a hard guy to impress and he has the kind of visionary building skills my uncle had.) I couldn't get enough of talking to him, this pilot who was suddenly a direct link to my no-longer-living uncle. He remembered Dan in his prime, and remembered vividly this place I could only describe to my friends.

I sat in the copilot's seat and enjoyed the incredible flight and view, yes, but mostly I enjoyed talking to someone who knew Dan, knew his place that held a sanctuary in my heart. It felt like Dan was reaching out from another world and telling me, somehow, I was doing well. That taking a day of luxury, to fly, to spend the money to enjoy a day just for fun and joy had been the right thing to do. If I hadn't, I would have missed this connection.

That Dan was remembered all those years later for how he faithfully flew into church on Sunday mornings also hit me—right on the guilt-o-meter (impossible to completely shake). In the summers I consider immersion in nature's beauty to be my "church". But I admire my uncle's steadfastness, his commitment to his faith. There was my wild pioneer pilot uncle—flying into church every Sunday.

To have this complete stranger remember that detail about Dan years after he died was remarkable to me. To be in my Canadian home hundreds of miles from Uncle Dan's fishing camp, to make the effort to book and pay for a flight, and then to receive this gift was a highlight of the summer. As I watched the white spray as we lifted off and then again as we settled from wings of air back to water, I felt Uncle Dan reminding me again that all things are possible.

"Reach for the sky," he would say. "Reach for joy; it's out there."

Chapter Twenty-Six

From Cavan-Blazers to Controversy

During one of the many years of my writing this book, a controversy broke out at the church I belong to, the Basilica of St. Mary's. The Minneapolis/St. Paul archbishop created a DVD that was anti-gay marriage and mailed it to 400,000 parishioners across the state. The artist in residence at my church, Lucinda Naylor, sent out a memo asking for the DVDs to be donated to her, in protest, and she would create a piece of art with them. She was immediately "suspended".

As stated in the Minneapolis *Star Tribune* of 9/28/10:

> She [Naylor] said her anger with the church's actions on gay marriage dates to the spring when three friends with gay children protested Nienstadt's interpretation of the Catholic position on homosexuality. She said the archbishop wrote back to all three, telling them that those who could not agree with "the teachings of the Catholic Church on homosexuality . . . ought not participate in the sacramental life of the church." The Archbishop added that the mothers' "eternal salvation" could depend on their adopting the church's position on homosexuality.

On TV news I heard this artist say, "There are many reasons for people to not come to church here. The archbishop has just given them one more." In the *Tribune* she was further quoted as saying, "I'm as Catholic as the pope. Why should I have to leave?" Her statements resonated deeply within me.

I worry about the mindset in homes where this DVD will be embraced. What message does this DVD send to young children?

The DVD, the reaction to Naylor's communications, have all the elements of Catholicism so many of us have run from and been hurt by—particularly judgment and shame. What is a fourteen-year-old who feels attraction to the same sex—unbidden, it's just there—to do with this? Being made to feel "wrong" or "less than" translates into shame. And for young ones whose families embrace this kind of judgment there is huge potential for holier-than-thou thinking and even bullying.

When my son was a teenager he went to an inner urban high school that celebrated and still celebrates differences. It was the same school where my husband taught for twenty-seven years. It was not a perfect place but there was an atmosphere of acceptance. And because of that acceptance in the artwork in the halls, the school plays, and in many other interactions, there was a richness and a daily celebration of life's diversity.

My son belonged to the gay-straight alliance. I was proud of him for this. He prefers girls himself but believes, strongly, his peers have a right to their own personal lives and choices. At his senior homecoming parade, guess which float took first place? Oh yes—the gay-straight alliance. Putting that stereotypical decorating ability to good use!

It is a public, secular high school. But it is my belief that God's work goes on there. Students are celebrated for who they are and the wide range of who they are creates a rainbow-infused, multiculturally rich experience. The difference between what was going on in this high school and what was going on in our church was striking. If the cornerstone of all major religions is compassion, which I believe, then it is striking to me when I see more compassion in an urban high school than from the political positions of my church's leaders.

But the people at the Masses I attend, the people whose religious practice I admire, my teachers in the world of prayer are compassionate people. My parents, Bernie, Gert, and Dan, the whole tribe were conduits of love. Who knows how many times their prayers, their hands moving over the rosary beads, helped so many of us? And they are still a part of why I still feel connected to the church.

And as my friend Michelle Porter was quoted in the Minneapolis *Star Tribune* on October 1, 2010, "But maybe someday it [the Church] will change if enough of us stay in it and speak up about it."

Sing it, sister. I'm with you.

And when I sit in church as the communion gifts are prepared at every Mass I am always touched by the words, "Only say the word and your soul shall be healed." These words are shortly followed by the "Lord have mercy" (repeated) which moves into "Grant us peace". Where there's a choir, the chord progression and resolution into "Grant us peace" settles into a deep place inside me, like many of the "Amens" do. My breathing and my bones feel the vibration. At the end of my twelve-step meeting we recite the serenity prayer (God grant me the serenity to accept the things I cannot change, the courage to change the things I can and the wisdom to know the difference), then we squeeze hands and say, "Peace."

Peace—isn't that what we are all seeking?

Epilogue

IN MY GENERATION we no longer have a central home or hearth to gather around. All of my siblings and I have left our hometown. Although seven out of eight of us live in Minnesota, we are twenty minutes to two hours away from each other. My mother is still living and we all visit her fairly regularly; we visit each other much less. Most of the women in my family are still working, in our fifties and sixties. We are busy. There is a separateness to our lives, and many factors feed into this.

I wanted to record my father's family because it is a way of living that is lost to us. I wanted to record its gifts and shed light on how I/we can carry some of these gifts into our lives and futures. I am so grateful for the journey that my near-death experience catapulted me toward. My anger could have been a cage I lived inside of forever; there are so many cages in this world.

For a while on Sundays I would go to the short Mass held in the assisted living place where my mom was. Unfortunately, this service was cut due to changes made in that parish. It was made for the old people—short and sweet. The front row was reserved for those in wheelchairs. The room was small but there was a piano and usually someone to play. Hymns were passed out and we sang—often weak and off-key. But we sang.

Again I was touched by the gathering of these people who were at the end of their lives and preparing for death. That Sunday Mass meant so much to them. I felt lucky to be there with my mother when I could. The words of the priest always fed me in some way. And if there was a prayer for the faithful about what it means to be truly married, I didn't respond. Take what you want and leave the rest.

In a wonderful full-circle way, my mother discovered the serenity prayer, a cornerstone of the twelve-step program, used to open and/or close most meetings. Through the services of hospice, she was meeting with a grief counselor, a kind woman who would come to my mom's apartment and talk. There was the grief of losing her husband of sixty-nine years and the grief of watching divorce in her family and her knowledge of suffering grandchildren. She said to me, "I am so glad your father is not around to watch this." The counselor gave her the serenity prayer, handwritten, and she kept it on her dresser held down by engraved stones that said "Peace, Wisdom, Hope."

Our spiritual worlds connected and overlapped.

I FELT MY FIRST writing impulse on the family farm and it is deeply fed in the months I spend on the island in Canada and all points in between. I am grateful for this way of making sense of my life. The twelve steps of Al-Anon keep me grounded and honest; in a weekly, daily way I am asked to look at myself, at the barriers I need to keep taking down in order to be who I truly am. And in church I am touched by music and by the shared intention of prayer and spiritual sustenance. I need all of these forces to live a spiritually vibrant life.

And nature. Nature has been a constant and steadfast connection to my spiritual life, my soul. Is there anything more hopeful in this world than the way the sun rises every morning, no matter where you are?

"There are things you can't reach. But
you can reach out to them, and all day long.

The wind, the bird flying away. The idea of God.

And it can keep you as busy as anything else, and happier."
–From Mary Oliver's "Where Does the Temple Begin,
Where Does it End?"

"Let the beauty we love be what we do. There are hundreds of ways to kneel and kiss the ground."
–Rumi

Acknowledgements

Deep wells of gratitude might begin to describe what I feel toward all the people who helped bring this book into being. North Star Press for the phone call telling me they "loved" my manuscript, and for all their efforts in editing and in making this book as beautiful and as perfect as it can be. A special thanks to Anne Rasset, who did so much of the editing and did such a beautiful job with the cover and layout. My last round of readers gave me crucial insights and support that encouraged me to keep going on the last leg of the marathon: Patricia Weaver Francisco, Jill Breckenridge, Beth Dooley, Fr. Michael O'Connell, Christine McVay, Patty Davies, and Mary Noreen. Other readers whose insights and encouragements over the long years of birthing this book were invaluable include: Mary Rockcastle, the editorial staff of *Water~Stone Review* in 2001, Charles Baxter for his vote of confidence in my first chapter "At the Hour of My Death" which they, as a team, named for Honourable Mention for the Brenda Ueland Prose Prize in 2001; the editorial staff of *Great River Review* for publishing a version of the chapter "Bernie, Gert, and BVG" and awarding it the first place for their Writers on Time contest in 2001. Thanks also to *Flight Training Magazine* for publishing an excerpt of my chapter about flying with Uncle Dan. You have no idea how much all of your support made my continuing work possible. Thanks to many of you who attended early readings I gave and received the material with open hearts; your enthusiasm helped me to continue to believe in this book. Deep thanks to the community at the Basilica of St. Mary who have welcomed me, and a special thanks to the choir which has provided me with an abundance of transcendent moments through the sharing of their gifts. Many thanks to the communities where I teach—Metropolitan State University and The Loft and my private groups—for the opportunity to teach, for all that I have learned from and with my students about the power of words and stories.

I also thank the many healers and loving friends in my life who help keep me moving toward wholeness in body, mind and spirit. Too many to name, you hold a grateful place in my heart.

To my siblings, cousins, nephews, and nieces: This is my version of our shared history. My perceptions are most likely not the same as yours but I hope you will receive these stories in the spirit of love, truth, and gratitude for our rich history with which they were written. Some of you have been very encouraging and I am eternally grateful for your support. I encourage you to take what works for you and leave the rest. A deep hope of mine is that these stories will open up conversations among us and further the sharing of both stories and questions. Special thanks to those of you who shared photos with me.

Finally, gratitude for those who have gone before us—for their courage and grace and their prayers.

Without the ongoing nudges from Chris, Caitlinrose and Kelly, this book would be in drydock instead of setting out to sea. Thank you, my loves.